THE PRAGUE SLAV CONGRESS OF 1848

LAWRENCE D. ORTON

EAST EUROPEAN QUARTERLY, BOULDER
DISTRIBUTED BY COLUMBIA UNIVERSITY PRESS
NEW YORK

1978

EAST EUROPEAN MONOGRAPHS, NO. XLVI

EAST CENTRAL EUROPEAN STUDIES
OF COLUMBIA UNIVERSITY

Lawrence D. Orton is Associate Professor
of History at Oakland University

143175

Copyright © 1978 by East European Quarterly
Library of Congress Catalogue Card Number 78-050549
ISBN 0-914710-39-7

Printed in the United States of America

To the Memory of Dwayne Orton

PREFACE

Pan-Slavism—few expressions have provoked such disparate emotional responses in Central and Eastern Europe since the Slovak scholar Ján Herkel first wrote of *verus panslavismus* in a linguistic treatise printed in Buda in 1826.* Since his writing, the term Pan-Slavism has been used to lavish praise or to instill fear, to inspire or to vilify. Yet among its advocates no less than its detractors, the term often has been misunderstood and abused. In 1846 in an article appropriately entitled "The Two Pan-Slavisms,"** Cyprien Robert defined Pan-Slavism as "the reconciliation, the fraternal rapprochement, and finally the reunion of all Slavs in a single moral body." On the ultimate aim of Pan-Slavism, Robert believed there was general accord; the confusion and disagreement concerned the means and conditions whereby union would be achieved. Here there were two fundamentally opposing approaches: the first, based on the principles of distinctive nationalities and voluntary federation, he termed genuine Pan-Slavism; the second, rooted in absolute governmental centralism and supranational uniformity, he called *Russian* Pan-Slavism. Robert's aim was to rectify the widespread belief among non-Slavs that tsarist agents and propaganda lurked behind the Pan-Slav strivings of the Danubian Slavs. (Although erroneous in 1846, this association of Pan-Slavism with expansionist Russian designs in East Central Europe would appear justified three decades later.)

When in the spring of 1848 the Danubian Slavs organized a congress in Prague to develop a common platform and policy to protect and enhance their national well-being, they expressly called their meeting a "Slav," not a "Pan-Slav," congress. The distinction was not merely semantic; the Slavs in Prague wanted to emphasize to their suspicious, indeed hostile, neighbors that their enterprise was not Russian-inspired or guided. But even before the delegates arrived in Prague, German and Magyar nationalists denounced in chorus the "Pan-Slav plotters in Prague" who they believed were embroiled in tsarist intrigue. These charges leveled at the Slavs assembled in Prague launched a century of divisive national conflict in Central Europe.

---

* *Elementa universalis linguae slavicae e vivis dialectis eruta . . .*
** In the prestigious Paris *Revue des Deux Mondes.*

In a series of essays on inter-Slav relations, Edvard Beneš suggested that the 1848 Slav Congress brought into sharp focus not only the bitter strife between the Slavs and their neighbors but also revealed the manifold strains and conflicts that have plagued relations among the Slavs ever since. Should the Slavs strive for the political and cultural union of all Slavs: Pan-Slavism? Or should they respect the existing state frontiers and forge lesser Pan-Slav unions: Austro-Slavism? Could union only be achieved by a radical revamping of political institutions, as advocated by the itinerant Russian revolutionary Mikhail Bakunin; or would the cautious, realistic approach, as propounded by the Czech historian František Palacký, bring success? Could any Slav union be achieved without prior resolution of the thorny Polish question? Would not the Poles' first loyalty always be to their own independence? And would Polish independence end the animosity between the Poles and their Slav neighbors—the Russians, the Ukrainians, and the Czechs? And was union possible among the kindred Slav nations—such as the Czechs and Slovaks, or the Yugo-Slavs—without first destroying the hegemony of the Magyars?*

Beneš, to be sure, conceded that the Slav Congress did not succeed in resolving permanently any of these questions, many of which still defy solution. The congress, in being the first body to bring these issues to the fore, made a contribution which the sudden rupture of its deliberations in no way diminished. The Slav Congress, poised between stages of national renascence and political maturation, stands as a watershed in the modern history of the smaller West and South Slav nations.

My study traces the genesis, organization, deliberations, and results of the congress. It focuses attention especially on those issues which joined and divided the Slavs in 1848, dominated contemporary evaluations, and which have influenced subsequent historical judgments of the congress.

The proper names but not the titles of contemporary newspapers and treatises have been adjusted to modern orthography (e.g., Václav for Wácslaw). Where proper names appear frequently in different languages, the form most consonant with the national predilection of the individuals is used (e.g., Josef Matyáš Thun, Pavel Josef Šafařík, Joseph von Lobkowitz). Common English equivalents for the names of cities have been

---

* *Úvahy o slovanství* (London [1944]), pp. 44-46.

used where suitable (e.g., Prague in lieu of Praha or Prag). In the case of
the nationally contested Galician city of Lvov, this present-day form has
been employed in preference to the Polish Lwów, Ukrainian L'viv, and
German Lemberg. But for the Silesian capital both German and Polish
forms are used, so that the author refers to the University of Breslau, but
to the Wrocław Polish Congress of May 1848.

Many persons and institutions helped in the preparation of this study.
The generous support of the Inter-University Committee on Travel Grants
made possible the means to sustain my research in Central European
repositories; the Institute on East Central Europe of Columbia University
kindly afforded me a semester's leave to complete the writing of this
study. I am indebted to the staffs of the Státní ústřední archiv and the
Archiv Národního musea in Prague, the Archiwum Główne Akt Dawnych
in Warsaw, and libraries in Europe and the United States too numerous
to mention here.

At different times several persons read versions or parts of this book:
the late Václav L. Beneš, Jerzy W. Borejsza, Istvan Deak, Charles and
Barbara Jelavich, Herbert H. Kaplan, Stanley Z. Pech, and Wayne S.
Vucinich. Their advice and encouragement has meant much to me, and
I am glad to be able to thank them here. Also, I wish to thank Professor
John Erickson, who kindly permitted me to read his unpublished manuscript on the origins and preparation of the Slav Congress. I owe special
gratitude to Professor Václav Žáček, who gave generously of his time
and vast knowledge of nineteenth-century inter-Slav relations during my
stays in Prague.

Acknowledgments are gratefully extended to the publishers of *Slavic
Review, Canadian-American Slavic Studies,* and *East European Quarterly*
for permission to reproduce portions of my previous work.

Special appreciation is given to Marian Wilson, editorial adviser to the
College of Arts and Sciences, Oakland University, for her sustaining faith
and encouragement and her help in preparing the manuscript. All shortcomings or errors are, of course, my responsibility alone.

Rochester, Michigan
June 1977

TABLE OF CONTENTS

PART I

BEFORE THE CONGRESS

A hundred times I spoke, but now I call
To you, O maligned Slavs!
Let us be one and not a splintered race,
Either we will be a whole, or nothing.

Slavs, you fragmented nation!
Union will give strength,
Or the untwirling currents will reveal
  but waste and barrenness.

—Ján Kollár, *Daughter of Sláva* (1824)

CHAPTER 1
PAN-SLAVISM, AUSTRO-SLAVISM,
AND THE SLAV AWAKENING

i

The provincial Thuringian town of Jena might seem unlikely as the birthplace of the modern movement for Slav unity. But it was in this German Lutheran university community that the leading early-nineteenth-century proponents of Pan-Slavism—Ján Kollár and Pavel Josef Šafařík—first experienced the lure of romantic nationalism. In the years after Napoleon's defeat, Jena had become the burgeoning center of the German student movement and of far-reaching intellectual inquiry, in marked contrast to the antiquated curriculum and system of education which prevailed in the Habsburg Empire.[1]

In contrast to the ideas of the French Revolution which imbued Frenchmen (*citoyens*) with the essence of the political nation, romantic nationalism in Germanic central Europe distinguished peoples or nations (*Völker*) exclusively in terms of linguistic affinities. Language, not political community, expressed the distinctive spirit of the nation. A major influence in Jena on Kollár and Šafařík was the historian Heinrich Luden, whose popular lectures on German antiquities and history stimulated the young Slovaks to ponder and probe their own Slav heritage.[2] A people, they came to believe, who lacked a codified language and literature to convey its common heritage could not achieve full nationhood. In order to bridge this gap, they devoted themselves to reconstructing the common past of the Slavs.

Kollár's stay in Jena inspired his epic poem of Slav patriotism, *Slávy dcera* (Daughter of Sláva), which unfolds as the poet's journey through the past and present homeland of the Slavs.[3] In Canto I the poet grieves at the ruins of the ancient Wendish-Slav settlements along the banks of the Saale near Jena, which medieval German crusaders had laid waste:

> Before my weeping eyes extends the land,
> my people's cradle once, their coffin now. . . .
>
> Blush, envious Teuton, neighbor to the Slav
> for all the crimes that lie upon your hands.
> No enemy has shed such blood—or ink—
> as Germany, to bring the Slav to grief.[4]

From this site of desolation the poet travels along the Elbe river to Bohemia, the scene of the past glory and the recent misfortune of the Czechs. In Canto III, "The Danube," the poet returns to his native Slovakia, which is ravaged by a different enemy of the Slavs: the Magyars. During his journey the poet invokes the mythical patron goddess, Sláva, whose corporate image personifies the unity of Slavdom: her head, Russia; her trunk, Poland; her arms, the Czechs; her legs, the Serbs. To make amends for her long suffering, the gods have given Sláva a daughter, Mína, whose beauty and strength epitomize for the poet the purity and perseverance of Slav womanhood. But Mína, the goddess who embodies the hopes for the reunion and regeneration of Slavdom, is also Frederike, daughter of a Lutheran German pastor in Jena, who is the object of Kollár's terrestrial love. This fusion of love with Slav patriotism permeates the poem and contributed to its immense popularity.

No less significant for the Slav awakening was Kollár's subsequent treatise, *On Literary Reciprocity Between the Various Branches and Dialects of the Slav Nation* (1837).[5] "Reciprocity" (German *Wechselseitigkeit,* Czech *vzájemnost*) meant to Kollár "the mutual sharing of all national branches [*Volkszweige*] in the spiritual output of their common [Slav] nation." Kollár saw fit to add that reciprocity "does not consist in a political union of all Slavs, nor in demagogic intrigue or revolutionary unrest against [established] governments and rulers." It was singularly a cultural movement. Through reading and discussion of works by other Slavs, "each [Slav] dialect ought to derive new vitality from the others to become rejuvenated, enriched, and to prosper." Kollár distinguished four principal Slav dialects—Russian, Illyrian (štokavian Serbo-Croatian), Polish and Czecho-Slovak—that *all* educated Slavs should learn; Slav scholars, however, should know "all Slav dialects without exception," even those no longer spoken, as well as the principal languages of the Slavs' neighbors. The Slavs need no longer strive for political unity, since mutual sharing would accrue benefits well beyond cultural bounds. Internecine squabbles and conflict with alien rulers would cease; understanding and harmony would prevail.[6]

Kollár made several suggestions for attaining this idyllic state: establishing Slav bookshops and libraries in the principal Slav towns; founding an all-Slav cultural journal; chairs in Slav studies in the universities and teaching Slav languages in the schools; publishing comparative grammars and dictionaries and compiling and translating Slav folklore and literature; purging the Slav language of foreign elements; and adopting a uniform orthography for Latin and Cyrillic usage. Further, Kollár urged the Slavs to alter their traditional national names and henceforce identify themselves as Slavo-Poles, Slavo-Russians, Slavo-Czechs, etc.[7]

Kollár's ideas were neither original nor far-reaching. Robert Auty suggests that it was Kollár's "enthusiasm and eloquence that caught the imagination of his contemporaries"; his widespread popularity derived foremost from an ability "to epitomise, exemplify and recreate the ideas of others."[8]

A major stimulus for Kollár, as for generations of Slav enthusiasts, was the German idealist philosopher and historian, Johann Gottfried Herder. In the celebrated "Slav chapter" of his *Ideen zur Philosophie der Geschichte der Menschheit* (1791), Herder depicted the Slavs as peace-loving agriculturalists of *one* nation who, since the time of Charlemagne, had suffered at the hands of their more warlike German neighbors. Particularly did Herder's prophecy of a bright future for the Slavs inspire Slav patriots:

> . . . these now deeply sunk, but once industrious and happy people, will at length awake from their long and heavy slumber, shake off the chains of slavery, enjoy the possession of their delightful lands from the Adriatic sea to the Carpathian mountains, from the Don to the Muldaw.[9]

Herder's influence is also evident in Šafařík's writings. After completing his studies in Jena, Šafařík returned briefly to Bratislava (Pressburg) before accepting a position in 1819 at the Serb Orthodox gymnasium in Novi Sad.[10] His training in classical philology led him to study comparative Slavic philology in the belief that greater awareness of the native language and literature would foster Slav patriotism among his contemporaries. In his first major study, *Geschichte der slawischen Sprache und Literatur nach allen Mundarten* (1826), he argued that the different Slav tongues were merely dialects of a common proto-Slav language. Šafařík echoed Herder's depiction of the Slavs' pacific nature, a theme which likewise permeates his pioneering study of Slav antiquities (*Slovanské starožitnosti*), which was published in Czech in 1837. The notion of the Slavs' agricultural, unwarlike character, though of dubious historical accuracy, became the watchword of the Slav awakening, especially as the German-Slav antagonism intensified.[11]

Šafařík's most significant contributions to arousing Slav consciousness was his study of Slav ethnography, *Slovanský narodopis* (1842).[12] The work's popularity derived largely from the detailed map that pictured the

Slavs' extensive area of settlement. The Slovene-Illyrian, Stanko Vraz, wrote to a Czech acquaintance that Šafařík's ethnographic cartography created more Slav patriots than all previous Slav literary achievements.[13]

It is noteworthy that both Kollár and Šafařík—the poet and the scholar of cultural Pan-Slavism—were of Slovak origin. Many Slovak intellectuals, in response to the menace of magyarization to their small nationality, instinctively identified with the larger Slav community.[14] Kollár also attributed the Slovaks' enthusiasm for Slavism to their geographical and linguistic position at the crossroads of Slav settlement.[15] Be this as it may, Kollár's and Šafařík's encounter with German romanticism in Jena stemmed from the Habsburg practice of allowing only Lutheran students in Hungary to study abroad at German universities.[16]

ii

Both Kollár and Šafařík wrote of the cultural communality of all Slavs regardless of religious differences or political frontiers. A parallel stimulus to the Slav awakening—Austro-Slavism—which antedated Kollár's and Šafařík's writings was already evident by the turn of the nineteenth century. The first expressions of this more limited theory of Slav unity are traceable to the Czech linguist Josef Dobrovský and the Slovene historian Anton Linhart. In a public address on the occasion of Emperor Leopold II's visit to Prague in 1791, Dobrovský emphasized the "devotion and attachment" to the House of Habsburg of the Slavs who by their "property and blood" had defended the monarchy and contributed to its greatness. Dobrovský pointed out that the Slavs not only outnumbered every other nation in Austria but were numerically equal to all other Austrian peoples combined.[17] In that same year, in the introduction to the second volume of a history of Carinthia and the South Slavs, Linhart maintained that, based on the Slavs' numerical preponderance, Austria should be seen as essentially a Slav state, just like tsarist Russia.[18]

The formulation of Dobrovský's and Linhart's observations into an Austro-Slav program was taken up by the Slovene, Jernej Kopitar, who had come to Vienna from Ljubljana to be curator of Slav books at the Court Library. In 1810 in an article in the Viennese periodical *Vaterländische Blätter,* Kopitar noted that, in contrast to Russia where only one Slav dialect predominated, Austria ruled over Slavs of *all* dialects and that Vienna was the natural point of union for all Slavs. The Slav apostles Cyril and Methodius had conducted their mission on Austrian soil ("auf österreichischem Boden") where the Old Church Slavonic tongue was born. In closing, Kopitar, borrowing words from a seventeenth-century

Austrian advocate of mercantilism, challenged that "herein as well, 'Austria over all, if it only wishes'" ('Österreich über alles, wenn es nur will').[19] In another article of that year in the same journal, entitled "Patriotic Fantasies of a Slav," Kopitar echoed the theme of the Slavs' numerical preponderance in Austria and called—twenty-six years before Kollár—for the establishment of a Slav academy and a chair of Slavic Literatures in Vienna.[20]

In large measure due to Kopitar's efforts, Vienna became an early center of Slav researches and the Austro-Slav movement.[21] Implicit in Kopitar's Austro-Slav concept is the theme that Catholic Austria must take the lead in appealing for the allegiance of its Slavs, no less than for those living under Turkish rule, lest they fall under the sway of Orthodox Russia. (This theme would recur poignantly in Palacký's celebrated reply to Frankfurt of April 1848.) Kopitar's russophobia is particularly evident in the effort he expended to bring to Vienna, "despite all sorts of Russian chicanery," a number of Old Slavic manuscripts discovered in the Mount Athos monasteries at the time of the Greek struggle for independence. Kopitar considered these manuscripts proof of his contention that the speech of the Austrian South Slavs was more faithful to Old Slavonic than that of Russian Slavs. Thus they were an asset in bolstering his attempts to root Austro-Slavism on a scientific basis, in what Professor Eduard Winter has called the "eigentlicher" (intrinsic) Austro-Slavism of the 1820's in contrast to the "taktischer" (tactical) Austro-Slavism of the Czechs and Illyrians of the 1840's.[22]

Though Kopitar's hopes for founding a chair in Slavic Studies at the University of Vienna (for which he probably had Dobrovský in mind) came to nothing, in the 1810's Vienna attracted numerous Slav students and scholars, notably the Czechs Václav Hanka, Josef Jungmann, and František Palacký, who briefly collaborated on the Viennese Czech-language newspaper *Videňské Nowiny,* and would play an outstanding role in the Czech national awakening.

At this time, Metternich and the Austrian government were far from hostile to the new Slav cultural awakening. Therefore, as censor for the government, Kopitar was able to assure publication of several journals and works in Slavic languages and of Dobrovský's last and major achievement, *Institutions of the Church Slavonic Language* (1822), a comparative historical survey, in Latin, of the evolution of the various forms of the ecclesiastical tongue among the Slavs. The real enemy for Habsburg Austria was German romantic nationalism and, later, Magyar strivings for autonomy. At first the Slav awakening was patronized by Metternich and

Austrian officialdom; later it was tolerated if only to counteract the more vocal and liberal-minded Austro-German and Magyar nationalists.[23]

A major influence in the spread of the Slav awakening was the establishment of literary foundations—the *maticas*—first begun in 1826 by the Hungarian Serbs and spreading among all the Austro-Slav peoples, which contributed greatly to fostering national consciousness especially through the publication of journals and ethnographical, literary and historical works.[24]

iii

Cultural Pan-Slavism found its strongest advocates among the Slavs in Hungary, who were subjected to magyarization; a more limited Austro-Slavism was supported by the Slovenes and Czechs (to counterbalance German cultural preponderance in the western half of the monarchy). A third, messianic strain of Slavism is evident in the works of Polish writers. In the years of political turmoil and decline preceding Poland's partition at the end of the eighteenth century, there appeared in Polish treatises and literature the recurring theme of Catholic Poland's liberating and civilizing mission among the Slav inhabitants of Europe's eastern borderlands stretching from the Baltic to the Adriatic and Black seas. This mission is evident in the appeal of the seventeenth-century poet Jan Gawiński. Not only the neighboring Lithuanians, White Russians, and Ukrainians, already joined to Poland as *gente Rutheni, natione Poloni*, but the Czechs and South Slavs should be united under Poland: "Come ye all who are of one speech, even though the same sky and the same country are not common to you; come, ye noble descendants of the courageous Czechs; the Pole (Lech) calls you all today into a common union."[25] However, Poland was destined not to unite others but to be herself divided.

Embittered by Napoleon's apparent betrayal of Poland's cause, many Poles in the first decades of the nineteenth century came to identify with the new "Slav tsar," Alexander I of Russia. This reorientation in Polish political thought was cemented in an address in 1815 to the Society of Friends of Science in Warsaw by Stanisław Staszic, a major contributor to the eighteenth-century Polish Enlightenment. In his remarks, entitled "Thoughts on the Political Equilibrium in Europe," he identified the German, who had turned Russian against Pole, as the real enemy of Slav unity and the principal villain in Poland's partition. Staszic implored the recently victorious tsar: "Do not suffer a stranger to tear apart our common consanguinal family. Strengthen it so that it shall be indivisible, quartered by nobody, a great political entity, a race of united Slav peoples! . . . The Poles are incapable of being your servants, but are prepared to become your brothers. . . . The unification and fraternization of the Slavs in the Russian Empire will lead towards the union of Europe, render wars impossible within it, and will bring everlasting peace to this part of the world! . . . Anyone who is against the Slavs is against Nature, and he can expect misfortune and destruction."[26] Federation with Russia, Staszic believed, was the only hope for a divided Poland, abandoned by the West.

The word messianism was first applied to the Slavs' mission by the Polish émigré philosopher Józef Maria Hoene-Wroński in an essay published in French in 1831. Twice the Slavs had saved Europe: from the Islamic onslaught and from the Jacobin scourge. Now it was their destiny to fuse the achievements of the French and Germans, to forge an "absolute union" of state and church. As Wacław Lednicki noted, in Hoene-Wroński's view Russia alone was "capable of giving the church her material power in order to bring about the Kingdom of God on earth." Russia must accomplish this union, however, before the West and South Slavs were drawn into a firm alliance under Austria.[27] Hoene-Wroński's views might foreshadow the later opinions of the Russian slavophiles, but with the important distinction that contempt for the "rotten West" is absent from his work. Another element of Polish messianism is the eulogy to the nation's sacrifice—"self-immolation" in Lednicki's words—for the future regeneration of humanity. This theme of national martyrdom, to be sure, is not present in the missionary fervor of the Russian slavophiles.[28]

After the harsh repression that followed the Poles' unsuccessful challenge to Russian rule in 1830-31, Hoene-Wroński's ideas, now branded as russophile, attracted few adherents. In the writings of Poland's greatest poet, Adam Mickiewicz, messianism now became synonymous with liberation from Russian despotism. In the biblical-style parables of *The Books of the Polish Nation and of the Polish Pilgrimage*, written soon after his arrival in France, Mickiewicz called Poland the "Christ of the Nations." She had been crucified for her belief in liberty and national brotherhood, which were anathema to the rapacious rulers of Europe. But Poland would rise anew, "And, as after the resurrection of Christ, bloody offerings ceased in all the world, so after the resurrection of the Polish Nation wars shall cease in all Christendom."[29] It was still the Slavs' mission to save humanity, but they must be led by the Poles, not the Russians, whom Polish Catholic messianists denounced as the antichrist in Slavdom.

Polish Slavism was above all an attempt to grapple with the thorny Polish-Russian relationship. Poles, after the debacle of Napoleon's schemes, wanted to believe that they would be accepted as an equal partner by the young, reform-minded Russian tsar to guide the well-being of all Slavs. After 1831 Polish messianism—an expression of "the moral imperialism of a vanquished nation which has renounced nothing"— redefined Poland's mission, and once-disillusioned compatriots again dreamed of the homeland's regeneration.[30] Polish Slavism was the achievement not of philologists and ethnographers, as among the Czechs and South Slavs, but of poets and philosophers, who cared little for the problems besetting the smaller Danubian Slav nations.[31] Moreover, after 1831 the Poles' principal concern with Slavdom was to counteract russophile tendencies among these other Slavs, whom they sought to enlist in the struggle for the restitution of the Polish state.

iv

As mentioned earlier, Kollár's and Šafařík's influence was particularly pronounced among the South Slavs in Hungary. As professor and director at the Orthodox Serbian Gymnasium in Novi Sad from 1819 to 1833, Šafařík nurtured the Serbian cultural rebirth. In 1820 he became acquainted with the Serbian poet and philologist Vuk Stefanović Karadžić, whose reforms paved the way for a standardized Cyrillic orthography and literary language based on the vernacular rather than the old Slavo-Serbian church tongue. In 1825 Šafařík cofounded the first Serbian cultural journal *Ljetopis,* and in the following year he joined in establishing the Serbian *Matica.*[32]

In Pest in 1829 Kollár met a young Croatian admirer, Ljudevit Gaj, who was striving to develop a program of South Slav unity to counteract the inroads of magyarization. Gaj called his movement "Illyrian," a term occasionally used to identify inhabitants of the former Roman province of Illyricum. Even after the dismantling of Napoleon's "Illyrian provinces" along the Adriatic, the term retained wide currency in Croatia. Gaj wished to establish a uniform literary language from among the three major Serbo-Croatian dialects: *što*kavian, *ča*kavian, and *kaj*kavian, derived from the word for "what" in each dialect. Gaj selected the *što*kavian dialect, the sole dialect of the Serbs, which had been used by the medieval Dubrovnik literati and was also widely spoken in Croatia. South Slav linguistic unity was a necessary precondition for a successful resistance to Hungarian efforts to introduce Magyar as the official language in Croatia. The struggle over language was for Gaj a "question of life and death, freedom or slavery for the nation."[33] In 1835 he founded *Novine Hervatske,* a newspaper with a weekly literary supplement, *Danica* (Morning Star), written primarily in *Što*kavian, which became the major forum for the propagation of Illyrism and Kollár's Pan-Slav theories.[34]

The heyday of Illyrism lasted until about 1843 when Gaj began to lose support among his more narrowly nationalistic and staunchly Catholic followers in Croatia, especially when he attempted to elicit tsarist Russian support for the cause of South Slav union. At the same time, the Habsburg authorities, informed by Russian officials of Gaj's overtures and fearful that his movement was becoming too revolutionary, forbade the use of the term "Illyrism."[35] Although the movement had failed to convert many Serbs (the *Matica* in Novi Sad would have nothing to do with it) or Slovenes (a notable exception was the Slovene lyric poet Stanko Vraz) and was bitterly opposed by the magyarophile faction (Magyarones) in Croatia, it did contribute enormously to the national awakening in Croatia. By the 1840's a politically mature Croatian national party was capable of challenging Magyar designs on Croatia. Like the Slovaks and Czechs, as we shall see, the Croats in the 1840's gradually shed their uncritical fascination with Kollár's Pan-Slavism and replaced it with a more limited program of national rights and autonomy within the Habsburg Empire.

V

Both Kollár and Safarik believed in a unitary Czecho-Slav (including the Slovaks) nationality. Though natives of Slovakia, both used the Czech language of the Králice Bible in their writings. But by the late 1830's a younger generation of Slovak literati challenged the linguistic domination of Czech. Though still believing in the concept of a common Slavdom, they rejected Kollár's division of the Slavs into only four linguistic units that treated the various Slovak idioms as essentially dialects of written Czech. How, the young Slovaks asked, could they bring enlightenment to their people and resist magyarization while employing an alien tongue? In the opinion of their leading spokesman, the Lutheran L'udovít Štúr, a distinct Slovak literary language was required. As in Croatia, the dialectical differences in the vernacular caused problems in establishing a literary language. At the end of the eighteenth century the Slovak Catholics' attempt to codify a literary language based on the Western Slovak dialect (termed *bernoláčtina* after its founder, Anton Bernolák) had not succeeded. Štúr and a small group of followers, notably fellow Lutherans J.M. Hurban and M.M. Hodža, in 1843 selected the Central Slovak dialect of the Liptovy and Zvolen regions as the basis for a literary language. They felt that the peasant speech of this remote area of Slovakia had been least corrupted by alien influences over the centuries and would best serve to unite all Slovaks.[36] To demonstrate their determination, in 1845 Štúr launched *Slovenskje Národňje Novini* in the new Slovak language. Like Gaj, he provided the newspaper with a literary supplement, *Orol Tatránski* (The Eagle of the Tatras).[37]

Štúr's actions were sharply criticized by the Czech literary establishment and by Kollár and Šafařík. In the press and in a tome specially prepared by the Czech National Museum, the luminaries of the Czech awakening chastised Štúr for delivering his people over to the Magyars (precisely what Štúr believed he was avoiding) by severing linguistic—and by implication cultural—ties with the larger Czech community.[38] Undaunted by criticism, Štúr persisted in his conviction that the Slovaks, despite their close cultural ties to the Czechs, would have to find a solution for their national well-being within the framework of the Hungarian state, and that only as a linguistically united nation could they resist magyarization.

Among the younger generation of Czech patriots as well, a reappraisal of Kollár's theories was evident. For many Czechs the oppression of the Poles after 1831 by the "brother Slav" Russians had been a rude awakening.[39] The plight of the Poles and the mounting tension between liberal European opinion and the reactionary Russia of Nicholas I led an increasing number of Czechs to a more realistic assessment of Russia. To be sure, for the older russophile generation of Czech "awakeners" (*buditelé*), such as Jungmann and Hanka as well as Kollár, the Polish situation did not alter their optimistic faith in Slavdom and spiritual allegiance to Russia. But in company with a few outspoken polonophiles, most Czechs became critical of both tsarist Russia and the volatile, self-centered Poles. Their Slavism was increasingly modified to apply primarily to the Habsburg Slavs. This change in outlook was not sudden; rather, it accompanied the growing political maturation of Slav scholars.

In the 1840's in the press and in polemical brochures, this "tactical" Austro-Slav orientation was advanced and debated. In 1842 the Bohemian noble, Count Leo Thun, in a work ostensibly in defense of Czech literature, sought to allay German fears that the Slavs, led by the Czechs, were bent on establishing a universal monarchy. Austria, however, to ensure the continued loyalty of its Slav subjects, should protect their national rights and provide means for the unfettered development of their nationality.[40] In the same year Thun prepared a memorandum for Austrian minister Kolowrat (thought to be more sympathetic to the Slavs than Metternich) in which he outlined his Austro-Slav thesis more candidly. The Czechs, he maintained, were in the forefront of the Slav movement in Austria, and through them influence on the other Slavs could be brought to bear. Prague was the intellectual center of the Slav awakening, but if the Slavs' needs were not heeded they might well turn someday to St. Petersburg or Moscow. To ensure the Slavs' continued loyalty and to make the Czechs even stronger supporters of the monarchy, Czech education at all levels should be established and cultural institutions encouraged so that Prague would remain the center of Slav intellectual activity.[41] In another brochure Thun took up the defense of the Slovaks in Hungary.[42] But his views were ignored by the intransigent Magyars, who considered their language and nationality the only viable one in Hungary. His opinions likewise received short shrift from the German centrist and increasingly inflexible regime in Vienna.

Thun's proposals contained the germ of the Czech Austro-Slav program that moderate liberals like Palacký would champion in 1848: the choice of the "lesser evil"—a constitutionally based, federalized Austria (Thun had not gone that far)—as a haven for the Danubian Slavs and an obstacle to Greater German and Russian expansionist designs.[43]

A fundamental tenet of belief among Austro-Slav proponents was that the Slavs comprised a clear majority of the population of the Habsburg monarchy. This argument was repeatedly advanced not only by Slav publicists but by some German writers as well, possibly in the hope of awakening their conationals to the "Slav danger." Such convictions flourished in the absence of any reliable ethnographic statistics by Austrian officialdom and contributed to the optimism, in some instances the arrogance, of Slav writers.[44]

One Czech who converted dramatically from an optimistic Pan-Slav to a skeptical Austro-Slav outlook was the journalist Karel Havlíček.[45] His lengthy personal encounter with Poland and Russia had "extinguished the last spark of Pan-Slav lore." In what he termed a "declaration of war" on the advocates of a unitary Slavdom, he rejected the idea that the Slavs comprised one nation. Challenging the fundamental precept of romantic nationalism, Havlíček charged that "nationality is determined not only by language but also by customs, religion, form of government, state of education, [and] sympathies," all of which rendered Poles and Russians "alien to us Czechs." The true sentiments of the Poles and Russians were not brotherly affection for their fellow Slavs, and nowhere was this more evident than in their shared rapacity toward the Ukrainians. In a passage that presaged Czech Austro-Slav policy in 1848, Havlíček contended that "only between the Czechs and Illyrians can there be more far-reaching sympathies, because under the present circumstances one cannot be dangerous to the other but on the contrary useful. The Austrian Monarchy is the best guarantee for the preservation of our and the Illyrian nationality, and the greater the power of the Austrian empire grows, the more secure our nationalities will be."[46]

Havlíček wrote as a nationally conscious Czech whose primary purpose was to caution his compatriots against an uncritical faith in dubious allies. Adam Mickiewicz had similarly warned the Poles in his polemical exchanges with Kollár and Thun. From the forum of the Collège de France in Paris, where he had been appointed to the newly established chair in Slavic Literatures, Mickiewicz inveighed against Kollár's naïve russophilism. Kollár, who had first sought Mickiewicz's friendship, now described him contemptuously as "that Polish defiler of reciprocity from Paris" ("ten nevzájemník z Paříže").[47] Mickiewicz also chastised Leo Thun's fidelity to an Austria which could not be trusted to protect the smaller Slav nations. The Czechs, Mickiewicz counselled (in a letter to Thun sent through the intermediacy of František Zach), should devote less energy to Austrian loyalism and more toward acquiring their own political freedom.[48]

The Poles' antipathy to Austria turned into bitter resentment in 1846 when the Galician peasantry (Polish-speaking peasants of Western Galicia, not Ukrainians as is often alleged) rose against their Polish masters— apparently encouraged by Habsburg officials—and aided Austrian troops in suppressing an abortive Polish uprising.[49] The Galician massacres also accentuated Polish mistrust of the Czechs, who were prominently represented in the Galician bureaucracy. The widespread Polish conviction of Austrian complicity in the jacquerie prompted the Polish noble, Margrave Aleksander Wielopolski, to send an open letter to Metternich in which he denounced Austrian duplicity and counselled his compatriots that they would surely fare better with Russia at the head of the resurgent Slav movement than in continuing their futile entreaties for support in the decaying West.[50]

But official Russia remained implacably opposed to the political no less than the literary expression of Pan-Slav ideas. Repression had intensified in 1847 following the discovery of the clandestine Ukrainian Brotherhood of the Saints Cyril and Methodius, led by the Ukrainian poet Taras Shevchenko and the historian Mykola Kostomariv, who had formulated a federalist program for Slav union based on popular representation. Tsarist authorities were particularly disturbed over the large number of teachers involved in the brotherhood. Count Uvarov, Minister of Education, immediately forbade any expression, written or spoken, that advocated the annexation or union of foreign Slavs with Russia.[51]

Restrictions on the travel of Russian scholars to the West were imposed (an endeavor which received official Austrian support), and when in early 1848 the "revolutionary disease" spread across Europe, official Russia redoubled its efforts to impose a "moral quarantine" on its subjects.[52]

vi

On the eve of the revolutionary year 1848 it would be difficult to speak of a unified Slavdom. The gradual politicization of Slav scholars and "awakeners" during the 1830's and 1840's led many away from vague Pan-Slav speculations to more pressing regional and national concerns. As scholars became better acquainted with their fellow Slavs, they discovered not only cultural and linguistic affinities but differences in customs, social conditions, and political outlook. National awakening had drawn the Slavs closer together, but it had also made them aware of their differences.

Even within the Slav linguistic groupings as defined by Kollár, sharp variations emerged: Illyrism fostered Croatian national consciousness but failed to attract the Slovenes and Orthodox Serbs. And Slovak intellectuals, despairing that written Czech could ever raise their people culturally, molded a Slovak literary language. In both instances the codification of a literary language based on the vernacular had defined the limits of a single nationality rather than cementing the communality of related nationalities. In their efforts to make available the learning of the recovered past, Slav scholars had forged the tools which in fact accentuated the differences among the Slavs.

Most Poles after 1831 became suspicious of their fellow Slavs, believing them to be, at worst, in collusion with Poland's enemies and, at best, their unwitting instruments. The Poles judged the Danubian Slavs by their attitude toward Russia. To remove them from tsarist influence and make them useful to the Polish cause, the émigré leader, Prince Adam Czartoryski, supposedly said, "Il faut poloniser le mouvement slave."[53] The program and politics of the smaller West and South Slav nations, however, had been determined largely by their deteriorating relations with their German and Magyar neighbors. In 1848 these different perceptions and national aspirations would be accentuated in an unprecedented tide of political and social unrest.

CHAPTER 2
THE MARCH REVOLUTION

i

The news in late February 1848 of the proclamation of a republic in France and of Louis Philippe's flight abroad sent shock waves across the continent. In the Prussian and Austrian capitals the old order yielded to popular wishes after little more than token resistance. In Vienna the court, hoping to appease the popular mood, readily jettisoned Metternich on March 13, only to be pressed in short order to abolish censorship, sanction a national guard, and permit students to bear arms. But these concessions merely led to greater demands. The universal clamor was for responsible governing institutions, summed up in the watchword, "constitution." Late on the afternoon of March 15 an imperial rescript proclaimed Emperor Ferdinand's intention to "grant" a constitution and convoke as quickly as possible the representatives of the provincial estates. This step sufficed to calm the Viennese crowd and temporarily slow the revolutionary momentum.[1]

Street scenes in Vienna were repeated in the provinces: after a brief intoxication with rallies, parades, and merriment, popular attention focused on Vienna. One after another, Austria's nationalities drafted petitions in the name of their nations and lands and besieged the court and government (once the old administrative apparatus was dismantled and a ministry was appointed) to reaffirm long-standing, but recently moribund, privileges and to establish locally responsible administrative institutions. When some requests met with success, other nationalities escalated their demands. After decades of bureaucratic centralism, centrifugal pressures threatened to disrupt the monarchy.

ii

The Magyars were the first to petition the court successfully. Encouraged by Lajos Kossuth's fiery speech in the Hungarian diet on March 3, which denounced the repressive and obsolete Metternichian system, the Magyar liberals formulated a national program that amounted to full independence for the Hungarian crownland, tied to Austria by only the personal union of the Austrian emperor and Hungarian king. On the very evening—March 15—that the Viennese crowd was acclaiming its "constitutional ruler," the deputation from the Hungarian diet arrived in Vienna. Through the intermediacy of the Royal Palatine for Hungary, Archduke Stephen (who informed the court that the Hungarians might well attempt to secede if their demands were not met), an imperial rescript, hastily issued on March 17, authorized the "loyal" Hungarian Estates to establish a responsible ministry. A government headed by Count Lajos Batthyány was formed, and the Magyar-dominated diet drew up a corpus of legislation which, after prolonged negotiation, was enacted by Ferdinand on April 11.[2] These "April Laws" fundamentally changed the social fabric of Hungary. The abolition of feudal privileges and the broadened franchise speeded the transfer of political power from the old feudal magnates to the middle gentry that had led the reform movement before 1848. A major effect of the April Laws was to legalize the concept of a unitary Hungarian state—a notion dear to the Magyar liberals. In particular, the new legislation reduced Croatia and the Military Frontier to several counties, directly subject to lawmakers and administrators in Pest.

The Magyars hoped to drive a wedge between the subject nationalities and the court in Vienna, which should no longer arbitrate internal Hungarian disputes.[3] Magyar fears of Habsburg meddling were not unfounded. The initial enthusiasm, especially of the Serbs in the Vojvodina and the Slovaks, for the Pest revolution had not passed unnoticed. The court's furtive nomination of Colonel Josip Jelačić as Croatian ban (governor) on March 23 was a case in point. The appointment was initiated by the Illyrian advocate Ljudevit Gaj and Prime Minister Kolowrat, who prevailed on Baron Francis Kulmer (a spokesman for the Croat nobility at court), the Palatine, and the conservative Hungarian magnates who were disaffected by the March events in Pest to secure Jelačić's nomination before the Batthyány government was formally constituted.[4] Jelačić's supporters in Vienna had correctly perceived in him both a rallying point for Croat nationalism and a loyal supporter of the dynasty.[5]

March unquestionably was the high point of the short-lived national fraternization in Hungary; the shared enthusiasm made it all the more difficult for Magyars to comprehend the subsequent turn-about of the subject nationalities. The Magyar liberals had thought that the national question would simply disappear with the promulgation of reform. They reasoned that past differences had stemmed from the archaic political and social institutions that weighed so oppressively on all Hungarian subjects alike. Now, to safeguard the newly gained freedoms from outside danger, it was necessary for all Hungarians to speak and act as one;

political unity must be reinforced by cultural and linguistic cohesion. This view was aptly summed up on April 5 in the liberals' newspaper, *Pesti Hirlap:*

> The prerequisites for the unity of the state are one political nationality and one state language. This language can only be that of the race which has conquered the fatherland by blood and, in its name, acclaimed it loudly throughout Europe. . . . Our citizens of other languages must therefore become Magyars where they are in contact with public institutions.

The author cited France as a model wherein one political language had forged a strong union of different peoples.[6] But the non-Magyar nationalities of the mid-nineteenth century were hardly willing to emulate the fate of earlier generations of Bretons, Burgundians, or speakers of Provençal.

Understandably, the first challenge to the Magyars came from the Croats who, unlike the Vojvodina Serbs and the Slovaks, could point to a long, though flawed, tradition of political autonomy, fostered by a native nobility. The revolution in Hungary evoked little joy among the Croatian liberals, who were locked in a bitter linguistic controversy with Magyar centrists. By the mid-1840's the Illyrian movement, remolded as the Croatian People's Party, had already articulated a national program. The Croats demanded legal sanction for the Croatian language in their affairs, and the union and full autonomy of the triune kingdom of Croatia, Slavonia, and Dalmatia. When the Croatian diet in 1847 unequivocally declared that Croatian (not Latin) was henceforth the official language in the country, the Magyars reacted swiftly. Legislation was drafted in the Hungarian diet to reintroduce Latin as Croatia's official language; but Magyar would have to be taught in Croatian schools and used in all dealings with the Hungarian authorities.[7]

Two days after his nomination by Vienna on March 23, Jelačić was also acclaimed ban by a hastily convened Croatian assembly in Zagreb, the diet not being in session. The assembly also issued a series of national demands, foremost of which was the union of all Croat lands (the triune kingdom plus the Military Frontier and the port city of Rijeka [Fiume]), governed by a ministry independent of Pest.

Few figures in the drama of 1848 have evoked such disparate judgments as Jelačić. Magyar and German radicals denounced him as a vindictive and heartless reactionary, a lackey of the court camarilla and the creature of Windischgrätz, with whom he shared an abiding loyalty to the dynasty. His supporters acclaimed him as the savior of the monarchy. Austro-Slav partisans extolled his leadership, even after his ruthless suppression of radical Vienna in October 1848. In Croatia he has traditionally been lauded as a national hero, an assessment now disputed by Marxist writers.[8] There is no doubt, however, that Jelačić solidified opposition to Magyar radicalism. The court obviously valued his service: in addition to his appointment as ban, Jelačić was promoted to general and, in early April, to field marshal. After the April Laws were passed, Jelačić instructed officials in Croatia to sever all ties with the Hungarian ministry, declared martial law in Croatia, and issued directives for convening a Croatian parliament (sabor) in June. Attempts to reassert control by placing Jelačić under the authority of the Palatine and the Hungarian General Hrabowszky when the court briefly withdrew support, due to its need for Hungarian troops to fight in northern Italy, were consistently resisted.[9] In effect, Jelačić exercised dictatorial powers in Croatia. Every effort at mediation with the Batthyány government failed, due to nationalist intolerance on both sides, and especially because the court camarilla seemed bent on bringing the Magyars to heel militarily.

Unlike the Croats, the Serbs in southern Hungary had lost almost all the national and religious privileges granted them at the turn of the eighteenth century by Emperor Leopold I when the Habsburgs were encouraging resettlement of lands recovered from the Turks. The initial Serb requests were quite moderate: a group in Pest, emboldened by radical gains there, hastily drafted a list of seventeen demands on behalf of the Serbian nation. Though acknowledging the primacy of the Magyar nationality and language in Hungary, they insisted on formal recognition of Serbian nationality, the unrestricted use of their tongue, religious equality and freedom of worship for the Orthodox faith, and a Serbian national assembly with direct access to the king.[10] These demands were sharply criticized in the Magyar press and, by order of the Pest Committee for Public Safety, their publication was banned.[11]

A similar series of Serbian demands drafted by a popular assembly in Novi Sad was summarily rejected by the Hungarian diet in Bratislava.[12] The Magyar liberals were particularly incensed at the Serbs' insistence on dealing directly with the monarch. Djordje Stratimirović, who headed the Serbian delegation to Bratislava and only weeks earlier had ostentatiously displayed the Hungarian cockade, got into a heated argument with Lajos Kossuth on this issue. The Magyar leader rejected out of hand the Serbs' claim to nationhood and threatened that if the nationalities did not desist their meddling they would have to cross swords with the Magyars, a challenge, Stratimirović assured Kossuth, the Serbs would surely not shirk.[13]

This exchange is frequently cited as the turning point in Magyar-Serbian relations. The Magyars were clearly unwilling to extend to Serbs the same rights within Hungary that the Magyars themselves sought from the Habsburgs.[14] Failing to gain redress from the Magyar-dominated diet, the Serbs turned to the Croats and the court. In late April they announced a national congress, which convened on May 13 in Sremski Karlovci. This city, just across the Danube in Croatian Slavonia, was selected in place of Novi Sad because the Hungarian government had declared martial law in the Vojvodina, ostensibly due to peasant disturbances in the wake of the March Revolution.[15] On May 15 the congress issued a ten-point program that declared the Serbs a free nation and the Vojvodina a separate political entity.[16] To solidify this regained independence the congress elevated Metropolitan Josip Rajačić to patriarch and designated Stepan Šuplikac vojvoda (governor), both positions that had long remained unfilled due to Magyar pressures. A significant point in the declaration was the Serbs' wish to see the Vojvodina joined in political union with the triune kingdom. To symbolize the spirit of reconciliation among South Slavs, Rajačić journeyed to Zagreb to take part in the ceremonies installing Jelačić as ban.[17] The Magyars vigorously opposed this demonstration of Serbian independence and dispatched a military force under Hrabowszky to Sremski Karlovci to disperse the rebels.[18]

In contrast to the South Slavs, the Slovak national leadership was fragmented and lacked a common center of political activity.[19] The two best-known Slovak spokesmen, L'udovít Štúr and Ján Kollár, differed sharply over means to enhance national well-being. Kollár, who opposed Štúr's efforts to fashion an independent Slovak literary language, continued to use Czech.[20] No Slovak petition reached the Hungarian diet in March and April, although there were several cases where patriots and local assemblies formulated demands. On March 28 a group in Liptov petitioned the county dietine to permit the use of Slovak in local schools and government bodies. Štúr and his close associate Jozef Miloslav Hurban publicized the Liptov petition and suggested that other Slovak communities follow suit.[21] Although the Slovak requests were largely limited to questions of language rather than political matters, they nevertheless enraged the Magyar authorities. At Batthyány's insistence, the officers of the Liptov dietine, who had accepted and agreed to forward the Slovak demands, were forced to refuse.[22] Other petitions, notably one drafted by Hurban at a popular assembly in the town of Brezová on April 28, were similarly ill fated. In this instance the envoys who conveyed the petition to the authorities were in fact arrested.[23]

As was the case in the Vojvodina, scattered outbreaks of rural violence in Slovakia after the March Revolution were exploited by the Magyars to discredit the national movement and to forbid further public assemblies. But on May 10 a group of Slovak patriots gathered clandestinely in the remote northern Hungarian town of Liptovský Svätý Mikuláš (Liptó-szentmiklós) to draft the first all-Slovak national program. Although insisting on the free use of the national tongue—a feature common to all national programs in 1848—and a measure of local autonomy, the Slovaks conceded the political unity of the Hungarian crownland.[24]

The Magyars, however, made scant distinction between the secessionist agitation by the Croats and Serbs and the "loyal" demands of the Slovaks, which were equally treasonous in the eyes of the Batthyány government. Arrest orders were issued for Štúr and his associates, who were forced to flee their homeland. The Magyars saw in their "Pan-Slav incitement" the handiwork of their main enemies, the Habsburg bureaucracy and reaction- ary Russia. They believed that the Slav nationalities were bent not only on reversing the hard-won revolutionary gains but on obliterating the Hungarian state as well. In such a struggle, the use of extreme measures was more than justified from the Magyar point of view.[25]

iii

As the wave of revolution spread eastward, it rekindled Polish hopes, kept alive through two decades in romantic verse and conspiratorial activities, that their hour of deliverance was finally at hand. The Poles in the Austrian monarchy shared with the Magyars both deep distrust of Habsburg officialdom and fear and loathing for tsarist Russia. Galician Poles still seethed with resentment at what they deemed Austrian complicity in turning Galician peasants against their Polish masters in 1846 to abort a Polish uprising. The failure of the 1831 insurrection in the Congress Kingdom had left Poles convinced that Tsar Nicholas would never willingly countenance the restitution of Polish independence. Since then, Polish patriots had based their aspirations on a common European struggle against Russia.

A principal casualty of 1846 had been the former free city of Kraków, which, following occupation by Prussian and Austrian forces, was formally annexed to Austrian Galicia. When reports of the March demonstration in Vienna reached Kraków, they touched off a popular cry for the release of the 1846 political prisoners. After the emperor proclaimed a general amnesty, Krakśw quickly filled with former prisoners and political émigrés, especially after the Prussian government refused them admittance to Poznań. The radical-minded émigrés assumed a key role in the newly established Krakśw National Committee and began to lay plans for a march into Russian Poland. The anxious Austrians responded by sealing off the city, and when the enraged townspeople began to construct barricades, they were ousted by a prolonged artillery bombardment on April 26. The émigrés were expelled, and Krakśw, subjected to military rule, became the first victim of counterrevolution in 1848.[26]

Lacking telegraphic communication with Vienna, the Galician capital of Lvov was the last provincial center to receive word of Metternich's dismissal and the concessions made by the court. Following the usual scenes of street jubilation, a group of townspeople and Galician nobles drafted a petition to the emperor. Signatures were hastily gathered—including a number from Jews and Ruthenes, although Ukrainian writers maintain that the latter were coaxed.[27] On March 19 the document was conveyed by a large crowd to Galician governor Franz Stadion. When the group's spokesman, Prince Leon Sapieha, began to read the petition in French, presumably for the benefit of the governor, who had met the crowd before the city hall, there were cries demanding that he speak Polish. In addition to the customary demands that Polish replace German in Galician schools, courts, and administrative agencies, the petition raised several political matters, most notably the request that administrative positions as well as high army posts be filled by only native-born Galicians.[28] This was a clear indication of Polish mistrust of the Germans and Czechs who predominated in the Austrian bureaucracy in Galicia.

Distasteful as the Polish demands were to Stadion, he had no recourse but to agree to forward the petition to Vienna. The Lvov Poles decided, however, to reinforce their case by dispatching a delegation to Vienna to convey the petition personally to the emperor. The delegates took several days, stopping off in the towns along the way to distribute copies of the petition, harangue the crowds of well-wishers, and collect additional signatures.[29]

Once in Vienna, the Poles realized the full magnitude of the revolutionary events. And after learning of the Magyars' gains, they escalated their own demands. A new petition was drafted and the Poles were granted an audience with Emperor Ferdinand on April 6. The Poles now asked for full autonomy. A national committee should be authorized to oversee the political and national reorganization of Galicia, and the Poles demanded a national army. In effect the Poles were asking the emperor to acknowledge the injustice of Poland's fate and to repudiate the partitions.[30] The moronic emperor, reading from a text handed him by Austrian Interior Minister Franz Pillersdorff, accepted the petition and promised a speedy reply. Nevertheless, the Poles were made to cool their heels in Vienna for over a month, after which Pillersdorff rejected most of the demands out of hand.[31]

The Galician petitions had contained no reference to the province's Ukrainian populace. The Poles believed that they themselves constituted the sole "political nationality" in Galicia, not unlike the Magyars' attitude in Hungary. The only concession to the Ruthenes in the April 6 petition was an oblique reference that instruction in primary schools be in the prevailing "dialect" of the locality.

It came therefore as a considerable surprise to most Poles when on April 19 a group of Uniate clerics, headed by the Lvov bishop Hrihorii Iakhymovych, submitted a separate petition to the emperor on behalf of the "loyal Ruthenes," who, they alleged, comprised half of Galicia's populace.[32] In marked contrast to the assertive Polish petitions, the Ruthenes opened with an expression of profound gratitude to the emperor, whose benevolent reign had witnessed a "flowering of our [Ruthenian] homeland" since Austria's "revindication" of Galicia. The Uniate clerics were in fact describing the economically most depressed crownland in the monarchy. The Ruthenian requests were limited to language rights and made no reference to the peasant question. The issue of partitioning Galicia administratively into Polish and Ukrainian districts, a plan that the Austrians had toyed with after 1846, was not mentioned, although by June this would be the major plank in the Ukrainians' program.

The newly formed Polish National Council in Lvov countered with a series of paternalistic appeals to their "Ruthenian brothers," alleging that the April 19 petition reflected only the narrow viewpoint of the reactionary Uniate consistory in Lvov.[33] But when these attempts to win over the Ruthenes failed, Polish writers became less conciliatory. In an article on May 9 in the leading Polish newspaper in Lvov, *Dziennik Narodowy*, Józef Supiński derided the presumptuous Ruthenes, whose language, after all, was merely a "rural dialect," a sort of "Polish *patois*."[34] Supiński asked, "Who really is a Ruthene?" He could not be defined only as one who used this Ruthene dialect, certainly, since the high Uniate clerics spoke and wrote Polish among themselves. (This was in fact still the case in early 1848.) And if a Ruthene was one who had been raised on old Ruthenian lands, then practically all Galicians were Ruthenes. Nor did the author believe that religion was sufficient to define nationality just because some Galicians went to the *cerkiew* (Greek Catholic church) and some to the *kościół* (Roman Catholic church). If that were a basis for nationhood, then one would have to talk about a Lutheran *nation* or a Ruthenian *religion*. Sophistic arguments of this stripe appeared throughout 1848 in Polish writings.

The Poles immediately suspected that Governor Stadion was behind the Ruthenian action. The Poles certainly had good cause to mistrust Stadion. Even after censorship had been abolished by Vienna, he obstructed the publishing of Polish newspapers. And when the Poles established a National Council, he instructed officials to have no dealings with it and in fact set up a rival Beirat (advisory council) composed of Austrian officials, conservative Polish magnates, and Uniate priests. The Poles most resented Stadion's preemptive abrogation, in the emperor's name, of peasant servitude, well prior to its official pronouncement, to assure the Galician peasant's loyalty to the dynasty and to upstage a similar emancipation plan by the Poles.[35]

Although the Polish charge, invoked almost as a litany in 1848 and long after, that Stadion actually "invented" the Ruthenes is absurd, there is abundant evidence that he fostered the nascent Ruthenian movement to strengthen the government's hand against the Poles. In a memorandum he sent to Vienna on May 3, Stadion indicated his intention to use the Ukrainians "to paralyze Polish undertakings."[36] The Poles were convinced that Stadion, or possibly his deputy (later, Galician governor), Count Agenor Gołuchowski, first conceived the idea of creating a Central Ruthenian Council (Holovna Rada Rus'ka) in Lvov to rival the Polish National Council.[37] The Ruthenian clergy consulted Stadion regularly on the best course of action and the governor subsidized from state coffers the free distribution in the Ruthenian countryside of the Ruthenian Council's newspaper *Zoria Halytska*.[38]

In an attempt to counteract the influence of the Ruthenian Council and *Zoria Halytska*, a group of polonized Ruthenes, *gente rutheni, natione poloni*, established a rival Ruthenian assembly (Rus'kyi Sobor, in contrast to the Rada Rus'ka of the Uniate clergy) and laid plans to publish their own newspaper. One genuine Ruthene whom they did win over was Ivan Vahylevych, who had been a member of the so-called Ukrainian triad of "national awakeners" in the 1830's. Vahylevych agreed to edit *Dnewnyk Ruskyj*,[39] but the newspaper lasted for only nine issues. The main reason for its failure, aside from its pro-Polish stance, was its use of the Latin alphabet with Polish phonetics for Ukrainian. The Uniate priests who regularly read *Zoria Halytska* to their peasant parishioners, were more accustomed to its modified old Slavonic script.

The main aim of the Polish émigrés who returned from France in March 1848 was to reach the Grand Duchy of Poznań, which had fallen under Prussian rule in the second partition of 1793. Poland's plight evoked considerable sympathy in German liberal circles. One of the most dramatic expressions of this *Polenrausch* (pro-Polish intoxication) was the release from the Moabit prison of the Polish veteran of the abortive 1846 insurrection, Ludwik Mierosławski, to be greeted by a throng of cheering Berliners.[40] A leading supporter of the Poles was the new Prussian foreign minister, von Arnim, who encouraged them to prepare an armed strike across the border into Russian Poland. He strongly intimated that the Poles could count on Prussian and, in all likelihood, French backing in their struggle with Russia.[41]

The Poznań Poles had reacted swiftly to the news of street fighting in Berlin on March 18 and of King Friedrich Wilhelm's bowing to popular demands. A National Committee was quickly formed and on March 20 proclaimed its dedication to the "great and holy goal" of "complete liberation of our Homeland."[42] The committee dispatched to Berlin a deputation headed by Poznań Archbishop Przyłuski to petition the court and government to effectuate the "national reorganization" of the grand duchy. The Prussian army would be confined to the citadels and barracks, and Polish commissioners would supplant the district administrators (*Landräte*). The shaky government in Berlin readily acceded to most of the Polish demands, insisting only that the Poznań Germans share in this reorganization. However, they did refuse to appoint the pro-Polish General Wilhelm von Willisen as royal commissioner to oversee the changes.[43]

But the Polish National Committee already had started to assert administrative control in Poznania. Lacking instructions from Berlin and momentarily intimidated by the Poles' show of strength, the local Prussian officials scarcely resisted. Polish émigrés were returning at such an alarming rate that the French minister in Berlin, de Circourt, reported that Poznania would soon be transformed into "a recruiting center, a training ground, an arsenal, a supply base" for the anticipated Polish strike into Russia.[44]

The local Germans concentrated largely along the province's northern and western fringes, alarmed at such a display of Polish nationalism and incensed at what they believed was their abandonment by Berlin, banded together, often with the connivance of the anti-Polish military commander General Colomb, to form their own voluntary corps.[45] By the first week of April the grand duchy was an armed camp of two hostile national forces, and incidents of violence were common. At this point Berlin relented and dispatched Willisen to Poznań.

Upon arriving in the province on April 5, Willisen realized that before national reorganization could be initiated it was necessary to disarm the warring factions. He reached an understanding with the Poles, known as the Jarosławiec Agreement, which, though reducing their forces under arms by removing irregulars and non-Poznanians, authorized a Polish Poznanian detachment of three thousand men with its own officers, colors, and language of command.[46] In granting a separate Polish force, Willisen overstepped his authority, and this concession, coupled with his expected proclamation of national reorganization (polonization in the eyes of the Poznań Germans), caused the Prussian military to commence its own "pacification" of Polish villages and military camps. Powerless to halt the spread of the fighting, and no longer supported by Berlin, Willisen left Poznania barely a fortnight after his appointment, his mission a failure.[47] The Poles under Mierosławski's command, although vastly outnumbered, successfully resisted several Prussian assaults before capitulating in early May.

In the meantime, on April 14, the king had decreed that "national reorganization" not be carried out in those districts having a German majority. The thorny problem of drawing an ethnic demarcation line was exacerbated by the dilemma the Poznań issue posed for the self-appointed architects in Frankfurt of German unity, because the grand duchy lay outside the boundaries of the German Confederation of 1815. Although the Frankfurt Pre-Parliament (Vorparlament) in March had issued the customary resolution decrying the "shameful injustice" of Poland's partition, its successor, the Committee of Fifty, reacting to prompting from irate Poznań Germans who feared exclusion from the new empire, decided to grant provisional representation to Poznania in the upcoming federal assembly, based on a demarcation line to be worked out by the Prussian government. Although the 1843 census indicated that Poles outnumbered Germans in Poznania by two to one, the Berlin government eventually settled on a line which assigned two-thirds of the province's population and territory, including the fortress and town of Poznań, to the new Germany.[48]

The German liberals had recovered quickly from their March *Polenrausch*. Von Arnim, the Poles' staunchest supporter in March, wrote just a few months later of the need to combat "the perfidious Polish onset" to disrupt the peace in Europe.[49] Betrayed by their erstwhile German supporters, and isolated from their compatriots in Kraków, the Poznań Poles now looked southward toward the Czechs in Austria,[50] who by April had also become embroiled in their own conflict with German nationalism emanating from Frankfurt.

iv

In its initial phase the revolution in Prague developed independently of events in Vienna. The first summons was sounded by a group of young Czech and German radicals, members of Repeal, the clandestine reform society modeled on O'Connell's Irish organization.[51] The Prague "Repealists" called a public meeting for March 11 to review the reforms to be submitted to the emperor. Despite official harassment—Metternich was still in power and the old order as yet unscathed—the gathering drew a large attendance. Prior to the meeting the Czech lawyer, František August Brauner, persuaded the radicals to moderate their social demands to ensure broad middle-class support. In addition to the stock-in-trade liberal tenets of 1848—public lawcourts, a free press, freedom to assemble and petition, religious liberty, and abolition of feudal (*robot*) duties—Brauner's proposal reaffirmed Bohemian state rights (*Staatsrecht*) which central bureaucratic rule from Vienna had increasingly abrogated. He called for the union of the Czech crownlands—Bohemia, Moravia, and Silesia—with a common diet based on broadened suffrage, to meet annually, alternating between Prague and Brno; a central administration for these lands in Prague, staffed by native, bilingual officials; and full equality of Czech and German nationality in schools and public office. The March 11 assembly overwhelmingly endorsed Brauner's draft, and a committee (known as the St. Václav Committee from the location of the meeting) was chosen to convey a final version to Vienna.[52] But when the committee convened on March 13, Brauner's already moderate version of the radicals' program was still further toned down. The passage reasserting Bohemian state rights was now merely a call for a joint meeting of the pre-March Bohemian and Moravian "estates" diets, and the section on abolishing serfdom was only a vague statement on reforming peasant conditions.[53]

Before the committee could complete arrangements to present the petition at court, word reached Prague of Metternich's downfall. The news unleashed such popular excitement that the St. Václav Committee reconsidered the petition, whose tone now seemed too subservient. But, anxious to place its demands before the court quickly, the committee opted to submit both Brauner's draft of March 11 and the watered-down committee version. This ambivalence helps to explain the court's high-handed response to the Prague delegation. The emperor's reply, delivered on March 23 by Interior Minister Pillersdorff, carefully sidestepped Brauner's essential points. The vague and noncommittal answers reaffirmed the already existing arrangements governing the Czech lands.[54]

Not surprisingly, when the delegates returned to Prague on March 27 with the court's reply, there was widespread disappointment and dissatisfaction, especially in the Czech community. The St. Václav Committee decided to prepare a new petition and called on Brauner to reformulate his demands. His new draft differed more in tone than in substance from the earlier version; the language was more emphatic, directly challenging the court's earlier response. The demands of March 11 were reasserted, but the emphasis was now essentially on separate autonomous political institutions for the united Czech crownlands.[55]

The second Prague delegation, composed exclusively of Czechs, found the Vienna government more conciliatory and willing to make real concessions. The intervening weeks since its first reply had seen a dangerous separatist trend in Hungary and Northern Italy, and the embattled government could ill afford disaffection on yet a third flank.[56] The Cabinet Rescript of April 8 granted most of the Czech requests. Only the demand for union with Moravia and Silesia was denied, the government insisting that this step could only be undertaken by the forthcoming imperial parliament, in which all three crownlands would be represented. The rescript did agree to convene a new Bohemian diet not based on the old estates, and granted Bohemia a separate administration (though not a responsible ministry as in Hungary). Particularly important to the Czechs was the passage stipulating full autonomy of the Czech language with German in all administrative and educational facilities.[57]

If the Cabinet Rescript of April 8 represented the highwater mark of Bohemia's political gains in 1848,[58] it also symbolized the breach between Bohemia's Czech and German liberals who in March had cooperated in formulating political demands. The second petition, with its accent on restoring Bohemian *Staatsrecht* and affirming equal rights to the Czech language, caused considerable anxiety among Bohemia's Germans. The calls for German unity issuing from Frankfurt gave them heart, since Bohemia's Germans had momentarily been startled into silence and acquiescence by the sudden display of Czech political initiative. Even while the second Prague delegation awaited a reply in Vienna, a group of Sudeten Germans there submitted a counter petition to Pillersdorff on behalf of their compatriots in Bohemia, Moravia and Silesia, who, they maintained, comprised over a third of the population and by whose "intelligence and industry" alone these lands had prospered. The Sudeten Germans vehemently protested any separation of their homeland from the other Austro-German provinces. Although not specifically mentioning Frankfurt, they called for the *Anschluss* of these territories to Germany.[59]

It is noteworthy that the two individuals most often identified with the Czech national movement in 1848, František Palacký and Karel Havlíček, played little part in the petition campaigns. Both in fact entered the national spotlight largely as a result of their bold resistance to Frankfurt. Palacký's celebrated reply of April 11 to Frankfurt, rejecting the offer of membership in the Committee of Fifty, symbolized the determination of Austria's Slavs to resist the inclusion of their homelands in a German national state. In Palacký's judgment, only an independent, federally structured, and politically reformed Austrian state could protect the smaller Slav nations—positioned between obscurantist tsardom and an alien German nationalist movement—from absorption by these stronger neighbors. For Austria to merge with Germany was in fact asking Austria to commit suicide and the Slavs to forego their quest for national equality.[60] Here, then, was the first political application of Austro-Slavism that had evolved from pre-March cultural Pan-Slavism.

Already in March Havlíček had offended German sensitivities with a brash call in the press for Czech merchants to replace the German signs in their shops with Czech ones. But when this unleashed indignant protests, he modified his request to bilingual signs. Later, in April and May, as editor of the first Czech national newspaper, *Národní Nowiny,* Havlíček led the opposition to holding elections to Frankfurt in the Czech lands.[61]

The Czechs' refusal to share in the forging of a greater Germany provoked first dismay, then bitterness and contempt in German nationalist circles. In an attempt to convert the obstinate Czechs, the Committee of Fifty dispatched a mission to Prague in late April. By their own account, the Frankfurt representatives—Ignaz Kuranda, a native of Bohemia and editor of the Leipzig weekly journal *Die Grenzboten,* and Karl von Wächter, a South German liberal—were shocked by the change in the Bohemian capital. The familiar German city had been transformed into a strange and hostile Slav encampment, where Germans seemingly feared to express their national convictions.[62] On April 29 the Frankfurt delegates met with the Czech leaders in the foreign affairs section of the National Committee. (This body had evolved from the March St. Václav Committee, less many of the German members who had withdrawn over the second petition.) The delegates based their case for full representation in Frankfurt on Bohemia's long-standing tie to the Germanic Confederation and earlier Roman empire. The Czechs calmly refuted this historical claim, but when Ernst Schilling, an Austrian member of the Frankfurt Committee and a rabid Pan-German, unexpectedly joined the meeting, a heated debate ensued. In Schilling's opinion, the "Austrian patriotism" that Palacký espoused was delusory: "Austria would certainly disintegrate if it failed to remain German." In a clear affront to the Czech patriots, Schilling charged that "Prague was a completely German city, both in its spirit and learning. Czech literature was incapable of advancing the cause of liberty, for this concept was alien to the Slavs." If the Czechs sincerely desired freedom, then they must join with Germany. Schilling's claim to a "German monopoly of the principle of freedom" incensed the Czechs, and the acrimonious exchange broke off without issue.[63] The Germans returned to Frankfurt convinced that the recalcitrant Czechs, led by the "fanatic historian [Palacký] and his impetuous followers," were bent on turning Austria into a hostile Slav empire.[64] Soon after this meeting the last Germans withdrew from the National Committee in Prague, which had in effect already assumed a Czech national character.[65]

v

The Slovenes, spread over several crownlands in Southern Cisleithania, lacked a unified national movement in 1848. Only in Carniola did the Slovenes comprise a clear majority; in Styria and Carinthia they were outnumbered two to one by German-speakers. In the spring of 1848, Slovene national initiative actually arose outside Slovene-inhabited territories per se, in Graz and Vienna, and only later in the year did Ljubljana become the leading Slovene national center.[66] Although the Slovenes could not match the Czechs' zeal in thwarting the Frankfurt elections, their boycott was partially successful in Southern Styria and Carniola.[67]

Unlike the Czechs, the Slovenes could not fall back on historic rights to base their national program; instead, early in 1848, Slovene spokesmen advocated replacing historical crownland frontiers by new lines based on ethnic claims. In an address of April 22 to the emperor, the Graz Slovenija society made this its first point: "The abolition of the historical crownland frontiers and the union of our Slovene territories according to linguistic boundaries into one land and one nation."[68] The court, however, had no intention of acceding to such a radical revamping of its territories (not even later at the Kroměříž Reichstag), and paid little

heed to the Slovenes or even to the moderate Slovenija society in Ljubljana, which limited its demands to linguistic rights and the creation of
national cultural institutions.[69]

vi

It was hardly surprising that the February Revolution in Paris had
spread into central Europe. The cracks in the old system were apparent,
and Metternich's grip on affairs quickly weakened when unrest and dissatisfaction intensified at the news from Paris. What the liberals had not
anticipated, however, and what is still fascinating with 1848 in central
Europe, was the suddenness with which political aspirations were over-
taken and swallowed up by the unprecedented tide of national sentiment
and chauvinism. Within weeks of Metternich's fall, the initial enthusiasm
of Slavs and non-Slavs who had celebrated together in the streets of
Vienna, Prague, Berlin, and Poznań dissolved into suspicion and recrimination. What Lewis Namier so aptly termed the "acid nationalisms"
of 1848 was the real specter that haunted Europe.[70]

Within a remarkably short time , two hostile axes crisscrossed central
Europe: one running from Frankfurt in the west through Vienna and
Pest; the other from Poznań in the north through Prague to Zagreb. The
first line joined the liberal and radical advocates of greater German unity
and Magyar independence; the second, the Slavs seeking to escape German
and Magyar hegemony and distant bureaucratic rule. To the east the
Galician Poles, torn between the Slavs and Magyars and ignoring the
province's Ruthenes, clung to their hope of restoring Polish independence.

This atmosphere of mounting enmity engendered the Slavs' search for
a common program to ensure their national well-being. To trace the
genesis of the Slav congress, we turn our attention to Vienna, where the
various Slav delegations converged with their grievances.

PART 2

THE CONGRESS

L'Autriche est évidemment en voie de décomposition, mais les Slaves spécialement sentent la nécessité de se rapprocher pour n'être pas dévorés, soit par la Russie, soit par l'Allemagne.

—František Zach to Prince Adam Czartoryski,
June 9, 1848

i

In the capital the Slav delegations were warmly received by the Viennese Slav community. Prior to the March Revolution the Vienna Slavs had enjoyed an active social life. An array of national clubs and societies arranged social gatherings, concerts, and theatrical performances. Large numbers often gathered at the Sperl hall in the city's Leopoldstadt suburb. After one festive occasion on November 6, 1847, a Czech visitor, František Ladislav Rieger, noted in his diary that the flower of Viennese Slavdom had been present. Among the guests were the family of the Russian Prince Trubetskoi; the young Czartoryskis; Michael Obrenović, the son of Serbian Prince Miloš; the Serb bard Vuk Karadžić; and M.F. Raevskii, the cultural emissary attached to the Russian embassy in Vienna.[1]

An air of heady excitement accompanied the arrival of the delegations in Vienna.[2] There, for the first time, Slavs met as political spokesmen of their respective nations and shared viewpoints on the burgeoning issues of the day. On Sunday, April 2, several thousand Slavs gathered at the Sperl for an evening of speechmaking, singing, and earnest discussion.[3] Galician Polish, Czech, Slovak, Croat, and Serb representatives were present. Observers agreed that the evening reached a high point when the Slovak L'udovít Štúr addressed the gathering. Decrying the "diabolical policies" that sought to foment discord, Štúr urged the Slavs to reconcile their differences and assist one another in the common struggle for just national rights: "When we join forces in this way, bind ourselves together, then no one can resist us, and our enemies will drop in fear and terror." The Moravian Jan Ludmil Stájský felt his "heart bursting" with gladness as he followed Štúr's words: late in the evening when the guests departed, "each [left] with a feeling of pride in being a Slav."[4]

In private conversations Štúr reportedly let it be known that the Slovaks were prepared to break with Hungary and join with their brother Czechs and Moravians.[5] Štúr's Pan-Slav stance was also noticed in Viennese anti-Slav circles. An Austro-German reporter charged that "Russian money and influence" were contributing to the unrest among the Slavs, and that Štúr's earlier differences with the Czechs over a literary Slovak language had been merely a pretence: now Štúr fancies that the Slovaks would prefer death to continuing under Magyar oppression and openly calls on his people to unite with the Czechs.[6] In fact, Štúr's wish to draw closer to the Czechs did not actually mean that the Slovaks were prepared to sever all ties with the Hungarian crown. His position was clarified shortly after in his Bratislava newspaper, *Slovenskje Národňje Novini:* despite the Magyars' persistent efforts to spread dissension, the Slovaks still trusted that an understanding could be reached with Magyar ruling circles.[7]

Although the individual Slav delegations had arrived in Vienna with their own regional and national demands foremost in their minds (the Poles in particular had given scant thought to the problems besetting their fellow Slavs in a monarchy), the Sperl meeting on April 2 had deepened interest in further inter-Slav exchanges. The Viennese police, charged with keeping an eye on the Polish delegates in particular, became alarmed over the mounting Slav patriotism shown at these meetings. A report to the minister of interior on April 6 foresaw that "Shortly we will be locked in a life and death struggle with a Pan-Slav movement that embraces Russia and that fosters separatism from Germany and an uprising of Slavs in Hungary."[8]

As the delegates awaited replies to their petitions, they had ample opportunity to continue their discussions. The initiative came especially from the Hungarian Slovaks and Croats, for in early April the most immediate threat to the Slavs still lay with the Magyars, not the Germans.[9] An important meeting of Slovak, Croatian, and Galician Polish spokesmen was held on April 7 at the Sperl to determine the Polish attitude on the Hungarian question. Although traditional Polish sympathy for the Magyars was well known, Polish cooperation was imperative if accord were to be reached. By all accounts the discussions were both frank and inconclusive.[10] When the Croats and Slovaks reproached the Poles for flirting with the Magyars, the Galician Floryan Ziemiałkowski retorted that Polish sympathy for the Magyars was of long standing and was deeply rooted in the similar social and political heritage of the two nations. The Poles should not be asked to choose between the Magyars and the Hungarian Slavs. If war with Russia developed—and Ziemiałkowski believed this was a certainty—the Poles surely must seek support among the Magyars and Germans. A break with the Magyars would be political folly for the Poles. The Croats obviously were not impressed with this reasoning. Recalling the meeting in his memoirs, Ziemiałkowski sensed the mistrust of Ljudevit Gaj, who merely shook his head in silence during the discussion.[11]

Ziemiałkowski's remarks on Štúr were particularly unflattering: "[He is] a typical representative of our good-hearted neighbors—straightforward and naïve as a child."[12] Elsewhere in his memoirs Ziemiałkowski was more candid on the subject of the dilemma that the Hungarian question posed for many Poles: "Our situation with respect to the Slavs is dreadful. Broadly speaking, it is very hard to sympathize with them. What sympathy have they shown us? The Magyars have never sought to hide theirs. . . . We can be certain of the Hungarians, . . . but we still don't know whether the Slavs will support us. And even if they wish to assist, what would come of their intentions? They themselves are powerless."[13]

On that same day the Galician Poles also met with the Czechs, who feared that a separatist movement by the Galician Poles would impair the security of all Slavs in the monarchy. The most assurance that the Poles were prepared to give, at least for the time being, was that they would continue to work within the Austrian framework.[14]

Not all Galician Poles shared Ziemiałkowski's antipathy for the Slav movement. Prince Jerzy Lubomirski, who had studied in Prague in the 1830's, and Karol Malisz, a Lvov lawyer, had close acquaintances among the Czechs and had helped in arranging the Vienna meetings. Yet in all probability, their pro-Slav sentiments reflected a minority attitude in the Galician delegation.[15] When another meeting was called for April 12, Ziemiałkowski insisted that "we shall attend [only] privately."[16] He did not wish to convey the impression that the Galician Polish delegation as a whole endorsed these exchanges. However, the arrival in Vienna on April 13 of representatives from the Polish National Committee (Komitet Narodowy) in Poznań had the immediate effect of broadening the Polish discussions. The Poznanian Poles were concerned foremost with halting German national designs on their province and had little sympathy for the conservative social policies of many of their Galician compatriots. On the Hungarian question they joined in urging Polish mediation between the Magyars and the Hungarian Slavs.[17]

The Vienna setting had allowed the Slavs to meet informally and exchange views on a variety of problems affecting their national well-being and political aspirations. While no consensus was reached, a determined effort had been initiated to overcome narrow regional and national interests. Although there is no evidence that the idea of a congress of Slavs was aired publicly at this time, the possibility may have been raised in private.

ii

The first formal suggestion for a Slav congress came from Croatia. Writing in Gaj's newspaper, *Novine Dalmatinsko-Hervatsko-Slavonske,* on April 20, Ivan Kukuljević-Sakcinski charted specific guidelines for political cooperation among the Slavs.[18] Kukuljević, a member of Gaj's Illyrian circle, had accompanied Gaj to Vienna in late March and had taken part in the inter-Slav discussions.

Kukuljević prefaced his proposal by urging the Slavs to follow the example of the Germans and Italians, who were striving to unite their co-nationals in a single political body. Just as the Germans were calling representatives to Frankfurt, so leading Slav spokesmen should meet together in a common assembly. Such a gathering might be an effective counterweight to the aggressive national policies issuing from Pest and Frankfurt. The different languages and states that divided the Slavs should not deter them. He proposed a meeting of Slavs living in the Russian, Ottoman, and Austrian empires and those from Serbia and the German lands. He further suggested that such an assembly would be best held in Prague. Finally, he reminded the Austrian Slavs that they must continue to recognize and, if necessary, defend the ruling Habsburg dynasty. In return for their loyalty, the Slavs had every right to expect concessions.[19]

Before Kukuljević's proposal could reach Prague, steps were already being taken there to convene a congress of Slavs. The guiding figure in developing the congress idea was L'udovít Štúr. Following the Vienna meetings Štúr went to Prague to put his case for inter-Slav cooperation before the Czech leaders; in his native Slovakia Štúr was no longer allowed to speak freely.[20] He reached Prague on April 20 and that same evening met with members of the Czech student association Slavia.[21] The following day the students staged a public burning of the 1846 anti-Slovak pamphlet sponsored by the Czech museum at the height of the linguistic quarrel over written Slovak.[22] Smoothing over this earlier controversy, it was hoped, would facilitate Štúr's efforts to win the Czechs to the congress idea.

Štúr's work received the support of several influential Slav enthusiasts in Prague: Dr. Josef Frič, a Prague lawyer, and his student son Josef Václav Frič; Vilém Gauč, a leader of the pre-March political association Repeal; Witalis Grzybowski, a Galician Pole and lecturer in Polish at Prague University; Jan Petr Jordan, a Lusatian writer and editor of the Leipzig journal Slawische Jahrbücher; and, surprisingly, Štúr's old opponent in the linguistic quarrel, Karel Havlíček.[23] Štúr's dominant role in developing sentiment for the congress in Prague was evidenced as early as April 22 in a letter that Dr. Frič sent to the Czech writer F.L. Čelakovský in Wrocław: "Štúr is still in Prague; all has been won and the otherwise frightful beast of Pan-Slavism is taking on the most lovely appearance."[24] The younger Frič was even more enthusiastic in his praise of

Štúr: "[The Czechs] could not long resist the eloquence of our L'udovít; in short order he succeeded in captivating them for the long-yearned-for Slav theme."[25]

While Štúr was soliciting backing in Prague, encouragement for a Slav assembly reached Prague from Polish Poznania. On April 23 Jędrzej Moraczewski, acting at the behest of the Polish National Committee, wrote to a Czech acquaintance, František Brauner, reminding him of an earlier conversation in which both had expressed a desire to serve the Slav cause. Such a time had now come: "My dear Doctor; take this matter to heart. . . . Choose some city where, without obstructions, we could hold a [Slav] assembly. From among us Poles many will attend and we hope that we will encounter in you [Czechs] our true brothers."[26] Moraczewski suggested that Czechs, Poles, Moravians, Illyrians, and Serbs should attend, and hoped that the Hungarian Slovaks and "some Ruthenes" might be there also. His démarche came at a time when the Prussian government was proceeding with plans to partition Poznania to the disadvantage of the Poles. The Poznanian initiative seems to have been independent of the measures undertaken by Kukuljević and Štúr. It is not known, however, what bearing, if any, Moraczewski's proposal had on the congress plans in Prague. In his brief account of the congress, Moraczewski claimed to have received a favorable reply to his letter to Brauner, through there is no trace of this alleged answer. Moraczewski also credited himself with the main responsibility for initiating the congress.[27] His overture was clearly designed to secure broad Slav support against German encroachments. He made no reference to the Magyars, nor did he envisage a gathering limited to Austrian Slavs.

In Prague, Štúr also emphasized the need to impress upon the Germans, especially those now gathering in Frankfurt, the Slavs' determination to defend their national welfare. By April 29, talk of convening a Slav congress had become widespread in Prague. Count Josef Matyáš Thun learned of the idea at the rancorous meeting between the foreign affairs section of the Bohemian National Committee and the deputation from the Frankfurt Committee of Fifty, which had shown how deep was the gulf between the German and Slav points of view.[28]

In Prague the groundwork was being laid for the favorable reception of the congress plans. On April 29 and 30 Havlíček's influential *Národní Nowiny* carried articles by Vilém Dušan Lambl exhorting the Slavs not to shrink from the idea of Pan-Slavism: they should be prepared to carry "the holy idea of Slav reciprocity" into the political arena. Only in common struggle could Slavs hope to right the injustices they had suffered at foreign hands: from "the vulgar Magyar in their midst, the barbarous

Tartar in the East, the arrogant Turk to the South, and the shameless German to the West." Lambl reminded the Slavs of their numerical hegemony in the Habsburg empire and urged a close union of all Austrian Slavs.[29]

Prague was a natural site for a gathering of Slavs. The city had been a center of the Slav re-awakening. Slav scholars had chosen Prague as a place to study, conduct their researches, and publish their findings. Indeed, a mythology had grown up about Prague as a citadel of Slav history and culture. The Slovene-Illyrian Stanko Vraz, writing in 1844 to a Czech acquaintance, K.J. Erben, extolled this city "where, from each street, each palace and home, yes each stone, Slav history speaks forth in golden tongues and in which. . . Slav reciprocity, accompanied by a genial erudition, ascends to its golden throne."[30] From a practical standpoint the city stood at the communications crossroads for the West and South Slavs.

Students of the Slav Congress have differed sharply in weighing the various individual contributions to the congress idea. Nationally minded historians have invariably overrated the roles of their own compatriots.[31] Of the three men—Kukuljević, Štúr, and Moraczewski—who specifically proposed the convening of a congress, only Štúr actively pursued the idea. Throughout April it was he whose name was most often associated with the advocacy of Slav political cooperation. In Prague Štúr worked tirelessly to solicit effective backing for his plan. It was hardly coincidental that, on the evening of April 29 when several men gathered to discuss plans for a congress in Prague, Štúr was called upon to draft the announcement. The responsibility, however, does not rest with one person alone. The initiative came from several quarters but was linked by a common insistence on the need for the Slavs "to deliberate [forthwith] the means whereby their subjugators in Pest and Frankfurt could most easily, quickly, and surely be confronted."[32]

iii

Preparations for a Slav congress were formally launched on Sunday morning, April 30, at a meeting of prominent Czech intellectuals and political leaders. Kukuljević's article, which appeared that same morning in Czech translation in *Národní Nowiny,* was read and enthusiastically discussed. Štúr presented his draft of an announcement that was tentatively adopted, after a brief debate, contingent on the endorsements of Palacký and Šafařík as well as representatives of the pro-Czech Bohemian nobility.[33] Baron Jan Neuberg immediately informed Šafařík, who was in

Vienna, of these developments. Neuberg's remarks echoed the sentiment of "a nucleus of reliable patriots" in Prague. The immediate danger was to Austria, not just to the Slavs. A new force must be fashioned to save Austria, and "this force can only be found among the Slavs. . . . The congress will establish a strong counterweight to Germany. [It] must guarantee the integrity of Austria and the Slav nationality [and] provide a solution advantageous to the Slavs and Austria for the important and difficult Polish question."[34]

At another meeting that afternoon, a committee was selected to guide the preparations.[35] From the outset this Preparatory Committee was dominated by the politically cautious Czech liberals. The several Bohemian aristocrats on the committee lent prestige but added to the overall conservatism.[36] Although Štúr had not been elected to the committee, he continued to attend its meetings until he left Prague on May 7.

The following day, May 1, the Preparatory Committee broached the controversial question of the congress' composition. Karol Malisz, representing the Galician Poles, hoped the Poles would be permitted to participate fully. The Czechs' answer was: "We must stand firm on the principle of preserving Austria."[37] No agreement was reached, and the committee decided to await word from Šafařík before proceeding. This brief exchange foreshadowed the major debate over Polish participation later in the month.

Šafařík's reply was read at the next committee meeting on May 2. He insisted that non-Austrian Slavs should not be specifically invited in the announcement, although they could attend as guests. The committee should also issue a separate statement on the Slavs' loyalty to Austria. In its original form the announcement "could be interpreted as Pan-Slavism of the worst kind." Šafařík had discussed the matter at length with Minister Pillersdorff, who was concerned over the reaction the congress would provoke in the Austro-German community.[38]

On the basis of Šafařík's suggestions, Štúr's original wording was altered to provide a clearer Austro-Slav direction to the congress. Štúr's closing sentence, "We attest that all other Slavs living outside our empire are cordially welcomed to our gathering, at which, we earnestly urge and fervently trust, they will participate in all our meetings," was changed to read, "Should other Slavs living outside our empire wish to share our company, they will be sincerely welcomed as guests."[39] The committee then formally approved the text and agreed to prepare copies in Czech, German, Polish, Illyrian (Serbo-Croat), and Lusatian.

In its final form the announcement briefly stated the considerations which moved the Slavs to join in common assembly.[40] Ignorance and particularism, which had so long divided the Slavs and contributed to their misfortunes, were yielding to a recovered awareness of their common heritage. But recent actions by their neighbors now raised new dangers, foremost of which was the attempt of the Frankfurt assembly to join the non-Hungarian Habsburg lands to a new Germanic empire. "Such a step would destroy not only the unity of Austria, but also the affinity and independence of its Slav peoples." To counter this threat the signatories invited all Austrian Slavs "possessing the trust of their peoples. . .to assembly in the venerable Slav and Czech city of Prague on May 31."

Surprisingly, the announcement made no mention of the Magyar threat to the Slavs. It was addressed as much to official Vienna (a tactical necessity which Šafařik repeatedly emphasized in his letters from Vienna), whose acquiescence the Czech leaders deemed necessary, as to the Slavs themselves. Its formulation was couched in guarded terms to secure the broadest possible support. The task of developing both a format and an agenda for the congress would have to be worked out by the Preparatory Committee.

Debate in the committee meeting on May 3 arose first over the form of the congress. Palacký thought small private sessions would be best, but the Czech writer Jan E. Vocel favored the looser organizational pattern of the pre-March German academic and scientific conferences.[41] Eventually, the committee again followed Šafařik's advice. He proposed two types of sessions that would function jointly—round-table meetings of the principal national groupings: (1) Bohemians, Moravians, and Slovaks; (2) Poles; and (3) South Slavs; and general sessions for all participants. For the latter he foresaw the possibility that a non-Slav language, either German or Latin, might have to be used.[42]

At their May 3 meeting the committee belatedly chose its officers. Count Josef Matyáš Thun, a leading supporter among the Bohemian nobility of the Czech cultural revival, would serve as chairman, with Baron Neuberg acting as vice-chairman. The committee chose the Czech writer and former Austrian official in Galicia, Karel Vladislav Zap, to handle the secretariat.[43]

Further communications from Šafařik enlarged on his conversations with Pillersdorff—now minister-president. Pillersdorff was particularly anxious over the possible attendance of "foreign Slavs," a prospect that caused him to exclaim: "So Russians too!" Šafařik believed that Pillersdorff would not raise major objections as long as the congress did not become the occasion for an Austro-German counter-demonstration. For this reason Šafařik reiterated that an open invitation to non-Austrian

Slavs "could produce a calamity." Prague would be inundated by "German irregulars [*Freischaaren*] from Vienna. . . . Privately, by letter, we can invite foreign Slavs. . . , even Russians, and then, at the opening of the congress, announce in the press that they are there as guests." Šafařik concurred that "a couple of old Bohemian aristocratic signatures [on the announcement] would have a positive effect."[44]

In another letter Šafařik urged the Preparatory Committee to issue simultaneously with the announcement an explanation to the Austro-Germans and Magyars regarding the Slavs' intentions that would emphasize:

(1). . . our loyalty to the dynasty and our unalterable determination to remain in the Austrian Empire [despite] public accusations in the Germanic press of Pan-Slavism, separatism, and Russianism;

(2). . . that we do not desire to oppress any nation in Austria smaller than ourselves, but to preserve vigilantly equal rights [for all] in accordance with the principle of justice;

(3). . . that we wish to maintain in their entirety the rights of Slav nationalities which are constitutionally guaranteed to our people, to defend ourselves when necessary against the attacks of our opponents with all our strength, and that we desire to consult together on means to achieve these goals.[45]

The committee readily adopted Šafařik's proposal, and an appropriate statement was drafted by Palacký. However, when the Pole Grzybowski asked to have the Austrian emphasis played down "if [the committee] did not want all Poles to stay home," Count J.M. Thun replied, "Then let them stay home."[46]

Although he closely followed Šafařik's outline, Palacký concluded with his own candid assessment of the Slavs' aims:

Thus our national independence and unity can only be served by the continuance of the integrity and sovereignty of the Imperial Austrian state. It is evident that this entire endeavor is of an essentially conservative nature and presents nothing that should disturb in the slightest our just and liberal [*freisinnig*] non-Slav fellow citizens.[47]

Palacký's *Erklärung* was widely publicized in the non-Slav press.[48] But whereas this disclaimer of hostile intentions helped to reassure cautious officials in Prague and Vienna, it aroused further suspicions of a Slav conspiracy among the Austro-German nationalists.

Nevertheless, Neuberg glibly informed Šafařík on May 6 that Palacký's statement "should paralyze any talk of Pan-Slavism." Unfortunately, not all of Šafařík's recommendations had been followed. "The announcement," Neuberg regretted, "stemmed from the pen of Štúr, and not from . . . Palacký." But should Šafařík see fit to return from Vienna, "the direction [of the congress preparations] would be placed in his hands."[49] With his letter Neuberg enclosed a statement of his own which he planned to address to "Austria's Eighteen Million Slavs." Neuberg's appeal, like the earlier announcement, cited only the threat to the Slavs from the German west and urged the Slavs to dispatch their finest representatives to the Prague congress. Speaking to the Slavs, Neuberg never doubted that "your hearts are beating for a great constitutional Austria. . . . Austria is in danger, [and] you must save her; Austria must be more firmly rooted [and] secured from foreign domination."[50] Palacký also reassured Šafařík that his recommendations were receiving careful attention. But Palacký doubted that the pressure of other affairs would permit him to devote much time to the congress preparations.[51]

From his vantage point in Vienna, Šafařík continued to deluge the Preparatory Committee with suggestions. The committee must see to housing arrangements for the delegates. It should avoid the word "Pan-Slavism," which was easily misunderstood; it was better to speak of "Slavdom." Regarding individuals to be invited, Šafařík believed they should have a mandate from a Slav organization if they were not personally known to the organizers. Under no circumstances should Jews be invited. Šafařík hoped the committee would be specific on this point. In his opinion, "Jews failed to constitute a nation in the true sense of the term because they neither possess land nor work as farmers or soldiers— which are the fundamental criteria of nationhood." Šafařík's anti-Semitic views were shared by many Slav intellectuals, who associated the Jews with German interests. In another letter to Neuberg he charged that "Jews had taken control of the German press and German politics." Viennese press reports of recent disturbances in Prague greatly disturbed Šafařík. Were the congress actually to be convened, it was absolutely necessary that "peace and order" be maintained in Prague.[52]

iv

By May 10 Šafařík could write that the congress announcement was attracting considerable attention in Vienna. "The Russian minister," he had learned, "was [already] making discreet inquiries."[53] As news of the congress plans reached Vienna, the strident hostility toward the Slavs in the Viennese press, which Šafařík noted with increasing alarm in his letters to Prague, erupted in an outpouring of contempt and denunciation.[54] But, Šafařík wrote his wife Julia, "it was still not so bad that the Slavs here might have to flee."[55] The radical daily, *Die Constitution,* which Šafařík singled out for its "enraged" stance, greeted the announcement with an article ominously entitled "Pan-Slavism at the Threshold." Its author, a certain Dr. Franck, concluded that the only alternative to Austria's *Anschluss* with greater Germany would be "slavization."[56] A similar conviction was expressed in a series of articles in the *Oesterreichisch deutsche Zeitung:* there were but two avenues open to the Austrian Germans—the Germany being molded in Frankfurt, or Slav domination. The correspondent urged his readers to ponder "Germanic Prague"; what was happening there was a foretaste of Vienna's fate if the Slavs succeeded.[57]

The principal object of German anger was Palacký. On May 8 the Austrian government offered him the portfolio of Education. Although he eventually refused the appointment, news of the offer raised furious protests in the Viennese press. Minister-President Pillersdorff was accused of patronizing the congress plans and of flirting with the politically ambitious Slavs.[58]

In the Ministerial Council the matter of the Slav Congress was first raised on May 10 by the Minister of War, Count Latour.[59] The following day, Pillersdorff, in an inquiry to the newly appointed governor of Bohemia, Count Leo Thun, voiced his concern that the Slavs' desire for equality might develop into a more aggressive move to secure hegemony within Austria at the expense of the non-Slavs. Ignoring his earlier conversations with Šafařík, who had sounded out the minister as early as May 2 on the congress plans, Pillersdorff maintained that he first learned of the congress through the press. Under no circumstances should Thun permit the congress to evolve into a "Slav parliament" that would rival established governing agencies. Pillersdorff's principal fear, however, was that this latest action by the Slavs would further exacerbate national tensions within the empire.[60] In a subsequent letter to Thun on May 13, Pillersdorff urged the governor "to move decisively" should the planned congress develop in a direction hostile to the best interests of the state.[61] However, the increasingly strained relations between the central government and the Bohemian governor, particularly following the radical insurgency on May 15 in the imperial capital, greatly diminished whatever influence Vienna may have wished to exert on developments in Prague. Thun simply ignored Pillersdorff's repeated requests for information on the congress preparations.[62] Though under pressure from the Austro-German liberals in the capital to break with the Slavs, Pillersdorff did not care to risk losing potential Slav allies for the cause of maintaining the monarchy. But while Viennese officialdom adopted a somewhat ambivalent stance on the forthcoming congress, the Viennese press, with rare exceptions, continued to ridicule the Slavs.[63]

The Hungarian ministry displayed none of the equivocation that had characterized the Vienna government. Although the congress announcement had not specifically cited the Magyars' national policies, they clearly understood that a united Slav front would threaten their political and national hegemony in the eastern half of the empire.[64] On May 19 the Hungarian ministry entreated the Pillersdorff government to have the Slav Congress reduced to "a provincial gathering of the Czech nation." The Magyars hoped to separate the Galician Poles from the Slav camp. Trying to capitalize on traditional Polish sympathy, they also interceded on behalf of Galician demands for greater provincial autonomy, which were pending before the Vienna cabinet.[65] The Magyars reasoned that, if the Galician demands were met, the Poles would be unlikely to seek further aid among the Slavs. Pillersdorff rejected the Magyar intervention on the belief that the Magyars were merely exploiting the Polish issue to attack the Slav Congress.[66]

Though rebuffed in Vienna, the Magyars expected a more sympathetic hearing in Frankfurt. On May 14 the Batthyány ministry dispatched envoys to Frankfurt to seek closer German-Hungarian ties. In particular, they were to emphasize the common danger to both peoples should the Slavs prevail in their efforts "to transform the previously German provinces of Austria into Slav states."[67] The Magyars were convinced that the creation of "a [Danubian] Slav empire and the extinction of the Magyar state would go hand in hand."[68]

The Magyars' belief that a conflict with the Slavs was inevitable was widely shared in Germany. As in Vienna, hostility toward the Slavs was inflamed by the nationalist press. Typical of German anxiety over the Slavs' intentions was a report in the *Breslauer Zeitung* on May 14.[69] The Slav Congress would be the launching point for the creation of "a vast Pan-Slav republic" that would be extended to include both Poland and Russia.

A prestigious journal of opinion in Germany, *Die Grenzboten,* followed closely the preparations in Prague. In the pre-March years this liberal weekly had consistently supported the efforts of Austrian Slavs for increased national and political rights. But by the spring of 1848 it favored the immediate *Anschluss* of the Austrian "provinces," including Czech and Slovene territories, with a greater Germany.[70] In its first reports, *Die Grenzboten* denounced the attempts to create a "Slav Frankfurt in the heart of German soil."[71] In a series of articles, "Prague and the New Pan-Slavism," Ignaz Kuranda echoed the theme of Germany's ultimate civilizing mission among the Slavs:

> Austria had sense and meaning only as a German power; the destiny of Austria was to elevate the primitive Slav peoples [*Naturvölker*] to the level of German civilization, and to offer them as a dowry to Germany. From the moment when the Austrian government, through weakness or lack of self-confidence, is no longer able to fulfill this calling, Austria [will] collapse and deserves to disintegrate. Then only one power can take over the mission which Austria has let fall from its hands: it is the German Empire which is being forged in Frankfurt.[72]

In Vienna, Pest, and Frankfurt forebodings of a far-flung Slav conspiracy had taken root. The Austrian cabinet feared Bohemian separatism; radical-democratic circles in Vienna feared Slav reactionaries; Frankfurt resented the Slav rebuff to a greater Germany; and the specter of a united Slavdom shadowed Pest. All of this malaise focused on Prague, ranging in emotional content from cautious misgivings to outright hatred.

Initially, the congress idea developed among the Hungarian Slavs and Poznanian Poles, who envisioned a gathering of all Slavs regardless of state frontiers. The idea was picked up in Prague by the Czech liberals, who molded it into the framework of their own political ambitions and carried it to fruition. But to the hostile observer in Vienna, Pest, or Frankfurt the motives for calling a congress of Slavs were of little consequence. The Magyar and German nationalists saw only a reactionary threat to the realization of their long-cherished dreams of political independence and national unity. However lucid their refutations, the Slavs hardly received a tolerant hearing. Their sole recourse was in numerical strength and unity of purpose. Despite their many differences, it was toward this goal that the congress organizers proceeded during the remainder of May.

CHAPTER 4
THE PREPARATIONS

i

The organizers had allowed less than a month to complete their preparations for convening the congress. The immediate task was to publicize the announcement so that a large and representative attendance would be assured. Although the Preparatory Committee kept no formal record of invitations, two tentative lists of names are preserved in the congress files.[1] The first, drawn up by Václav Hanka, comprised mostly Slav academics, in particular Russians, with whom Hanka was personally acquainted. The Russians included Count S.S. Uvarov, tsarist minister of education, and M.P. Pogodin, a leading proponent of cultural Pan-Slavism. Adam Mickiewicz also appeared on Hanka's list. On May 3 the committee had decided to invite Mickiewicz despite his anti-Austrian, revolutionary activities in Italy.[2]

The compiler of the second list is unknown.[3] It included editors of several Slav newspapers, and with few exceptions was limited to Habsburg subjects. The two lists were probably intended to complement each other: the formal announcement to Austrian Slavs would be handled by committee secretary Zap, while the invitation of non-Austrian "guests" would be conducted in a more private manner, as Šafařík had suggested.

The committee also debated whether to include non-Slavs in the congress. Considerable time at the May 11 meeting was expended on the question of inviting Austro-Germans. Although this idea received some support from committee members who wished to see the congress broadened into a sort of Austrian pre-parliament, it was eventually rejected.[4] But given the rapid deterioration of Slav-German relations since the March revolution, it is doubtful that Austro-Germans would have attended. The possibility of inviting Magyars was not even raised.[5]

In conversations, letters, and newspaper articles the congress plans were widely disseminated. The patriotic Czech press took the lead in propagating the congress. Karel Havlíček's *Národní Nowiny* reported extensively on the preparations and printed the enthusiastic replies of Slav associations in Austria and abroad. The *Slavische Centralblätter*, which Jan Petr Jordan and Karel Kašpar founded on May 21, quickly became the principal vehicle in Prague for presenting the Slav position to the German-speaking public.

Secretary Zap appealed to the burgeoning Slav press that had blossomed in Austria since March. On May 5 he wrote to several editors, asking them to print the announcement.[6] His letter to the editor of the Kraków daily, *Jutrzenka,* stressed that the national well-being of all Slavs, and no less the Poles, was threatened by the "German usurpers": "We call upon all Poles (not just Galicians) to attend."[7] A clearer statement of Zap's views was expressed in his letter to the Ukrainian Iakiv Holovats'kyi, a close acquaintance from Zap's pre-March government service in Eastern Galicia: "To defend ourselves against the German bureaucracy . . . , our sacred task is to transform Austria into a Slav state, free and independent of any foreign influence."[8]

From Vienna Šafařík tirelessly labored to convey the congress message. On May 10 he wrote Ljudevit Gaj to reinforce Zap's invitation: although the congress might coincide with the convening in June of the Croat Sabor (diet), Šafařík nevertheless hoped that the Croats would be well represented in Prague.[9] Šafařík also wrote his son Jan, a teacher at the Royal Lyceum in Belgrade, urging him and "a dozen or so Serbs, especially from the Serbian principality" to attend.[10] It was Šafařík who first informed Jan Kollár of the congress.[11] Both Zap and Šafařík in their letters encouraged the participation of foreign Slavs and played down the Austrian/non-Austrian distinction in the announcement.[12]

ii

Czech response to the news that a congress of Slavs would shortly assembly in their capital was understandably favorable. The leading Czech cultural and political societies in Prague readily supported the preparations and selected delegations. Měšt'anská beseda (Civic Forum) chose several prominent burghers and merchants. Svornost, the Czech component of the city's national guard, also appointed representatives, as did the student association Slavia and the new Slovanská lípa (Slav Linden Society).[13] Founded in Prague on April 30 and soon spreading throughout the Austro-Slav lands, Slovanská lípa fostered national and political consciousness among the Slavs. The society's program, issued on May 24, emphasized the defense of newly won constitutional liberties and the securing of national equality for Slavs in education and government and pledged itself to promote commerce and industry in predominantly Slav regions in the monarchy.[14]

The reaction of the Moravian Czechs to the congress announcement was similarly positive. Jan Ohéral, editor of the Brno *Týdenník,* welcomed Zap's invitation and suggested the names of several additional Moravians.[15] The branch of Slovanská lípa in Olomouc, headed by Professor Jan Helcelet, also pledged its support.[16] A rare instance of grass-roots support for the congress stemmed from Moravia. Several Western Moravian communities joined in endorsing Matěj Mikšíček, their most noted patriot, as their representative to Prague.[17] Yet throughout May, congress agitation in Moravia was over-shadowed by the elections to the provincial diet, which were strongly contested between the Czech- and German-speaking populace.[18]

In a couple of instances prominent Czecho-Slovaks were forced to forego attending the congress from fear of German or Magyar reprisals. The Czech ethnographer, František L. Čelakovský, believed his participation in Prague would cost him his academic position at the University of Breslau. In a letter to Dr. Josef Frič he remarked, "The Germans are keeping a close watch on me now, [and] after [the congress] they would surely stone me."[19] Threats by ardent Magyar nationalists in Pest on Jan Kollár's life also dissuaded him from attending.[20]

The Lusatian Serbs in German Saxony already had a spokesman among the congress planners. Jan Petr Jordan translated the announcement into Lusatian and dispatched copies to the Maćica Serbska in Bautzen (Budyšin). But diffidence and the fear of German retaliation precluded formal Lusatian participation in Prague.[21] In the Lusatians' absence, Jordan assumed the duty of dramatizing their plight before the congress.[22]

The small Slovak national leadership was united in its support. Although the Mikuláš petition of May 10 had indicated the Slovaks' continued willingness to retain their ties with Hungary, the Batthyány ministry steadfastly refused to consider their demands. Instead, political reins were tightened in Slovakia and the more outspoken Slovak patriots were forced to flee. Several found refuge in Prague, where they eagerly enlisted in the congress effort. Jozef M. Hurban arrived there on May 22, followed shortly thereafter by Michal M. Hodža and L'udovít Štúr, the latter having made a dramatic escape from the Hungarian authorities.[23]

Unlike the Slovaks, the Croats sought a complete break with Hungary. The congress would afford a ready opportunity to solicit broad Slav support for their struggle with the Magyars. Already by May 11 the Croat Skupština (assembly) in Zagreb had selected its congress delegation, which included the journalists Maksim Prica and Josip Praus (both close associates of Jelačić), Baron Dragutin Kušljan, and the Slovene veteran of the Illyrian movement, Stanko Vraz.[24]

The Vojvodina Serbs, who had been meeting since May 13 in Sremski Karlovci, chose a delegation headed by the Orthodox priests Nikanor Grujić and Pavao Stamatović.[25] The Principality of Serbia also sent observers to Prague, though not as many as Šafařík had hoped for.[26]

Slovene interest in the congress was greatest in areas where German nationalist agitation was most intense: in Carinthia, Southern Styria, and among the Slovenes in Vienna. The Graz "Slovenija" society, though it strongly endorsed the congress, displayed considerable reluctance to enter into formal political discussion with foreign Slavs.[27] The Vienna "Slovenija" also adopted a narrow Austro-Slav posture in its reply to Prague. But despite their considerable interest in the congress, the only Slovenes to attend, in addition to Vraz, were Anton Globočnik and Alojsij Šparovac from Vienna.[28]

Although no delegates journeyed from Dalmatia, the Preparatory Committee received enthusiastic letters of support from Slav associations in Zadar and Šibenik.[29]

iii

While the Czecho-Slovaks and South Slavs were showering Prague with heartfelt endorsements, the Preparatory Committee by mid-May was entirely preoccupied with the matter of Polish participation. At its May 13 meeting, committee chairman J.M. Thun expressed concern over questionable Polish loyalty to Austria.[30] Palacký cautioned the committee, however, not to lose sight of the few Austro-Slav partisans among the Poles. He relayed the impressions of Karel Havlíček, who, during a recent trip to Kraków on behalf of the Preparatory Committee, had found that "our adherents" there were "terrorized by the émigrés and old nobility who yearned for the Poland of yore." Palacký advised "extending a hand to the well-meaning Polish faction." Leo Thun, who had served in Galicia prior to assuming his post in Prague, contrasted "solid and well-educated Kraków" to "the lamentable rest of Galicia" where political obscurantism still prevailed among the provincial gentry. František Brauner ventured to suggest that the Galician Poles might "learn a reasonable policy here [in Prague]." Jordan reminded the committee that the Czech position was receiving a sympathetic hearing in Poznania. The Czechs apparently regarded the anti-German Poznanian Poles as more zealous Slavs than the ambivalent Galician Poles, and this preference may have contributed to their later willingness to broaden the congress to include non-Austrian Slavs as regular participants. Of the various speakers on May 13 (no Poles were present), only F.L. Rieger, a long-time polonophile, grasped the ramifications of the Polish question. He speculated that both the Poznanian and Galician Poles would support the Czechs only if there were a strong likelihood that the Slavs' efforts at the congress would lead to greater autonomy for the Polish provinces.

The Polish debate evinced the Czechs' limited acquaintance with Polish affairs. Austro-Slavism was the sole criterion by which the Czechs measured Polish intentions. Unable to comprehend Polish preoccupation with regaining independence, the Czechs were alarmed over apparent Galician equivocation toward Austria.[31]

Czech misgivings were reinforced by the letters from compatriots that were reaching the Preparatory Committee. On May 9 several Czech residents in Vienna warned the organizers of the Poles' dubious loyalty. They pointed out that the Polish students in Vienna were among the staunchest proponents of Austria's *Anschluss* with Germany. The students seemed convinced that splintering the monarchy would lead to independence for Galicia.[32] A spokesman for the Czech community in Lvov, František Jachim, cautioned Palacký to beware of "false friends," citing Polish-Magyar amity and the Poles' indifference to "the holy idea of Slav reciprocity."[33]

In a lengthy article in *Národní Nowiny* on May 12, Karel Havlíček reported on his recent visit to Kraków.[34] Havlíček had sounded out various Polish political factions on the congress plans. Although the radical Polish émigrés remained intransigent, political moderates, he found, were willing to attend and discuss inter-Slav concerns. But they could not be expected to share the Czech point of view on all matters. Most Poles still believed that the Czechs were acting in league with the tsarist government. From his conversations, Havlíček believed that the principal "obstacles to understanding between the Poles and the other West Slavs are Polish pride, impatience, and ignorance of the state of affairs":

> The Pole . . . knows only his native country and the French. Already he has mistaken notions about Germany; but he is completely ignorant of conditions among the West Slavs. . . . Pride does not allow the Pole to speak or think of anything but the total renewal of Poland as it was of old . . . . The greatest misfortune is that in Poland only those persons without a calling, that is, the gentry, who are continuously without work, reflect and act upon politics.

Polish mistrust of the Czechs was no less manifest. "The Czechs and Their Aspirations," an article in the Kraków newspaper *Jutrzenka* on May 18, though probably written without knowledge of Havlíček's report, elucidates well the views of the Polish moderates.[35] The author, a certain "K. Ch." who claimed extensive acquaintance with the Czechs and their country, observed that of all the Slavs the Czechs, though closely related ethnically, evoked the least sympathy in Poland. The Serbian and Russian languages were pleasing to the Polish ear, but Czech sounded ridiculous. The author believed that the source of Polish antipathy lay in the fact that the Czechs had only recently emerged as a nation and were still largely imbued with Germanic traits. Furthermore, the average Pole's only acquaintance with Czechs was in their bureaucratic role as Austrian officials in Galicia.

Poles also looked askance at the Czech intellectuals' flirtation with political Pan-Slavism. For most Poles, Pan-Slavism and the "muscovite knout" were synonymous. The writer for *Jutrzenka* did not completely agree. He applauded those Czech writers who were defending their people against germanization. He felt sure that the prevailing attitude in the Czech lands was anti-Muscovite. The two leading russophiles—Hanka and Kollár—gave scant cause for concern; Hanka had no "political" influence in Bohemia, and Kollár was taking no part in the current developments.

What then was the purpose of this congress? Was it still the specter of Pan-Slavism? These were the questions that Poles asked. The author agreed that it was indeed Pan-Slavism, but only in the sense of fostering political liberty, mutual assistance, and the amity of all Slav peoples. But there remained a deep gulf between the Czech and Polish views on Austria's future. The Czechs' preoccupation with the security and preservation of Austria (one of the partitioning powers) offended Polish opinion. The Czechs "still did not aspire to their own independence"; instead, they comprised "a nation of diplomats." How then could these few million Czechs, "swamped among Germans," dare claim to lead the Slavs when "we, a nation of twenty million, famed as a preeminent military people throughout enlightened Europe, could not shake off the yoke [of oppression] despite every possible sacrifice and endeavor"? Nonetheless, the author urged the Poles not to boycott the Prague congress; "If we are worried that the Russian spirit may get the upper hand at this assembly, that is all the more reason that we also be there."

When the Preparatory Committee reconvened on May 19, the acrimonious Polish debate of a week earlier was not resumed.[36] This was due in part to the presence of the conservative Galician Poles, Prince Leon Sapieha and Antoni Walewski, both intimate associates of Prince Adam Czartoryski. František Palacký introduced Sapieha to Count J.M. Thun and played a mediatory role in bridging Czech-Polish mistrust. By his own account Sapieha left Prague with every intention of returning to attend the congress. His brief stay there eased his doubts and convinced him that the Czech leaders wanted nothing to do with either Russia or Russian-inspired Pan-Slavism.[37]

To clarify the congress' aims to the Poles, the Czech organizers turned to Witalis Grzybowski, their sole Polish colleague on the committee. Unfortunately, the resultant message was an Austro-Slav panegyric. Grzybowski appealed only to those Poles who were "prudent, moderate, and not given to violence or disruption" to attend. Echoing sentiments which Poles found so reprehensible in the Czechs, he reminded his compatriots how much their excitable temperament had cost the Polish cause in the past. "Today moderation and legality constitute the only policies which can raise us from our sorrowful ruin."[38] Czechs who hoped to dissuade Polish revolutionaries from attending were apparently unaware that Grzybowski was quite unknown and without influence in Poland.[39]

The Galician democrat Floryan Ziemiałkowski exemplified this revolutionary Polish temperament that Grzybowski did not wish to have in Prague. Already hostile to the Slav encounters in Vienna, Ziemiałkowski scorned the congress, which he believed a threat to radical political change in Central Europe. In words remarkably similar to German and Magyar denunciations of the congress plans, he accused the Prague reactionaries of seeking to "Czechicize" Austria and to transform Vienna into a Slav city. He compared the Czechs to a "Slav Ulysses" defending Austrian integrity as "the staunchest ally of the Metternichian system," while actually hoping to rule Austria some day. Ziemiałkowski was especially contemptuous of his fellow Galician Karol Malisz, who had signed the congress announcement in the name of the Polish delegation to Vienna of which Ziemiałkowski was also a member.[40]

The Poznanian democrats did not share Ziemiałkowski's hostility to the congress. At the conclusion of the Polish assembly in Wrocław on May 9, several Poznanian leaders and Jerzy Lubomirski addressed an open appeal to fellow Poles, regardless of political frontiers, to attend the Prague congress in great number.[41]

The Galician Poles' response to the congress announcement was more deliberate. Only after considerable debate and prompting by the local press[42] did the Rada Narodowa in Lvov decide to authorize sending a delegation to Prague.[43] Detailed instructions were drafted to guide the delegates' activities. Since the congress was not an officially constituted, representative assembly, the Rada's delegates were to participate as individuals and not give the impression that they were a formal deputation. Their main task would be to convince those assembled in Prague that Polish desires to regain independence in no way hindered the interests of the other Slavs. On the contrary, the fulfillment of Poland's aims would place her in a better position to aid the Slavs. Specifically, the delegates should mediate the Magyar-Slav dispute and develop close ties with fellow Poles at the congress. The Rada Narodowa wanted daily reports on the delegates' activities, and therefore its secretary, Seweryn Celarski, would also attend.[44]

The cautious guidelines emphasized defending provincial Polish and Galician interests rather than fostering a broad political coalition of Slavs. For this reason, Jerzy Lubomirski, although he had been appointed to the Rada's delegation, opted to attend privately.[45] A number of other Galician Poles, notably Maurycy Kraiński and Prince Sapieha from the conservative camp, also decided to attend privately. From Kraków, which was under Austrian military rule since the abortive uprising of April 26, the only representative was Antoni Helcel, a professor of law at the Jagiellonian University.

iv

The Polish émigrés followed developments in Prague with interest. Reaction to the congress plans varied considerably between the democratic and conservative wings of the *emigracja*. Whereas the Polish radicals in general scoffed at the plans of the Prague Slavs, the conservative émigrés tried to utilize the congress to further their political goals.

An active center of the democratic *emigracja* in 1848 was the Komitet Emigracji Polskiej (Polish Emigration Committee, but commonly referred to as the "Dwernicki Committee" after its founder, General Józef Dwernicki). Based in Paris, the committee attempted to unite the splintered émigré forces under a common banner and serve as a liaison to the new French republican government.[46] The driving force in the organization was its secretary Henryk Jakubowski. The Dwernicki Committee's sympathies clearly lay with the Germans and Magyars, not with the "reactionary" Austrian Slavs. Word of the congress first reached the committee from its informant in Frankfurt, Józef Reizenheim, who contended in a letter to Jakubowski that the Austrian government was probably supporting the congress in order to impede the absorption of Habsburg territories into a Greater Germany.[47]

The committee declined to reply to the congress announcement, reasoning that the Austrian Slavs were thoroughly under Russian and Habsburg influence and that any favorable gesture, even the simple statement of fraternal greetings which Jakubowski proposed, could harm Polish relations with the Magyars.[48] An even harsher anti-Slav stance was taken by Franciszek Gordaszewski, a committee member in Amiens: it was high time to cease toying with the Slavs, who were in disarray and resourceless and in whose lands Muscovite intrigue and religious obscurantism were rampant.[49]

The Towarzystwo Demokratyczne Polskie (Polish Democratic Society) in Paris also refused to have any dealings with the congress. At a meeting of its policy board, the Centralizacja, concern was voiced that the Czechs' Austro-Slav program might irrevocably bind Galicia in yet a new Austrian combination.[50]

Outside Paris the democratic émigrés took a more tolerant view of the congress. From his exile in Brussels, Joachim Lelewel, the noted Polish historian and scion of the democratic camp, sent greetings to Prague and regretted his inability to attend.[51] An émigré association in Switzerland, the Dozór Genewsko-Polski (Polish-Geneva Watch), also replied to the announcement, but cautioned the Slavs that tsarist Russia would surely try to influence the proceedings.[52]

From his base at the Paris Hôtel Lambert, Prince Adam Czartoryski, leader of the conservative wing of the emigracija, adopted a flexible policy toward developments in Prague. Thanks to a network of agents spread throughout Europe, Czartoryski remained well informed on the rapidly changing political situation in Central Europe. Whereas the democratic émigrés saw in the congress only a further opponent in the forthcoming struggle between enlightened Europe and reactionary Russia (the outcome of which they were convinced would lead to Poland's renewed independence), Czartoryski saw in the Austro-Slav federative schemes the opportunity for an autonomous Galicia to form the nucleus of a regenerated Poland. Although by late May he no longer placed much hope in German support for his plans, Czartoryski still wished to avoid antagonizing the Magyars, whose aid neighboring Galicia needed.[53]

Czartoryski's principal informant in Prague was Antoni Walewski. The Czech leaders had made a positive impression on both Walewski and Czartoryski's brother-in-law, Prince Sapieha, and Walewski urged Czartoryski to come to Prague and take a direct hand in guiding affairs. At all costs, though, the prince should cancel his plans to visit Frankfurt, which would greatly harm his stature in Prague.[54]

Czartoryski's plans to visit Frankfurt also ran counter to the counsel of the Polish legionaries who had assembled in Germany in anticipation of war with Russia. Since the Poznanian events in April, the Polish soldiers no longer believed that effective Polish-German cooperation was possible. They advised Czartoryski to pull his agents out of Paris and Frankfurt and transfer his headquarters to Prague: given the present political situation, "we can hope for the salvation of Poland only in the Slav movement."[55] Czartoryski eventually abandoned his trip to Frankfurt and proceeded directly to Dresden, where reports of the June Uprising cut short his plans to reach Prague.[56]

A Czartoryski-sponsored "circle" of former representatives of the 1831 Polish diet (Grono Członków Sejmu) also decided to participate. The émigré diet, which had met sporadically in Paris during the 1830's, was revived by Czartoryski in May 1848 with the eighteen remaining members. The circle's delegation, headed by Bogdan Zaleski, was delayed in leaving Paris and had only reached Dresden when news of the congress' premature closing was received.[57]

A sympathetic proponent in Paris of the Slav cause was Cyprien Robert, Mickiewicz's successor at the Collège de France. With Czartoryski's financial assistance, Robert formed in March 1848 a Paris Slav society, composed mostly of Polish émigrés with a sprinkling of Frenchmen, Czechs, and South Slavs, whose program called for the federal union of the non-Russian Slavs built around a nucleus of a regenerated Poland. On June 1 Robert launched *La Pologne, Journal des Slaves confédérés*, which reported sympathetically on the congress.

v

Absorbed in their hopes of restoring the Poland of 1772, the Poles in their preparatory counsels for the congress had paid scant attention to the mounting national aspirations of the Galician Ukrainians. A meeting of the Central Ruthenian Council (Holovna Rada Rus'ka) on May 12 decided to table discussion of the congress announcement until it could be ascertained that the congress was not an illegal, anti-Habsburg undertaking. The loyal Ukrainian prelates sought the approval of Governor Stadion before agreeing at a meeting on May 16 to accept the Prague invitation. The council's delegation consisted of three Uniate priests, Ivan Borysykevych, Aleksei Zaklyn'skii, and Hryhorii Hynylevych.[58] Czech officials in Lvov made special efforts to introduce these Ukrainians to the congress organizers and to assure their cordial reception in Prague. Writing to Zap, František Jachim described each delegate: Borysykevych was vice-president of the Ruthenian Council; Zaklyn'skii, a theology student "intelligent beyond his years and probably the most brilliant hope of the Ruthenes"; and Dr. Hynylevych, a canon from Przemyśl.[59]

Stadion provided the Ukrainian delegates with a letter of introduction to his counterpart in Prague, Count Leo Thun.[60] On their way to Prague they stopped over in Kraków where they duly reported to the city's new ruler, Austrian General Schick. In reply to his inquiry regarding the purpose of the congress, the Ukrainians purportedly maintained that they were proceeding to Prague to thwart Polish designs for Galicia.[61]

In addition to this "official" Ukrainian delegation, several Ukrainian residents of Vienna, as well as a small delegation of the Polish-sponsored Ruthenian Assembly (Rus'kyi Sobor), headed by Kaspar Cięgliewicz, attended the congress. But the Uniate clerics from the Central Ruthenian Council would have nothing to do with these dubious compatriots.

Zap's close Ukrainian acquaintance, Iakiv Holovats'kyi, had already broken with the Ruthenian Council, which he considered merely a tool of the Austrian bureaucracy. After receiving the announcement from Zap, Holovats'kyi assembled several Uniate priests from the Czortków (Chortkiv) district of Eastern Galicia to select their own delegate to Prague. The group chose the priest Tadei Virskyi and requested the Uniate metropolitan in Lvov to release Virskyi from his clerical duties to attend the congress. As it turned out, Virskyi did not go to Prague, though the reason for this decision remains obscure.[62]

vi

Hanka's list included a preponderance of Russian academics and officials. Although there is evidence of only two invitations from Hanka to tsarist subjects, the fate of other invitations may be inferred.[63] On May 8 Senator A. Ia. Storozhenko, a director of the State Commission for Internal and Spiritual Affairs in Poland, received from Hanka a bundle of Slav newspapers with a covering letter announcing the congress:

> We have lived to see times which were never expected; everything would have gone well with us but for the cursed Germans! It is a pity that you do not have our papers, for then you would know with what wiles they want to entice us. . . . Read the goings-on of the fifty Frankfurt impostors in regard to our protestations. We do not want union with this Great Germany. We are Slavs and we will remain so to the last drop of our blood. It would be very gratifying to see our brothers the Russians, too, at our Congress.[64]

Storozhenko, who was well acquainted with official Russian policy on the Pan-Slav question, cautiously informed the Russian governor in Warsaw, General I.F. Paskevich, of Hanka's letter and mentioned that he had made Hanka's acquaintance in Karlovy Vary. Paskevich forwarded the papers to the tsar, who directed that no reply be made to the invitation. The Slav Congress, the tsar remarked, "was not our affair."[65] Nicholas looked with only disfavor on such entreaties of the meddlesome Austrian Slavs.

Another invitation, to Professor F.S. Tsytsurin in Kiev, was also turned over to the authorities. The military governor of Kiev, D.G. Bibikov, forwarded it to Paskevich, mentioning that he knew of several other individuals in Kiev who had also received invitations.[66]

Thus Russia was not formally represented at the first Slav Congress.[67] Those invited could not afford to ignore the tsar's implacable hostility to Pan-Slavism. The Czech organizers, however, were certainly familiar with official Russian policy, and it is probable that Hanka invited the Russians out of courtesy, knowing that under the circumstances they could not attend.

Perhaps the clearest statement of the tsar's fear of Pan-Slavism as a potentially disruptive force is in his marginal notes on the deposition of the Russian slavophile, Ivan Aksakov, following his arrest in 1849:

> Under the guise of sympathy for the Slavic tribes supposedly oppressed in the other states, there is hidden the criminal thought of a union of these tribes, in spite of the fact that they are subjects of neighboring and in part allied states. And they expected to attain this goal not through the will of God, but by means of rebellious outbreaks to the detriment and destruction of Russia herself.... And if, indeed, a combination of circumstances produced such a union, this will mean the ruin of Russia.[68]

Nicholas' aversion to the agitation of the Austrian Slavs stemmed not only from his desire to preserve quiet within Russia but to sustain the European balance of power, a policy which implied maintaining the integrity of the Habsburg monarchy. Nicholas' correspondence in summer 1848 with Count Nesselrode, however, indicated that the tsar reckoned on the possible disintegration of Austria, in which case Galicia would have to be annexed.[69]

Ironically, Nicholas' fears of a new Slav combination were echoed in the German nationalist press. The *grossdeutsch* Viennese newspaper, *Der Freimüthige*, on May 10 warned of the ambitions of the Prague Slavs:

> The Slav leaders are counting with certainty on the outbreak of a revolutionary movement in Russia, on the transformation of that monstrous empire into various linguistically divided states (*Dialektstaaten*), and then on the founding of an almost limitless Slav republic which will rule from the shores of the Arctic Ocean to the banks of the Bosporus.[70]

Although for quite different reasons, both official Russia and the German nationalists saw in the Slav Congress a source of grave concern and ascribed to it goals which the congress planners would scarcely countenance. Of the congress participants, only the itinerant Russian revolutionary Mikhail Bakunin might possibly have entertained such grandiose and imaginative aims as the opponents of the congress foresaw.

vii

The Preparatory Committee had managed with remarkable success to promote the congress. Despite short notice, long distances to be traveled, the opposition of the tsarist government, and the harassment by German and Magyar nationalists, the hoped-for large assemblage in Prague was assured. There would be representatives of all the Slav peoples in Austria and a number of foreign Slavs, most notably Prussian Poles. And, though several Slav luminaries would not be present, the delegates comprised an impressive array of acknowledged spokesmen.

But the period of preparation had also made evident the considerable division of opinion among the Slavs. The vision of the pre-March cultural Pan-Slavs of a unitary Slavdom appeared remote when confronted with the political aspirations and fears spawned by the revolutionary changes in Central Europe. The Poles did not share the Austro-Slav convictions of most Czechs and South Slavs. Even moderate Poles envisaged Galicia's continued association with Austria as only a temporary tie. The Poles' disinclination to join an anti-Magyar crusade was certain to lead to a confrontation with the Hungarian Slavs. And the mounting Polish-Ukrainian controversy in Galicia would likely carry over into the congress deliberations. Indeed, a key measure of the success or failure of the congress would be the degree of understanding and cooperation attained between the Poles and the other Slavs.

CHAPTER 5
THE CONGRESS CONVENES

i

While Zap concentrated on ensuring a broad Slav participation in Prague, others on the Preparatory Committee attended to the local arrangements. For the festive opening ceremonies the large concert hall on Žofín Island was reserved, while working sessions would take place at the Czech National Museum. A special committee meeting on May 20 was devoted to the matter of housing the many expected participants. It was decided to appeal to the patriotic Czech citizenry to make available "individual rooms, with the necessary furnishings, for the lodging of one or more guests for a period of two to three weeks."[1] The notice appeared in *Národní Nowiny* on May 23 and was posted on street corners and in bookshop windows. The costs of the congress were met by private subscription to which the pro-Czech nobility made the principal contribution. A major portion of the expenses for the preparations was borne by Baron Neuberg.[2]

But scarcely a week before the congress was scheduled to convene, the planners had still not settled on an organizational format or an agenda for the deliberations; in effect, though the first delegates were arriving in Prague, the congress still lacked a stated definition of goal and purpose. Since the committee's sessions had demonstrated the difficulty of drafting policy in large meetings, these two remaining tasks were assigned to individual members.

On May 24 J.P. Jordan submitted to the committee a draft of procedural rules to govern the congress. Closely following Šafařík's earlier recommendations, he proposed dividing the congress into three regional/national sections: 1) Czechs, Moravians, Silesians, and Slovaks; 2) Poles and Ukrainians; and 3) Slovenes, Croats, Serbs, and Dalmatians. Each section would select its own officers (chairman, deputy chairman, and secretaries), and designate sixteen representatives, who, together with the designees of the other sections, would form the Plenary Committee. In addition, each section would nominate a candidate for the congress presidency. On the eve of the congress' opening the Plenary Committee would elect the president from among the three nominees, the other two becoming vice-presidents. An executive committee comprised of the

section and congress officers would also be established to monitor the
sections' deliberations and coordinate congress dealings with outside
parties. The two committees—executive and plenary—were given the task
of resolving differences of opinion which arose among the sections. Jordan
further proposed an elaborate scheme whereby each section could keep
abreast of the discussions in the other sections. Each section would
appoint two representatives to observe the deliberations in the remaining
sections and clarify their own section's position. In addition to meetings
by the sections, the congress would assemble periodically in general
session to ratify agreements commonly reached by all three sections.[3]

The most controversial feature of Jordan's proposal was the considerable autonomy allotted to the national sections, especially in their formation. F.L. Rieger questioned this entire concept. How, he asked, would
uninvited guests be handled? Rieger wanted some means of excluding
unknown or undesirable persons from admission; the specter of anti-
Austrian, Polish revolutionaries taking over the congress apparently still
haunted the cautious Austro-Slav zealots on the committee. To forestall
such a possibility, Rieger proposed that the Preparatory Committee
"appoint" three "trusted" individuals to initiate the selection of delegates in each section. They would admit one member, then the four would
admit another, and so forth, a procedure the committee accepted.[4] But
although Rieger's intervention considerably complicated the admission
procedure, it did not appreciably alter the principle of sectional autonomy.

The congress program or agenda was drafted by František Zach and
submitted to the Preparatory Committee on May 27, just four days prior
to the scheduled congress opening. Zach's intimate acquaintance with the
three major national groups attending the congress likely explains why
the committee selected him for this delicate task. A Moravian by birth,
Zach had briefly taken part in the 1831 Polish uprising. Since 1843 he
had lived in Belgrade, while serving as Czartoryski's emissary.[5]

Zach's program was divided into four topics, each of which concluded
with a question for deliberation by the delegates.[6] The Austrian Slavs
would seek to further cooperation and union among themselves and
would discuss, in this order, their relations with the non-Slav peoples
in the empire, with Slavs living beyond the frontiers of Austria, and with
the remaining European nations. The congress would also determine if it
wished to inform the emperor of its decisions. The immediate question
was how the Slavs could best meet the threat to their national well-being
posed by the Magyar and German national movements, but the underlying theme of the agenda was the matter of federative union. Zach

purposely stopped short of phrasing his questions in direct political context—such as a union of only Austrian Slavs, all Slavs, or all Habsburg subjects. This imprecision would be a principal source of dissatisfaction with the program in the early sessions.

The cumbersome and cautious agenda reflected the moderate Austro-Slav orientation of the congress planners. An ailing Austria should be reanimated by injecting fresh Slav blood. Of the possibility of forming an independent, federal state of West and South Slavs the program made no mention.[7] The passage dealing with Austrian/non-Austrian relations among the Slavs, which confined itself to the "safe" subject of promoting the exchange of books and learning and carefully sidestepped the possibility of political cooperation, was clearly unsatisfactory to most Polish delegates.

Although Zach's proposal was eventually allowed to stand as submitted, it provoked in the committee (now broadened to include several non-members) a heated exchange that foreshadowed later disagreements during the actual sessions. Governor Leo Thun precipitated the debate when he called for assurances that the congress would not infringe on his administrative prerogatives. He reminded the committee that the Slavs were gathering for "intellectual purposes" (*duševní sesílení*), not political ones; "the congress was not a legislative body," though hopefully the forthcoming Imperial Parliament would weigh its findings. Neuberg took issue: "We have a guiding principle: national equality. With intellectual matters we are not concerned here, only with political ones!" Karel Havlíček regretted the excessive stress on legalistic niceties: "We must now act as Slavs, as free peoples, not as Austrians." František Brauner concurred: "Discretion has been our failing," he maintained. But Šafařík, as he would often do during the sessions, urged caution: "We [Slavs] are strong in numbers, but till now not a compact body." He recalled the Slavs' dependence on West European sympathy. But Havlíček had the final say: "For the time being let us not be so scrupulous regarding distant nations. 'The shirt is closer than the coat' [*košile bližší nežli kabát*]."[8]

The discussion had brought into focus several strands in Czech political thought. From the left, Havlíček (who would be supported during the sessions by the Slovak Štúr) pressed the planners to move decisively to safeguard Slav, not merely Austrian, interests; from the right, the moderates—Neuberg, Palacký, Šafařík, and Rieger—had to contend with the bureaucratic- and legalistic-minded Leo Thun. Despite Polish assumptions, the Czechs were by no means in agreement on the purpose of the congress which they were about to convene.

ii

The congress had been scheduled to open on May 31, but the delays in the preparations and the late arrival of some delegates caused its postponement until June 2. Well before that date, however, delegates and observers began to converge on the Bohemian capital.[9] On May 30 a number of participants arrived by special train from Vienna. That morning *Národní Nowiny* announced their expected arrival, ensuring a large turnout of well-wishers at the railway station.[10] Members of Svornost and Slavia escorted the delegates to the assembly hall on Žofín Island, where they were welcomed to the accompaniment of singing and a fervent exchange of greetings. The ecstatic Czech press reported that "each [guest] spoke in his mother tongue, and we all understood one another"; "for all true Prague Czechs," it had been a day of "heartfelt delight."[11]

The Czechs were understandably excited by the appearance of their colorful Slav guests. The variety of national attire—particularly the long, dark brown coats and red Greek caps worn by the Hungarian Serbs—attracted considerable attention. The garb worn by the Orthodox Serb priests reminded a Polish visitor of the Jews in his land.[12] A Prague reporter, observing the city's main thoroughfares, likened the sight to a stroll on an Italian corso.[13] But not all observers found this scene appealing; the Moravian German, Alfred Meissner, who passed through Prague en route to Frankfurt, had a quite different impression:

> How changed I found the old, well-known city! It had become a gaudy, big caravansary, boasting of strange foreign guests from the East. . . . What a swarm of odd figures! . . . Wherever one looked—un-European uniforms, rattling swords, fluttering feathers of the Slav tricolor. . . . How did these lovely barbarians get to civilized German Prague? . . . It gave everyone the impression of a bad masquerade.[14]

A correspondent for the Heidelberg *Deutsche Zeitung* speculated that such "theatrical pomp" and "so-called national dress" seemed to have been found in an old theater-costume attic.[15] The reporter for the Augsburg *Allgemeine Zeitung* was shocked by such "ghastly, barbarous figures with swarthy faces from the southern lands."[16]

However, time was not given over completely to festivities and merrymaking. On May 30 the Preparatory Committee met for the last time. A public announcement posted in Prague on May 31 called on the delegates to register at the Czech National Museum with their designated section representatives: for the Czechs and Slovaks, Václav Hanka, Jan Helcelet, and J.M. Hurban; for the Poles and Ukrainians, Jerzy Lubomirski, Maurycy Kraiński, and Ivan Borysykevych; and for the South Slavs, the Serb Pavao Stamatović, the Croat Dragutin Kušljan, and the Slovene Stanko Vraz.[17] Following Rieger's suggestion, the committee carefully selected these individuals, recognized as spokesmen for their nations; and in the case of the Poles and Ukrainians, all three men were Habsburg subjects.

The Polish section held its first organizational meeting on the morning of May 31. The session was chaired by the three designees, under the watchful eye of secretary K.V. Zap of the Preparatory Committee. Immediately a question arose over the seating of three Silesians who, according to the rules, should have joined the Czecho-Slovak section. However, they opted to join the Polish section because their "language and native traditions, as well as the material interests of their homeland, . . . were closer to those of the Poles than the Czechs." When Zap raised no objection, the three Silesians were duly admitted.[18]

The two Russians attending the congress, the itinerant revolutionary Mikhail Bakunin and the Orthodox priest Olimpi Miloradov, also joined the Poles and Ukrainians, since no particular section had been allotted to the Russians. Bakunin brazenly justified this decision, saying: "[Russian] affairs are closely tied to the Polish question; for only through the liberation of Poland can Russians secure national and political freedoms."[19]

The tide of the revolution had drawn Bakunin eastward, first to Frankfurt, then to Berlin. His goal was Poznań, whence he aimed to carry the banner of revolution to Russian Poland. The Prussian authorities, however, permitted him to travel only as far as Breslau, where in early May he learned of the forthcoming Slav Congress from the Czech Slavist F.L. Čelakovský. Disillusioned for the moment with the course of revolution in German Central Europe, Bakunin was aroused by the vision of Slav unity. In the words of his British biographer, E.H. Carr, "In the gloom of Breslau, it was a brilliant ray of light."[20] He hastened to Prague hoping to find an alternative springboard to revolution.

The local press singled out Bakunin as "one of the celebrities attending the Slav Congress."[21] Like many of the delegates, who stayed with Czech patriots, he was lodged with the Prague brewer František Vaňka.[22] During his first days in Prague, Bakunin kept company with the Poles, for they were his only acquaintances among the assembled Slavs. The priest Miloradov belonged to an Old Believers' monastery in Austrian Bukovina.

Shortly before the congress, the monastery had been closed, apparently at the request of the tsarist government. Miloradov, in the company of his metropolitan, journeyed to Vienna to seek redress, and having learned of the congress he proceeded alone to Prague.[23]

When the Polish section reconvened on the afternoon of May 31 to elect its officers, there was a lengthy discussion on whether Austrian subjects alone could hold official positions. When the question was put to a vote, it was decided that any member, regardless of his geographical origin, could serve as a section officer. The section then elected its chairman, Karol Libelt from Prussian Poznań, and its deputy chairman, the Ukrainian Hrihorii Hynylevych. Libelt's first official act was an attempt to dampen the smoldering national controversy in the section by reassuring the Ukrainians that "Poland no longer wishes to be as in the past; instead, she [now] seeks to be but one part in a free federation of Slavdom."[24]

Although a marked departure from the organizers' intentions, Zap had not interfered to block the choice of a non-Austrian chairman. Apparently Libelt's reputation for radical politics was a source of greater concern, especially for the conservative Galicians.[25] In the 1830's Libelt had studied philosophy in Berlin, where he came under the influence of the Young Hegelians. Later he had been sentenced to twenty years' imprisonment for alleged contacts with Paris-based Polish revolutionaries. In March 1848 he was released from Berlin's Moabit prison, along with Ludwik Mierosławski.[26]

Technically there were no Poles in the section. A list of sixty-four names appended to the protocol of May 31 identified each delegate by only the old regional designations: "R" (Ruthene), "M" (Mazurian), "W" (Wielopolak, from western Poland), and "L" (Lithuanian).[27] Thus Libelt from Poznań became a Wielopolak, and Prince Lubomirski from Galicia a Ruthene. This deception blurred not only the distinction Austrian/non-Austrian but diluted the genuine Ukrainians with an infusion of several polonized Ruthenes. The procedure had no place in a congress organized along national lines and belied Libelt's earlier pledge to the Ukrainians.

On June 1 the Poles and Ukrainians again met to choose their remaining officials. Even the relatively simple procedure of choosing representatives for the Poles and Ukrainians in the other sections was time-consuming. Eventually it was decided to select one representative on the basis of his knowledge of Galician affairs. As their candidate for congress president they chose Jerzy Lubomirski.[28]

The South Slavs also held their organizational meeting on May 31. The Serb writer from Novi Sad, Pavao Stamatović, was unanimously chosen section chairman and Stanko Vraz deputy chairman. However, when Vraz later became the South Slav candidate for the presidency, František Zach, whom the Preparatory Committee had appointed to oversee the South Slav section, replaced him as deputy chairman.[29] The South Slavs completed in one session the organizational tasks which had taken the Poles and Ukrainians two full days of meetings. By the afternoon of May 31 the South Slavs had already begun to consider the agenda.

Of the thirty-eight delegates enrolled in the South Slav section by June 1, only three were Slovenes. In a letter to Josip Muršec in Vienna on that day, the Slovene Alojsij Šparovac observed that only the "Illyrian" (Serbo-Croat) language was being used in the South Slav meetings. Šparovac was troubled that Slovene interests would not receive a fair hearing in the section, now that Vraz had official congress duties to perform. He appealed to the Vienna Slovenija society to send additional representatives to Prague immediately.[30]

As the minutes of the Czecho-Slovak organizational meetings are not preserved, the procedures by which the section's officers and representatives were chosen cannot be traced.[31] From other sources we know that Šafařík was elected chairman and the Moravian Jan Dvořáček his deputy. As expected, František Palacký was the Czecho-Slovak candidate for the presidency.

The Czecho-Slovak section was by far the largest of the three. According to the semi-official *Zpráwa o sjezdu slowanském* (Report on the Slav Congress), there were 237 Czecho-Slovak participants, as opposed to 42 South Slavs and 61 members of the Polish-Ukrainian section, a total of 340 delegates. However, the list appended to the *Zpráwa* includes only 318 names.[32] Zdeněk Tobolka and Václav Žáček, editors of a compendium of congress documents, have identified an additional 45 unofficial participants, guests, and signatories of congress pronouncements.[33]

A majority of the congress leadership—section and congress officers, and members of the Plenary Committee—can be classified as intellectuals (writers, editors, lawyers, or academics). Nobles and members of the clergy made up the remainder, with less than a handful from commerce or the military. Although no peasants attended the congress, many Slav intellectuals had their roots in the countryside. Several delegates had served the Habsburg bureaucracy in some capacity. There was a considerable variation in age among the leaders. Whereas Šafařík, Palacký, Neuberg, and J.M. Thun were all in their fifties, the relative youth of most delegates was striking: Havlíček was 26, Jordan 30, Hurban 31, and Štúr 32. Bakunin had just turned 34 in May, and the Polish candidate for the presidency, Lubomirski, was 31.

While all three sections managed to organize and choose their officers, the greatest difficulties arose in the Polish section. In addition to the mistrust between Poles and Ukrainians, the Poles themselves were politically divided. Barely a third of the Poles in Prague had gained admittance to the congress, since the section had been unable to agree on many candidates.[34] Among those not admitted were some radical Polish students from Vienna and a group of Polish émigrés who had come to Prague after the Wrocław Polish Congress in early May.[35]

Within the section, division was keen among the national and regional organizations, which jockeyed to place their representatives in key positions. Seweryn Celarski, who was charged with sending reports to the Rada Narodowa in Lvov, regretted that the Rada's delegates had not reached Prague several days earlier. With the exception of Lubomirski, they arrived too late to figure prominently in the congress committees. On the other hand, Celarski charged that the Ukrainian representatives from the Central Ruthenian Council, who had been in the city for several days, were actively scheming with the Czechs against the Poles.[36]

Celarski's suspicion of Czech meddling was not entirely unfounded. The choice of the Ukrainophile K.V. Zap to assist in setting up the Polish section was hardly reassuring to the Poles. And on June 1, when the Plenary Committee visited Leo Thun to inform him officially of the congress opening the next day, the Bohemian governor made a point of ignoring the Poles, including Prince Lubomirski with whom he was personally well acquainted.[37] The Plenary Committee also called on Prince Josef von Lobkowitz, the commander of the Prague National Guard. Palacký reportedly proposed a visit to Austrian military commander Prince Alfred zu Windischgrätz, but received no support for his suggestion.[38]

After visiting Thun and von Lobkowitz, the committee returned to the National Museum and unanimously elected František Palacký to preside over the congress.[39] That evening at an informal outdoor reception held for the delegates on Hunters' Island (Střelecký ostrov), L'udovít Štúr, who had just returned from Slovakia, delivered an impassioned anti-German harangue.[40]

iii

The Slav Congress was officially inaugurated on Friday, June 2, 1848. At 9:00 a.m., the delegates assembled at the National Museum and proceeded to the Týn Church near the Old Town Square for a religious service. Following the service the procession moved through the city to the Žofín Hall.[41] Curiously, the march was subdued and, despite the large number of onlookers, there was little sign of jubilation. The reporter for the Czech weekly *Pražský Posel* (Prague Messenger) thought the "magnitude of the occasion" perhaps left everyone a little breathless; yet "Prague on that day should have worn a happier countenance."[42] The correspondent for the German-language daily, *Constitutionelles Blatt aus Böhmen*, regretted that such "an unforgettable day in Prague's annals did not begin more joyously; [he] as well as the greater part of [his] fellow citizens remained quite indifferent while the long, almost endless procession passed slowly and quietly."[43]

In the large hall, conspicuously decorated with a huge black and yellow Austrian banner, the delegates took their places: the South Slavs occupied seats on the right, the Poles and Ukrainians those on the left, and the Czechs and Slovaks took places toward the rear. On a raised dais sat the members of the Preparatory Committee and the newly elected congress officials.

The assembly was opened by Jan Neuberg, the deputy chairman of the Preparatory Committee, in lieu of Chairman Josef Matyáš Thun, who presumably was ill. By one account, Thun's illness actually stemmed from the increasingly radical tone which several so-called "guests" were giving to the congress.[44] Thun later maintained that on May 29 he suffered a serious attack of gout, which incapacitated him for several days.[45] Thun had mentioned his gout to Palacký several days before the congress opened, at which time Thun declined to be considered for the presidency. What impression, he asked rhetorically, would be made if the president were obliged to welcome the Slav guests in German?[46] Here may well be the real reason for Thun's absence from the opening ceremonies. Though a Bohemian aristocrat and an ardent supporter of the Czech cultural re-awakening, he could barely speak Czech.

After welcoming the delegates on behalf of the Preparatory Committee, Neuberg turned the chair over to the president. Palacký's eloquent opening address set the tone for the serious business ahead. He cited the renewed spirit of liberty, fraternity, and harmony that had finally drawn the Slavs together, and he charged the delegates to proceed with the task of securing equality and justice for their peoples. Palacký's remarks were carefully measured; due gratitude was expressed to the "gracious" Emperor Ferdinand, under whose scepter the Slavs would surely attain a brighter future.[47]

The secretaries then read the names of the officers, the rules, and the agenda, after which delegates were invited to address the assembly briefly.

The first to take the floor was Jerzy Lubomirski. In a warmly applauded speech he called on the Slavs to abandon their "separatist egotism" and to form a firm and holy alliance.[48] The next speaker, the Moravian Jan Dvořáček, directed attention to the relations between German Vienna and the Slavs. He refuted recent charges in the Viennese press that the Slavs were working hand in glove with the forces of reaction in the monarchy. He reminded the Slavs that the Viennese, despite their present national intolerance, stood as a bulwark for political progress. But the audience seemed unwilling to entertain any favorable words on the Germans, and Dvořáček's remarks were not well received.[49]

More successful was the Croat theology professor from Slavonia, Mate Topalović, who recounted the plight of the South Slavs at the hands of their Magyar rulers. No longer would the South Slavs take orders from either Vienna or Pest, but only from their chosen ban and king. A special plea on behalf of the Galician Ukrainians was made by Ivan Borysykevych. The Ukrainians had given as much to Austria as any people, but in return they had never been accorded the respect due a nation. As if in anticipation of Polish charges, he denied that his people entertained any desire to combine with tsarist Russia. The Slovak M.M. Hodža exhorted the Slavs to assume their rightful place alongside the Latin and Germanic peoples as one of the three great families of nations in Europe. If the Slavs could achieve real harmony and unity, then no force could withstand them.[50]

The final speaker was Šafařík. In marked contrast to his usual reserve, he made a passionate and inflammatory appeal: "What has assembled us here? It is the stirring of nations . . . such as has never been in human history, and under which the earth trembles . . . . The rule of bayonets and informers is sinking into the grave." He denounced the abusive German and Magyar judgments that "we are incapable of complete liberation, incapable of higher political life, solely because we are Slavs."

> Brothers! This state of affairs can no longer endure . . . . Either we in fact purify ourselves and demonstrate that we are capable of liberation or we will be transformed in a flash into Germans, Magyars, and Italians . . . . A moral death is the worst death, but a moral life is the noblest life . . . . The path from oppression to liberation is not without struggle: either victory and unshackled nationhood, or an honorable death and after death, glory![51]

Šafařík's words electrified the audience. Josef Václav Frič noted that he spoke extemporaneously. Šafařík's contemporary and later biographer,

Josef Jireček, maintained that "this was the most solemn hour of Šafařík's life."[52] But Prince von Lobkowitz was dismayed: "This is surely revolution! What is it coming to when a man like Šafařík uses such blood-curdling language?" he remarked to an acquaintance.[53] Describing the opening ceremonies to his wife, the Moravian delegate Jan Helcelet wrote that "each speech surpassed the previous one but Šafařík's closing remarks were worth more than a hundred Viennese barricades."[54] Following the opening ceremonies, the delegates attended a gala dinner, enlivened with singing and frequent toasts to the galaxy of famous Slavs.[55]

The festive congress opening was extensively covered in the Viennese press. While the politically moderate newspapers were content merely to ridicule the activities, the radical-nationalist press used the occasion to foment anti-Slav feelings.[56] Even before the congress opened, the German press commenced a barrage of taunts that the Slavs would be unable to understand one another's native tongues and would have to deliberate in German. The Heidelberg *Deutsche Zeitung* relayed this "priceless piece of news"; the meetings, the report alleged, evoked the impression of Slavs enmeshed in building their own Tower of Babel.[57] Other newspaper accounts falsely stated that Palacký's keynote address was actually delivered in German.[58] The *Wiener Sonntagsblätter* popularized such charges in a drama parodying the congress deliberations. In each of the first four scenes a different Slav pleads for unity. The other Slavs applaud with cries of "Slava!" (glory). In the final scene a Russian, a Pole, a Serb, and a Czech ask for a common resolution. To their consternation they realize that they cannot understand one another; hence they resolve to use German in their subsequent deliberations.[59] This libel was widely accepted outside Slav circles and persisted in later years despite repeated denials by Slav and German historians alike.[60] Close examination of the congress documents indicates that German was used only in those manifestos earmarked for the emperor or for distribution abroad.

The Austro-German nationalists rested their hopes on Frankfurt, from which they hoped for a suitable response to the Prague congress. The reports of the opening session and the agenda that reached the German representatives gathered in Frankfurt on June 7 touched off a stormy session concerning the Prague developments. Though a few speakers, notably the radical Arnold Ruge, urged moderation, the majority of the delegates favored immediate action against the troublesome Prague Slavs. A few even advocated sending German military detachments into Bohemia, forgetting in their enthusiasm that the parliament commanded no such forces. Eventually the matter was referred to a special

Austro-Slav committee to draft appropriate measures.[61] And there the issue rested until news of the Whitsuntide uprising reached Frankfurt.

With barely a month's planning the Slav Congress had come to life. Although the delegates managed to organize along lines laid down by the Preparatory Committee, within the Polish section the door had been opened for the full-fledged participation of non-Austrian Slavs. It is not clear whether the Czech overseers willingly sanctioned this departure from their Austro-Slav guidelines; perhaps they simply yielded to the pervasive intoxication with all things Slav which had seized the delegates in the Bohemian capital and had culminated in Šafařík's exhortation on June 2. A leading student of the Czechs in 1848, Stanley Z. Pech, points out that "Against this background, it would have appeared blasphemous and petty to quibble over the detail of a person's birthright—it was enough that he was a Slav."[62]

But once the Slavs retired to deliberate the agenda in their respective sections, parochial interests and traditional animosities would again surface. In the days ahead, under the skeptical and often hostile scrutiny of European opinion, could the Slavs advance beyond self-righteous homilies, overcome their provincialism, and fashion an effective common policy with which to confront their nationally minded opponents?

CHAPTER 6
THE CONGRESS DELIBERATIONS

i

Whereas June 2 marked the festive opening of the congress, the substantive deliberations commenced in the sections on the following day. Both morning and afternoon sessions were scheduled at the behest of the South Slav delegates, who wished to return home as soon as possible. The Croat Sabor was scheduled to open on June 5, and hostilities had already broken in the Vojvodina between Magyar and Serb forces.

The procedures governing the congress called for the national sections to deliberate separately Zach's program and make a recommendation on each of its four points. The Plenary and Executive committees would then draft a common resolution for approval by the full congress. In the Czecho-Slovak section disagreement immediately arose over the first agenda item on establishing means for defending the national well-being of the Austrian Slavs.[1] What in fact divided the Czecho-Slovaks were their different attitudes toward Austria. Dr. Frič reminded the delegates that they were deliberating merely in an advisory capacity and that the congress in its own right possessed little power. Only the established regional diets and the forthcoming Imperial Parliament could implement the findings reached at the congress. The most effective means to obtain results would be to petition those diets in which the Slavs were well represented. "Certainly," Frič added, "we are all agreed that our primary goal is the preservation of Austria; we differ only on the means."

L'udovít Štúr quickly challenged this exclusive reliance on Austria: "Our goal is self-preservation. First we must serve ourselves, then others. As long as Austria has existed, we have decayed. What will the world say to us if we stand for no more than the maintenance of Austria?" Štúr exposed the pitfalls in holding to a narrow Austro-Slav position. The Austrian government was still dominated by Germans, while the Slav lands were neither free nor united. Only the Poles, Czechs, and Moravians exercised a measure of autonomy; the Hungarian Slavs had already seen what reply their entreaties received in a Magyar-dominated diet. If the Slavs wished to pursue a constructive Austrian policy, then the hegemony of the Austro-Germans and Magyars must first be broken. "What would become of us," he asked prophetically, "if the Germans and Magyars united to maintain their ascendancy in Austria?" Referring to the agenda, Štúr proposed:

> Let us not say we want to preserve Austria or create an Austro-Slav empire. That way would deprive us of all sympathy from the European nations. Let us rather proclaim that we wish to stand as autonomous Slav communities within Austria, with the accent on the word "Slav." Then the Austrian government can live with us.

Karel Havlíček concurred: "The main thing is to be realistic. Legality has ceased, and legally we would not go far. No one is acting lawfully in these times." Havlíček also doubted that appeals to the diets would serve Slav interests. Jan Dvořáček exhorted the Slavs to proceed from talk to deed. The Magyar intrigues at the court to secure Jelačić's removal in return for military support in Italy and with the Viennese radicals must cease. As an immediate measure he suggested issuing a call for voluntary Slav brigades to aid the South Slavs.

As on the previous day, the temper of the discussion had become inflammatory. But at this point Šafařík cautioned the delegates that they were wandering afield of the question. In a professorial manner he outlined the constitutional advances in Austria since the March revolution. The fundamental goal of the Slavs was national equality, for a nation was free only when its administration, courts, and schools were conducted in the native language. Šafařík and the Czech liberals reasoned that in sustaining Austria's integrity they were preserving a secure base where the Slavs could continue to foster national development and achieve political equality. Štúr, not convinced, continued to chide the Czechs:

> What has Austria made of you? It has sent you into Poland as the instrument of a most vile régime. What has Austria done for you whose history testifies that there has not been a more noble and heroic people? You have now become infamous instruments of servility. What is then this Austria which you Czechs have served? It is the quintessence of servility, spying, and similar rubbish.

Štúr believed that only by acquiring political autonomy could the Hungarian Slavs break the Magyar hegemony. And as long as the Magyars wielded unbridled power in their half of the monarchy, the Austrian government was unlikely to accept any revamping of the state structure.[2]

After a brief recess three proposed replies to the first question on the agenda were placed before the section: Štúr's formulation that Austria be remolded into autonomous though allied Slav national communities; a motion by Hurban calling for the recognition of national equality for all peoples in the empire; and a similar proposal from Šafařík which also took account of the different levels of national and constitutional development among the Austrian Slavs (where a nationality was still denied equal rights, the Slavs pledged themselves to their realization, and where equal rights already existed, to their defense). It was this last proposal that the section endorsed, indicating the high esteem the Czech delegates held for Šafařík.

Štúr, however, could not support such a proposal, which in his judgment "did not go beyond the customary tearful petitions" that had brought the Slavs so little in the past. To this charge Šafařík retorted: What would be gained by attempting too large a step on paper if the results remained elusive?

Although solicitous of those Austrian Slavs who still had no sanctioned constitutional apparatus (Slovaks, Serbs, Slovenes, Poles, and Ukrainians), Šafařík's formulation was equally designed to safeguard existing provincial rights such as the Czechs had received in the Cabinet Rescript of April 8. It has been characterized as the Czechs' "minimal Austro-Slav political program": a secure Austria would mean security for the Austrian Slavs whose demands were limited essentially to securing linguistic equality by recourse to lawfully established agencies.[3]

The South Slav delegates had met immediately following the ceremonies on June 2 to prepare an appeal to the other sections to join them in organizing a special congress deputation to intercede with the emperor on behalf of their embattled compatriots in the Vojvodina and in Croatia-Slavonia.[4] The Serb assembly in Sremski Karlovci had drafted a petition to the emperor on May 24 requesting confirmation of the elevation of Rajačić to patriarch and the appointment of Šuplikac as vojvoda.[5] In addition to requesting support for the Serb petition, the South Slav delegates urged the congress to express its solidarity with Ban Jelačić's efforts to sever all ties with the Hungarian ministry and to obtain administrative autonomy for Croatia and Slavonia.

The South Slavs likewise deliberated the agenda on June 3.[6] A committee was appointed to study the first item and determine if Šafařík's proposal was acceptable to the South Slavs as well. On the second item, the question of how Austria might be recast into a federative state, the South Slavs took a compromise position between preserving the existing provincial boundaries and opting for a new division along ethnographic lines. In regions inhabited by one or two nationalities (as in Bohemia, Moravia, and Galicia), the territorial basis would remain unchanged; but where several nationalities lived (as in the Hungarian crownlands), the area should be broken up into its national components. Then two or more of these nationalities were free to merge if they wished.[7] To speed the deliberations Šafařík asked the Czecho-Slovak section to endorse this compromise also.[8]

In the Polish-Ukrainian section, the discussion on June 3 came to a standstill over organizational and sundry formalities and never reached the agenda.[9] The section debated at length the form of the protocols, the admission of new delegates, the question of public or closed sessions, and the setting up of a subcommittee on Galician affairs. The last of these matters brought the smoldering Polish-Ukrainian conflict into the open. When Deputy Chairman Borysykevych demanded a separate Galician committee composed solely of Ukrainians, Prince Lubomirski countered that only political-administrative matters, not national issues, would come before the Galician committee. The section eventually decided to have two committees, one Polish and the other Ruthenian (*ruska*), but with the stipulation that they speak as one on political matters. Six members were selected for each committee, but of those on the Ruthenian committee only three were genuine Ukrainians. The other members, all of whom had designated themselves "R" (Ruthene) when they enrolled in the section, included the "Polish" Ruthenes Prince Leon Sapieha— of the old polonized family of Lithuanian magnates—and Ludwik Stecki, who was actually a member of the Polish Rada Narodowa.[10] By confusing geographical origin with nationality, the Poles again demonstrated their unwillingness to share with the nascent Ukrainian national movement their claim to speak exclusively for all of Galicia.

During the afternoon session the Polish section came no closer to discussing the agenda. A heated exchange developed with the South Slav observers after Libelt read their request for a congress deputation to Innsbruck. From the outset it was evident that the Poles had little under-standing of the conditions prevailing among the Hungarian Slavs. Karol Malisz opened by inquiring "if the information circulating in the press was correct that the Croats were surrendering to the Magyars"? Baron Kušljan, one of the South Slav observers, denied these rumors, but several voices asked what practical results could be expected from sending a deputation while the congress was still in session. Seweryn Celarski reminded the Poles of their cordial relations with the Magyars and suggested that the Poles might be mediators in the current disputes, a view which Lubomirski strongly supported. Kušljan's patience was exhausted; he challenged the Polish delegates: "Gentlemen, do not deceive yourselves; the sympathy of the Magyars for you has long since evaporated. The Magyars despise Poland!" This baseless charge merely reinforced the Poles' reluctance to take part in denouncing the Magyars.

To extricate the section from this impasse, Prince Sapieha suggested forming yet another committee to study the problem. This new "Slav Committee," composed of the twelve Ruthenian and Polish members of the Galician committee and six Poles—mostly from Poznania—with Mikhail Bakunin as the nineteenth member, was charged to determine whether a Polish mission should be sent to Hungary to mediate between the Slavs and Magyars, or whether the Poles would participate in a joint congress deputation to Innsbruck. After considerable discussion the committee recommended approval of the South Slav request,[11] but on condition that the deputation also protest the oppression of the Poles and Ruthenes in Galicia by German officials. That the Poles had scant enthusiasm for this step became apparent when the section could not find a volunteer for the deputation. Eventually the name of Julyan Dzieduszycki, who was absent from the meeting, was proposed. The section's handling of the South Slav request had exasperated Chairman Libelt:

> Gentlemen! We are taking an erroneous position; I see that we have succumbed to pressure and pretense rather than acting from conviction. I cannot commend such behavior. . . . Indifference and insincerity are infecting us, though the fate of our country depends on the fate of all Slavdom. . . . We are taking little to heart the cause for which we have gathered.

Throughout the afternoon meeting the tension between the Polish and Ukrainian delegates remained acute. When Borysykevych objected to the Poles' manipulation of the Galician question, Antoni Helcel threatened a Polish walkout if the Ukrainian protest did not cease. Many Polish delegates shared the contempt of Edmund Chojecki for these Świętojurcy (a pejorative name derived from the Uniate Church headquarters in Lvov, the Saint George Cathedral), "who are all paid by the Austrian government to sow discord and proclaim with unimaginable impudence that their nationality is stronger in Galicia than the Polish."[12]

The first section meetings had been the scene of divided opinions and harsh exchanges, quite the reverse of the harmonious and exhilarating opening ceremonies. Although the South Slavs and Czecho-Slovaks had reached tentative accord on the first two agenda points, they did so only by resorting to general formulations that, although not endangering vested national interests, would hardly make the impression on European opinion

that the Slavs deemed so vital. More serious were the national divisions
which surfaced in the sectional deliberations. For the South Slavs, the
Magyar threat overshadowed all other considerations and inevitably led
to a clash with the Poles. The Slovaks faced a twofold dilemma: though
the narrowly legalistic orientation of the Czech liberals offered them little
hope, they were not as yet prepared to follow the South Slavs in open
defiance of the Magyars. Within the Polish-Ukrainian section suspicion
and national recrimination threatened to paralyze the deliberations.

Among the delegates there was a growing awareness that the original
program was too cumbersome and imprecise. The section meetings pro-
gressed slowly and there was a general feeling that, given the existing
procedures, the congress would have little to show for its efforts.

However, a brief note of harmony was introduced on Sunday, June 4,
when an Orthodox Mass was celebrated in the open square, Koňský trh
(today, Václavské náměstí), by the Serb priests Pavao Stamatović and
Nikanor Grujić. The Mass attracted a large number of Prague citizens
and was attended by many congress delegates.[13]

ii

The Plenary Committee convened on Monday, June 5, ostensibly to
act on the South Slav request for a congress deputation to Innsbruck.[14]
But before the meeting adjourned the members had agreed to abandon the
Preparatory Committee's original program and adopt the new agenda and
procedures proposed by the Polish-Ukrainian section chairman, Karol
Libelt.

At the beginning of the meeting Šafařík suggested postponing the
departure of the deputation until the congress concluded. Speaking
for the Hungarian Serbs, Jovan Subotić insisted that the deputation be
dispatched immediately. The Serb petitioners were expected shortly in
Innsbruck, and if the deputation delayed it would surely arrive too late.
The issue was left in abeyance,[15] for at this point Libelt rose to offer
his changes in the agenda. The congress, he argued, had three objectives:

1. . . . to make clear to the world whether we are friends of liberty
or despotism, we should issue a manifesto to all the European
nations.

2. . . . to express the desires of every Slav branch in the Austrian
empire and send a declaration to that effect to the emperor.

3. . . . to provide means for attaining our goals and maintaining
our union.

Libelt proposed setting up three committees to work on these tasks. Each would be allotted three days to complete its task, after which its findings would be discussed and acted on in one day by the full assembly. In this way Libelt anticipated that the congress could finish in six days.

Šafařík and Maksim Prica translated Libelt's proposals into Czech and Serbo-Croatian so that there would be no misunderstanding of their meaning. Discussion followed. Štúr endorsed the new program but asserted that the congress must reach beyond Austria and express its solidarity with all Slavs who suffered oppression. Hopefully the European manifesto would achieve this aim. František Zach, however, thought the changes were impractical: manifestos would do little to meet the real needs of the Slavs. (Zach, it will be recalled, was the chief architect of the original program which the changes would replace.)

Other delegates spoke in favor of the new program: Prince Lubomirski, the Croats Brlić and Prica, and Šafařík and Palacký. Palacký emphasized the importance of presenting the Slavs' wishes to the Habsburg authorities and of publicizing them beyond Austria's frontiers, which the new program would accomplish. But the Slovak Hodža still opposed any departure from the original agenda. He argued that any manifesto from the Slavs should be drafted only after long deliberation. Šafařík explained that the manifesto would not be published until the congress ended.[16]

On the whole, Libelt's plan was not radically different from the original program; it was hardly "a coup which altered the character of the Congress" as Lewis Namier maintains.[17] There is no evidence of surprise among the delegates when Libelt offered his proposals. The general consensus at the June 5 meeting can only mean that the changes were worked out well in advance in private discussions between Libelt and the Czech congress leaders.[18] The original program had included a plank on Austro-Slav union and had specifically raised the idea of presenting the congress findings to the court. Only the public manifesto was a novel feature, but such practice was quite common and offered the most direct means of presenting the Slav position to the world at large.

The changes sought above all to hasten the faltering deliberations and enable the congress to show tangible results within the brief period of its scheduled meetings. An implicit but important change was to transfer the bulk of the congress business from the unwieldy section meetings to smaller, select committees where the work could be expedited without endless discussion and wrangling.

iii

The congress now had a specific and manageable program. It was to issue a manifesto to the nations of Europe, draft a petition of the Slavs'

demands to the Habsburg emperor, and develop plans to promote cooperation and union among the Slavs. Following the Plenary Committee
meeting on June 5, Libelt prepared a detailed outline of his proposals
which, upon approval by the sections, would serve as guidelines for the
committees charged with formalizing the documents.[19]

The European manifesto would proclaim the Slavs' commitment not
only to national equality but to achieving justice and liberty in their own
societies. The Slavs pledged themselves to realize the following principles:
national sovereignty vested in a representative bicameral assembly chosen
by direct election; constitutional guarantees of freedom of the press,
speech, and assembly; an equitable judicial system to guard against illegal
imprisonment; freedom of trade and commerce; a national armed force
sworn to uphold the constitution; and free public education for all citizens
regardless of religion or nationality. Libelt proposed abolishing the death
penalty as well as the practice of seizing a convicted man's property. The
Slavs should commit themselves to bettering social conditions, especially
the miserable lot of the peasantry. An important passage in the manifesto
would "attest to the principle that an individual Slav people, presently
divided politically, ought to be reunited in a national whole, . . . [and]
that no non-Slav parliaments may arbitrarily impose their decisions on
the Slav nations." Lastly, the manifesto should call on all European
nations to resolve their disputes by peaceful means. Framed in this democratic spirit the manifesto would refute the charges that the Slavs
gathered in Prague did not desire liberty but only the preservation of
the old pre-March order. As one delegate wrote to an acquaintance,
"The manifesto will demonstrate to Europe that the Slavs are not
reactionaries."[20]

In the petition to the emperor each nation would state its demands.
A preamble would affirm the Slavs' desire to join in a close association
under the Habsburg scepter and would clarify their relationship to the
non-Slav peoples in Austria. With the wishes of his own countrymen in
mind, Libelt added the request that the emperor proclaim an amnesty for
all political émigrés who had been forced to flee their homelands in the
pre-March era.

The most far-reaching feature of the new program dealt with furthering Slav union. Libelt proposed semiannual Slav congresses modeled on
the present gathering, each to be held in a different Slav city. A permanent Slav council composed of representatives from the three sections
should be established immediately to coordinate future arrangements
and to see to the founding of an all-Slav journal, library, and academy.
In addition, Libelt recommended forming a league (spolčení) of the

Austrian Slavs under the Habsburg dynasty to provide for a common means of defense against the Slavs' enemies.

Libelt, though a Prussian subject, conceded the essentially Austrian character of the congress in return for a public airing of the Polish question in the European manifesto. But this would not resolve the status of Galicia. Although the province would be included in a new Austro-Slav league, Libelt still called for the restitution of a reunited and sovereign Poland. This apparent contradiction would create considerable confusion in his own section and hamper the drafting committee's efforts to devise a workable federative scheme.

The new agenda was ready for consideration by the sections on June 6. In the Czecho-Slovak section, Šafařík briefly reviewed what had happened the previous day in the Plenary Committee and requested that discussion focus only on general themes, since the details would be worked out by the drafting committees.[21] Despite this admonition, several delegates raised objections to certain points. Vocel feared that the second chamber of distinguished national elders envisaged in the Slav assemblies would fuel the charges of reactionary politics being leveled against the Slavs, since such a body would mitigate the effectiveness of the first, democratically elected chamber. Jan Helcelet assured Vocel that the second chamber also would be elected democratically, not appointed "as usual" by the court. Hurban saw no need for a second chamber. Would not the nation, he asked, be sufficiently mature to select its most eminent leaders to the first chamber?

Several delegates were displeased with the passage on the reuniting of Slav peoples who were politically divided. Šafařík pointed out that this paragraph applied primarily to the Poles, who placed great importance on its inclusion. Nevertheless, the russophile Václav Hanka recommended its deletion from the manifesto, since the issue was too delicate to risk offending Austria's neighbors. To avoid putting this matter to a vote, an alternative and less imperative wording was offered jointly by Šafařík and Štúr. The emphasis on social and political change in Libelt's proposals, however, was not challenged; the delegates were seemingly prepared to commit the Slavs fully to a policy of domestic reform.

The next day, June 7, the Czecho-Slovaks broached the remaining two agenda items.[22] There was some confusion regarding the stipulation that each Slav people formulate separately its demands in the petition to the emperor. Many Czechs believed that the Cabinet Rescript of April 8 and the recent formation of a provisional government for Bohemia had fulfilled their principal aims. Therefore their interest turned to the future relationship between Bohemia, Moravia, and Slovakia.

Jakub Malý, editor of the Czech weekly, *Poutník,* thought the main goal should be the political union of the Czech crownlands. Dr. Otto from Brno went a step further in suggesting a common Bohemian-Moravian-Slovak government independent of Vienna. Reaching far back into history, Václav Štulc proposed the revival of the ninth-century Great Moravian Empire. Although most Czechs believed that Slovakia should eventually be joined with the Czech lands, there was no consensus on either the means or the time for establishing such a tie. Vocel feared that an open declaration of union, however common an ideal, was politically ill advised at this time. The equating of ethnographic and political boundaries would only precipitate further conflicts with the Magyars and Turks (with practically everyone) and provide additional incentive to the Galician Poles to pursue a separatist course. In the long run, Vocel added, the question of Czecho-Slovak union had to be decided by the Slovaks.

Hurban assumed the delicate task of clarifying the Slovak position. He doubted that an "old tomb" like Great Moravia could be resurrected. The Slovaks had formulated their demands on May 10 at Mikuláš, and despite the adverse Magyar response they still adhered to that program. The Slovaks did not now seek union with the Czech lands, which was neither practical—the Slovaks could not possibly withstand the full Magyar onslaught that surely would follow a declaration of secession—nor was it easy to sever a thousand-year historical tie, however oppressive. If the Czechs were surprised by the Slovak attitude, the impression does not emerge from the session's protocol.

The remainder of the meeting was devoted to a preliminary airing of Libelt's proposals for Slav union. The political role of future Slav congresses and, in particular, their unclear relationship to the existing diets raised considerable concern. Despite their rhetorical assertions of Slav unity in the earlier sessions, the Czech delegates seemed hesitant at the idea of a permanent Slav council that might encroach on their newly acquired political foothold in Austria.

Libelt's agenda encountered the greatest opposition within his own section, where several delegates seemed startled by the precipitant action of the Plenary Committee.[23] Libelt defended his program as favorable to Polish interests. The addresses, moreover, would be discussed by the sections, carefully prepared in committee, and approved by the full congress before their release. Antoni Helcel insisted that the passages on Poland be carefully formulated by the section before they were used in a manifesto. To this end he proposed forming another special committee. His suggestion provoked an outcry from the Ukrainians, who feared that only Polish concerns would be noted in a small committee. Helcel countered that to raise both Polish and Ukrainian affairs in the manifesto would imply that only Galicia was involved, although the fate of the entire Polish nation was at stake. Jan Dobrzański fueled the flames when he asserted, though claiming himself to be a Ruthene, that the Ruthenes were not yet a nation and that they needed Poland's help to become one. Even when the Ukrainians' objections were voted down, the controversy did not subside. Hynylevych threatened that the Ukrainians would have to demand that the section be disbanded if the Poles continued to deny a distinct Ukrainian national identity and to block their demands.

Libelt attempted to calm the Ukrainians by pointing out that the section was discussing a political, not a national matter. The Ukrainians had no cause to take offense. Europe did not recognize a Polish-Ruthenian nation but only a Poland torn into three parts. "The Ruthenian arrogations could well arouse similar claims by Lithuanians, Mazurians, and other nationalities." The Ukrainians had to decide whether to stand by Poland or follow the Russian tsar. Zaklyn'skii replied that the Ukrainians wanted to show Europe that they were a distinct nation, not a Polish dependency. They had shared too much with Poland to wish to sever all ties, but they were determined to obtain full autonomy in Eastern Galicia. The increasingly acrimonious exchange and the threat of a Ukrainian boycott prompted Libelt to adjourn the session and turn the matter over to the Galician committees.

Again the Ukrainian question had completely immobilized the section. The Poles and Ukrainians had no more success in deliberating the new program than the earlier one. Most Poles dreamed only of separating Galicia from Austria and thereby establishing the first link of a restituted Polish state. At the least, they sought autonomy for the entire province under nominal Austrian sovereignty. The Ukrainians' demands for national equality and administrative autonomy in Eastern Galicia were an unwelcome annoyance, capable of disrupting these larger Polish aims.

A potential compromise between the Poles and Ukrainians had narrowly failed on June 4 when a member of the Ruthenian subcommittee, Zenon Pogłodowski, withdrew his support for a draft agreement that included a plank on the administrative division of Galicia.[24] It is unlikely, however, that the full Galician Committee (including six additional Poles) would have supported such an arrangement. Only by sidestepping the thorny issue of administrative division was the Galician Committee able to reach accord. The seven-point agreement provided specific guarantees of national equality for the Ukrainians in Galicia.[25] The language of administration in a given district would depend on the prevailing national-ity of the local populace, though either Polish or Ukrainian was allowable in dealing with the authorities. This meant that in areas of mixed nationality officials must be bilingual. The language of instruction in the primary schools would be determined in the same manner, but by the third year study of the other language must commence. The national guard would wear the emblems of both nationalities (the Polish eagle and the Ukrainian lion). Galicia would be governed by a single diet and central administration where both languages could be spoken. All official notices would appear in both languages. The agreement placed the Roman and the Greek Catholic rites on an equal footing, but made no mention of the Greek Orthodox Church. Nor did the agreement take into account the German- and Yiddish-speaking populace in Galicia. The key final point affirmed that only "a constituent assembly could determine the necessity and time for a division of Galicia into two separate administrative regions." Inclusion of this last point assured Polish support. The agreement was approved by the twelve-man Galician Committee on June 7, but with the reservations of four Polish members, including Lubomirski, to the first passages on equal language rights in the administration, which they believed properly fell within the province of a constituent assembly as well. They also objected to airing the Polish-Ukrainian polemic in the address to the emperor.[26]

It is difficult to judge the agreement, since it was never formally accepted by the Ukrainian Holovna Rada and the Polish Rada Narodowa in Lvov,[27] although several of the provisions favorable to the Ukrainians were later invoked arbitrarily by the anti-Polish government in Vienna. Historians have differed sharply in their assessments of the agreement, usually reflecting their national persuasions. For example, the Polish historian Władysław Wisłocki contended that the Poles acted in good faith, but the Ukrainian Ivan Bryk believed that most of the Polish dele-gates had no intention of abiding by the agreement.[28] An immediate result of the agreement was to push the divisive national question into the background and allow the section to concentrate on the new agenda. The Ukrainian delegates no longer intervened in the discussions at every mention of the Polish question, though this did not mean that the deliberations within the section became any less boisterous.[29]

Among the South Slavs Libelt's program provoked considerably less dissension than was the case in the other sections. The proposals for the European manifesto were speedily endorsed and the South Slavs drafted their respective demands for inclusion in the petition to the emperor, to which they added the request that the provinces of Dalmatia, Croatia, Slavonia, and the Vojvodina be united as an autonomous part of the federally restructured Austrian state. There was, however, no mention of the Slovenes.[30]

iv

A second meeting of the Plenary Committee was called on June 7 to assess the progress made by the sections on the new agenda.[31] The first to report were the Czecho-Slovaks. But barely had Hurban finished his presentation of the Slovak position when the Croat Dragutin Kušljan protested: If the Slovaks remained associated with Hungary—with the Magyar government—they would ineluctably strengthen the Magyar element against the Slavs. The Croats were set on breaking away, and if the Slovaks did not follow suit they would find themselves fighting against their Slav brothers. Štúr pointed out to the South Slavs that the Slovaks were obliged to use discretion and consider public opinion in voicing their demands:

> We had to be diplomatic in our declaration; we recognized the necessity of remaining for the time being within legal bounds. Our nation is not so well outfitted militarily as the Croat and Serb. . . . Our people still have not acquired full nationhood; we still cannot speak openly to them. We have patriots [in Slovakia], but if we expressed anti-Hungarian sentiments, thousands of them would oppose us. But rest assured, brother Serbs and Croats, we shall not lag behind.[32]

The South Slavs were not so easily reassured. Jovan Subotić argued that the situation of the Vojvodina Serbs was no less precarious. The best policy was complete frankness, not only for the effect on European opinion, but especially to one's nation. He warned that if the Slovaks stood by the Magyars they would have to fight the Serbs as well. Despite Šafařík's repeated attempts at mediation, the dispute persisted. Hurban perhaps best summed up the Slovak dilemma when he pleaded:

> Each nation acts according to its circumstances. . . . Our own weakness is to blame for the fact that we do not want to fight. Should the Magyars accord us our due, we could hardly extirpate them—draw our swords against them. . . . But if the Magyars refuse, then of course [there will be] war.

At this point Kušljan moderated his position: "There is no reason to tell the Slovaks that they must break away [from Hungary] ; [we ask] only that they not recognize the Hungarian ministry." Šafařík supported this compromise position, but the most Hurban was prepared to concede was that the Slovaks would consider the South Slav request. He reminded Kušljan that, though he was a delegate of the Croat assembly, empowered to act in its name, the Slovaks attending the congress had no such official mandate from their people.

Until now, the Poles had refrained from intervening, but the debate afforded them an irresistible opportunity to renew their offer to mediate the Magyar-Slav dispute. Karol Malisz cautioned the South Slavs not to foment a European war; rather, they should seek a peaceful resolution of their conflict with the Magyars. But the South Slavs were already committed to a complete break, even at the price of war. They were angered by the Slovaks' vacillation, which meant the loss of an ally, and they resented the Poles' meddling.

To bolster their spirits, in the evening the delegates were treated to a patriotic theatrical performance. A one-act piece, *Matka Sláva,* by the Czech dramatist Josef Kajetán Tyl, was premiered before the main show. A Pole, a Serb, a Slovak, and a Czech succeed one another on stage, and each recalls his nation's heroic past. The Czech calls on the mythical figure of Mother Sláva to help the Slavs unite and overcome their recent misfortune. In the closing scene, against the backdrop of a panorama of Prague, she leads her four offspring before a statue of Emperor Ferdinand, while an Austrian hymn plays. Despite its primitive appeal, the play was so well received that it was presented again after the main performance.[33]

A parody of Tyl's play later appeared in the *Wiener Sonntagsblätter.*[34] In the final scene of the Viennese version, the four Slavs, now including a Russian, discover that they cannot understand one another, and resolve to speak only German in future meetings.

Since the Plenary Committee had been sidetracked by the Slovak-South Slav exchange, the section members were afforded additional time to formalize their recommendations to the drafting committees. In the Czecho-Slovak section Šafařík prodded the delegates, whose endeavors had so far achieved only a moral impact, to shape a "genuine confed-eration" of Austrian Slavs.[35] The union must be constructed to receive the full support of the provincial diets. Šafařík believed that this would be no obstacle in Bohemia. He foresaw the greatest difficulty with the Poles, who envisaged any Austrian tie for Galicia as a temporary measure. But the way was open for them to join. The non-Slavs in Austria also posed a dilemma, but for the present Šafařík felt that only Slavs should be included in the union.

The Czech lawyer Alois Trojan disagreed, maintaining that essentially the congress did have only a moral purpose. Echoing the sentiments of Dr. Frič at the first section meeting, he contended that properly speaking the Imperial Parliament should take up the question of federation, and then only on the recommendation of the regional diets. As long as non-Slavs lived in the empire, a Slav congress had no authority to formulate Austrian political policy.

Šafařík did not rule out the importance of consultation at the Imperial Parliament, but personally he doubted that it would actually meet this year. Preparations had not yet begun in Galicia, and the Hungarian Slavs undoubtedly would not be justly represented. In such uncertain times it was folly for the Slavs to delay, a view with which the section concurred. The Austrian Slavs should first unite among themselves, and only later might the non-Slavs be invited to join. No mention was made of the non-Austrian Slavs.

The range of opinion in the Polish-Ukrainian section paralleled the discussion of the Czecho-Slovaks.[36] A legalistic view, reminiscent of Trojan's argument, was advanced by Jan Dobrzański. As a private gathering, the Slav Congress had no right to draft a plan to reorganize Austria politically. Helcel, perhaps the best informed of the Poles on constitutional matters, could not deny the correctness of Dobrzański's argument, but as patriotic spokesmen the delegates also had an obligation to chart means for furthering understanding and cooperation among the Slavs. The discussion was cut short when several members left to attend a meeting of the Plenary Committee.

Unfortunately, neither the protocol of the June 8 Plenary Committee meeting nor of any subsequent meeting of that body is preserved. From Seweryn Celarski's report to the Rada Narodowa we know that the sections were instructed to select their representatives for the deputation to convey the petition to the emperor, as well as for a permanent Slav council in Prague. At Helcel's request the committee formally agreed to include a passage in the European manifesto deploring the continued partition of Poland.[37]

Alone among the three sections, the Poles and Ukrainians had still not completed their recommendations to the drafting committees. The fact that several conservative Polish delegates were hostile to the new agenda, which they believed gave excessive power to the Plenary Committee, had not expedited the deliberations. The section eventually endorsed Libelt's proposals on June 9, but only after another stormy exchange on the future of Galicia and the Poles' attitude toward Austria.[38]

The greatest difficulty centered on the proposals for a union of Austrian Slavs. Helcel was for "enthroning the principles of federalism," but only on condition that special status be granted to Galicia. Lubomirski disagreed: the Poles should not impose stipulations which could hinder the effectiveness of the Slavs' plans. "Should we say that we are Slavs only out of egotism?" Łukaszewicz agreed; the other Austrian Slavs had not put restrictions on Polish participation and the Polish question had received a sympathetic hearing at the congress, so "Let us therefore proceed with trust and in good faith."

The non-Austrian Slavs were more skeptical. Józef Zalewski feared that a federation of only Austrian Slavs would bind Galicia in entangling commitments and impede the settlement of the broader Polish question. The Poznanian Janiszewski was more explicit: the section was forever embroiled with Galicia's affairs. He rejected Lubomirski's reasoning and would not endorse any sort of "Pan-Slavism": "I am first of all a Pole, only afterwards a Slav. Such a point of view is not egotistic."

Nor did all Galicians share Lubomirski's and Łukaszewicz's enthusiasm for an Austro-Slav union. Celarski doubted that anything would come of such plans: "Whether this union will really come about is hard to say; but so much is certain: each [Slav] tribe is pursuing only its own advantage in Slavdom." The Serbs and Czechs were the worst offenders. The Poles could not expect much help from a still weak Slavdom, but Polish participation would at least legitimize the project before European opinion. And though the Poles would have to follow the "hypocritical policy" of the Czechs, some gains might be made for Galicia.[39]

Before adjourning on June 9, the Polish section received two memoranda from the Silesian delegates, Paweł Stalmach and Andrzej Kotula. National consciousness among the Slav populace in both the Teschen (Těšín, Cieszyn) and Opava (Troppau) regions of Austrian Silesia was just emerging. Most thought of themselves as Silesians rather than as belonging to a particular Slav nationality. Czech national consciousness was limited to a few individuals scattered in the towns and villages of the Opava region. Polish consciousness was somewhat more developed, due to the efforts of Ludwik Klucki, a lawyer in Teschen, and his circle. One of Klucki's collaborators was Paweł Stalmach, who, while studying in Bratislava, had been deeply impressed by Štúr's efforts to overcome Slovak linguistic provincialism. Štúr introduced Stalmach to Prince Lubomirski, who took the young Silesian under his wing.[40]

The Czech congress organizers had not actively extended their efforts into Austrian Silesia. None of the Czech patriots there received the announcement, though Lubomirski saw to it that Stalmach and his friend Kotula attended. Thus Austrian Silesia was largely represented by nationally minded Poles.[41] The Poles favored their young compatriot Stalmach by electing him to the Plenary Committee and by appointing him assistant secretary of the section.

Kotula's memorandum, "Why Silesia, insofar as it is Slav, desires to unite with Poland,"[42] declared categorically that the Silesian Slavs were of Polish nationality, despite their unfortunate separation of over eight hundred years from the Polish crown. Even under foreign rule they had remained overwhelmingly Polish in sentiment and culture. Kotula recognized the difficulty in joining Silesia to Galicia at present, but insisted that the province must be eventually reunited with Poland, "only with whom its happiness can be found." He urged the Poles to lay claim to the region and asked the Czechs to accede to this natural union.[43] Kotula rejected the notion that thousands of Czechs lived in the Opava region and around the towns of Frýdek-Mistek. Actually these people spoke neither Czech nor Polish but a mixture of the two; nevertheless their sympathies were for Poland.

Stalmach's memorandum, though echoing Kotula's arguments on the national question and Silesia's return to Poland, also spoke of the political and social needs of the region. There must be constitutional guarantees to ensure freedom of speech and equality before the law, to improve the miserable lot of the peasantry, and, most importantly, to protect the Silesian Slavs from the abusive power of the ruling Germans.[44]

It is noteworthy that neither memorandum was incorporated in the petition to the emperor, which in fact contained no specific reference to Silesia. At the time of the congress, apparently neither the Poles nor the Czechs wished to pursue their claims on Silesia, though seventy years later the Silesian issue would paralyze cooperation between these newly independent nations.

v

During what proved to be the final days of the congress there were few formal meetings. Business shifted to the three drafting committees, where the pronouncements were prepared for final congress approval. Though the sections still met informally, there is scant record of what happened.

The last meetings took place on Whitmonday, June 12. The Plenary Committee formally approved a draft of the European manifesto and scheduled a final congress session for June 14 in the Žofín Hall. Although only two documents—the European manifesto and the petition to the emperor—were expected to be in final form, it was anticipated that action could also be taken on a plan for Austro-Slav union, even if some changes would have to be made later.[45]

The Plenary Committee meeting broke up shortly after noon; immediately after, street fighting broke out between a crowd that was returning from a Slav Mass at the Koňský trh and some Austrian soldiers. In the week of fighting which followed, the congress was unable to continue its deliberations. Most of the delegates fled the city and a few were arrested or expelled by the military authorities.[46] The Slav Congress, which had opened with so much enthusiasm and expectation, had fallen a hapless victim to the first counterrevolutionary assault in Central Europe.

i

The Manifesto to the Nations of Europe was the only pronouncement that the congress approved before the street fighting caused the deliberations to close. It was prepared by the Diplomatic Committee, which Palacký headed. The committee held several meetings before agreeing on the text, probably on June 10. The actual drafting of the manifesto was entrusted to Palacký, who drew on suggestions from Libelt, Zach, Šafařík, and Bakunin.[1]

In Palacký's final version, the manifesto stated the aims of the Slavs gathered in Prague. Recent revolutionary changes throughout Europe now impelled the Slavs—eighty million strong—to assume their rightful place among the peoples of Europe. The yoke of oppression, "raised and defended by brute force in collusion with fraud and malice, is collapsing into dusty ruin under our eyes. A fresh vital spirit spreading over wide expanses is creating new worlds: freedom of speech, freedom of action have at last become realities."[2] The Slavs, "among whom liberty was ever cherished," were determined not to embark on the course of oppression that had marred the history of the Latin and Germanic peoples:

[The Slav] demands neither conquest nor dominion but he asks for liberty for himself and for all others: he demands that liberty shall be unconditionally recognised as the most sacred right that man possesses. Therefore we Slavs reject and hold in abhorrence all dominion based on main force and evasion of the law; we reject all privileges and prerogatives as well as all political differentiation of classes; we demand unconditional equality before the law, an equal measure of rights and duties for all.

The manifesto then raised an even more vital concern: the desire for the free development of Slav nationality:

Not less sacred to us than man in the enjoyment of his natural rights is the *nation,* with its sum total of spiritual needs and interests. Even if history has attributed a more complex human development to certain nations than to others, it has none the

less always been seen that the capacity of those other nations
for development is in no way limited.

The manifesto denounced those nations which in pursuit of their own
aims infringed on the just rights of other peoples to nationhood:

> Thus the German threatens many a Slavonic people with violence
> if it will not agree to assist in the upbuilding of the political great-
> ness of Germany, and thus the Magyar is not ashamed to arrogate
> to himself exclusive national rights in Hungary. We Slavs utterly
> decry all such pretensions; and we reject them the more emphati-
> cally the more they are wrongfully disguised in the garb of
> freedom.[3]

The Slavs did not seek vengeance for these wrongs; they were prepared to
"extend a brotherly hand to all neighbouring nations who are prepared
to recognise and effectively champion with us the full equality of all
nations, irrespective of their political power or size."

As for Austria's political future, the Slavs were determined that "the
state must be fundamentally reconstructed, if not within new [geo-
graphical] boundaries, at least upon new principles." Foremost among
these principles was the transformation of the imperial state into a "confederation of nations, all enjoying equal rights."[4] In this new union the
Slavs envisaged "not only [their] own salvation, but also liberty, enlightenment and humanity in general." The Slavs trusted that the European
nations would recognize the justice of this new arrangement. But whatever
the case, the Slavs were committed to defending their national well-being
by all available means. The manifesto refuted the calumnious accusations
which the enemies of Slavdom were spreading, especially the "bogey of
political Pan-Slavism."

Turning to specific injustices, the Slavs condemned the unjust partition
of the Polish state and called on the "governments concerned finally to
remedy this old sin."[5] The manifesto also demanded that the Hungarian
ministry cease persecuting the Slavs and fully assure their just national
rights.

In conclusion, the Prague Slavs proposed that "a general European
Congress of Nations be summoned for the discussion of all international
questions," and, prophetically, urged that this step be taken in all haste
"before the reactionary policy of the individual Courts causes the nations,
incited by hatred and malice, mutually to destroy one another!"

Among students of the Slav Congress the manifesto has evoked disparate judgments. Its admirers, exemplified by the Czech historian Josef

THE ACHIEVEMENTS OF THE SLAV CONGRESS

Macŭrek, maintain that the manifesto went well beyond other liberal homilies of the day by its radical egalitarian spirit and supranational appeal, and was "an effective reply to the Germans and Magyars who abused and sneered at the Congress."[6] Other writers have made more critical assessments. The Bohemian German historian Anton Springer, who witnessed the events of 1848 in Prague, pointed to the political naïveté and the contradictions of the document as the discrepancy between the radical urgency of the closing sentence and Palacký's cautious approach to reform within Austria.[7] Recently, Stanley Z. Pech has contrasted the idealistic depiction of a pacific Slav character, which contributed to a prevailing theme of Slav goodness and German evil permeating the document, with the manifesto's failure to weigh the social cause of oppression.[8]

Essentially the manifesto reflected a compromise of views advanced during the congress. Although specific political proposals were confined to the Austrian Slavs, the manifesto nonetheless voiced concern for the Slavs beyond the Habsburg borders. But any reference to the Russians was deliberately sidestepped to avoid adding fuel to critics' charges that the Slavs were playing into tsarist hands.[9] Both the romantic theme of a common Slav heritage and the primacy of the concept of national sovereignty derived from the pre-March writings of the Slav reawakening. In issuing the manifesto the Slavs sought to clarify their position before an uninformed—if not misinformed—European opinion.

Although Palacký had at his disposal several alternative drafts, the manifesto remained both in stylistic formulation and subject emphasis essentially his own creation.[10] Nevertheless, a German commentator for *Die Grenzboten* could not fathom that this "liberal" manifesto was the work of Palacký: "[It] is completely foreign to the spirit of the Czech party. The manifesto aims at the bright plains of humanism, [while] the Czechs' policy looks back to the past. . . . The language of the manifesto preaches peace among nations, but the entire policy of the Czechs. . . has been maliciously to incite the Germans to anger and hatred."[11]

On many issues Palacký's views did not significantly differ from those of his collaborators. Libelt's draft dwelled at length on the uniqueness of pacific Slav character and the egalitarian basis of primitive Slav communal life. He likewise projected a messianic role for the Slavs in a rejuvenated Europe. Libelt paid less attention to immediate political issues—the dangers stemming from the Germans and Magyars—than appeared in Palacký's final version. A teacher of philosophy by vocation, Libelt foresaw the triumph of a sort of Christian socialism, wherein individual Christian love would guide the relations among nations as well.[12] As a manifesto, however, Libelt's draft was ill conceived, bearing in the opinion of one observer "an uncomfortable resemblance to a political tract."[13] Moreover, Libelt's draft contained none of the specific proposals for social and economic reform that he had outlined in the new agenda of June 5.

Zach's suggestions covered many points raised by Libelt and anticipated Palacký's text. The previously politically scattered Slav tribes were rightly following the lead of the Latins and Germans in striving to attain political liberty, national equality, and union. Zach echoed the theme of an inherent egalitarian spirit among the Slavs, but unlike Libelt he scrupulously applied his suggestions solely to the affairs of the Austrian Slavs.[14]

ii

The preparation of the address or petition to the emperor was entrusted to a second drafting committee. The individual nations' demands were compiled by Jerzy Lubomirski and Jan Helcelet and prefaced by a brief introductory statement which the Kraków Pole Antoni Helcel prepared.[15] When hostilities broke out on June 12, only final stylistic adjustments remained to be completed before presentation to the congress for formal approval. According to Jan Petr Jordan, Lubomirski and Helcelet were working in the latter's hotel room on the last corrections when the shooting started at the nearby military headquarters. The soldiers, charging that shots had been fired from the hotel, placed the guests under arrest. Lubomirski and Helcelet were detained at the military compound until the following afternoon (June 13), when they were released on condition that they immediately leave the city. Though some of their papers were seized by the military authorities, it was later possible to piece together the text of the address from notes in the possession of the other committee members.[16] The reconstructed text was published in the local press and released as a broadsheet after the uprising.[17]

Helcel prefaced the address with a brief survey of recent political developments. The Europe of 1815—that abusive and archaic edifice of arbitrary bureaucratic rule over both nations and individuals—was moribund; the rule of justice and national equality was emerging. Adherence to this new political spirit constituted the most effective means for Austria to weather the current upheavals. Fulfillment of the Slavs' demands would serve the interests of a revitalized Austrian state. The Slavs addressed the emperor "with complete filial confidence in [his] paternal grace."

The Bohemians (Czechs) spoke first, expressing their appreciation for the Cabinet Rescript of April 8, which had gratified their aspirations "to their complete satisfaction." They had no additional demands. The Moravians asked that their province be accorded the same political rights that Bohemia had already been granted. Moravia should remain autonomous, but under a central administration from Prague, not Vienna. It was hoped that the Moravian and Bohemian diets would be permitted to meet in joint session. Neither the Bohemian nor the Moravian Czechs broached the matter of relations with their German compatriots, preferring to leave this question for local determination. Similarly, an outright declaration of the union of the two provinces was sidestepped, since this issue should rightly be decided by the provincial diets.

The Galician Poles and Ukrainians likewise sought greater provincial administrative autonomy. The Poles noted their disappointment at the failure of the emperor to act favorably on their earlier petitions. They demanded the same rights the Bohemians had received, and called for the establishment of a new, constitutionally selected Galician diet empowered to legislate for the province. The Polish-Ukrainian national agreement of June 7 was appended with the wish that the emperor initiate steps to implement these joint recommendations. Since the Polish-Ukrainian agreement called for officials knowledgeable in the local languages, the Galicians urged the emperor to replace all officials (i.e., Germans and Czechs) who did not meet this stipulation. Should other employment not be found for those so released, the provincial administration would underwrite the costs of assuring them a suitable pension.

The Slovaks objected to the distorted view which the Magyars and the Hungarian ministry attributed to their national aspirations. Their demands were modest and in keeping with the Mikuláš petition of May 10, which asked essentially for national administrative autonomy to establish Slovak schools and institutions. Specifically, they asked the release of all Slovak prisoners being held for alleged "national" offenses. Lastly, there should no longer be a "ruling" nationality in Hungary.

The South Slavs reiterated their requests made at the opening of the congress when they first raised the question of sending a special congress deputation to Innsbruck. The Vojvodina Serbs asked the emperor to acknowledge the legal authority of the Sremski Karlovci assembly and the recently established provisional Serbian government. Similarly, the Croats urged recognition of Jelačić's position as ban and the legality of the Croat Sabor then meeting in Zagreb. But there was no mention of the South Slav union which had figured prominently in South Slav plans, nor any reference to the Magyars and the deterioration of national relations in Hungary. The Serbs and Croats appealed to the emperor in his capacity as king of Hungary and rejected the legitimacy of the Magyar-dominated ministry in Pest.

The Slovene demands, more far-reaching, had little chance of fulfillment. They asked that all Slovenes in Styria, Carinthia, Carniola, and the Littoral be politically unified in a Slovene kingdom with its capital in Ljubljana. Slovene would be the official language and a Slovene-language university should be established in Ljubljana.[18]

In a closing paragraph the Czechs, Moravians, and Slovenes jointly rejected incorporation of their lands in a Greater German state, a move "which [would] impair the sovereignty of the Austrian monarchy and make [the Slavs] dependent on a foreign legislative assembly."

The demands of the Austro-Slavs followed a common pattern. Those nations which already possessed a regional assembly sought to gain (in the case of Bohemia, to preserve) a greater measure of local determination in their national and provincial affairs. The less fortunately endowed nationalities—Slovaks, Slovenes, Ukrainians, and, to a lesser degree, Serbs—demanded the opportunity to determine their own national existence. They appealed to the emperor to intervene directly in their affairs, while the former sought less central administrative involvement in their affairs.

At no point in the address did the Slavs attempt to justify the legitimacy of the Prague congress to serve as a forum for expressing their joint concerns, nor did the individual national spokesmen defend their right to formulate demands on behalf of their co-nationals. These issues were not put to a test. In the confusion of the June Uprising the Slavs' demands were never sent to the emperor, and it is unlikely that a copy was even informally presented to the court.

iii

The third congress project—the plan for a federative union of the Austrian Slavs—was even less near completion when the deliberations were suddenly terminated. The committee on inter-Slav relations examined several proposals that went beyond the guidelines set by the congress sessions. As outlined by Šafařík, the federative plan applied initially to only Austrian Slavs. The status of foreign Slavs, as well as the Magyars and Austrian Germans, would be worked out later. Though there had been less consensus among the Poles on limiting the union expressly to Austrian Slavs, the Polish-Ukrainian section had eventually endorsed this limited federative scheme.

Proposals by Libelt and Bakunin were therefore unacceptable to the committee, since they encompassed the Slavs living beyond Austria's frontiers. Similarly, a proposal from František Zach was rejected because it envisaged a federation of all peoples in Austria.[19] A more modest proposal, known as the "Akt unji rakusko-słowiańskiej."(Act of Austro-Slav Union) was advanced by the Poles Jerzy Lubomirski and Antoni Helcel. Their plan, although not formally acted upon by the congress nor later circulated with the congress pronouncements, nevertheless reflected the most comprehensive formulation of congress opinion on the central question of inter-Slav cooperation.[20] The Austrian bias of the arrangement is explicit. At a time when a dangerously weakened Austrian government was tottering toward incorporation in a greater Germany, the Austro-Slavs were uniting under the scepter of the ruling Habsburg dynasty to defend their nation and their territorial integrity. An executive Council of Union Representatives (Rada Wysłańców Unji), comprising five members from each participating nation, would meet annually to resolve issues among the union members and coordinate common action. In times of war or crisis the council would meet in permanent session. The union would become effective when three or more nations joined.

Administrative and legislative powers remained in the hands of national or regional diets and the Austrian central authorities. The council's authority was primarily moral and depended on the cooperation of the individual members. The Polish authors also inserted special safeguards for Poland's interests. The second paragraph specifically stated that those nations where only a portion of the populace lived within Austria did not, by joining the union, sacrifice their determination to achieve eventually political independence for their entire nation. Polish interests were also reflected in paragraph 16, which authorized the Magyars to join the union if "by word and deed" they took action to improve measurably the national well-being and equality of their Slav compatriots. A similar paragraph was added permitting the Austro-Germans to join if they renounced their *grossdeutsch* aspirations.

Although it entailed little more than a forum to perpetuate the dialogue among the Austrian Slavs and to provide channels for meeting common danger, the plan illustrated the broadening awareness of Slav leaders. Only a few months earlier, many Slav spokesmen had had but limited knowledge of each other's problems and aspirations, and their initial response to the breakdown of the absolutist pre-March regime had been to achieve greater local privilege and determination of their affairs. The implementation of the federative plan would have provided a significant check on German and Magyar efforts to spread dissension among the Slavs. Like the address to the emperor, the plan for federative union was a casualty of the Prague uprising. Yet, despite the failure of the Lubomirski-Helcel scheme, the congress discussions on federative union contributed to later deliberations on the reorganization of the monarchy in the Vienna and Kroměříž Reichstag.[21]

iv

Among the proposals that the Third Committee did not consider, only one—a scheme advanced by Bakunin—has been preserved. In his confession to Tsar Nicholas I,[22] written in 1851 while he languished in the Peter and Paul Fortress in St. Petersburg, Bakunin discoursed at length and with remarkable candor on his experiences at the congress.[23] He was "carried away by the sincerity and warmth of simple yet profound Slavic feeling" in Prague. Politically, the Slavs behaved like children, but he found in them "incredible freshness and incomparably more natural intelligence and energy than in the Germans." The "childlike delight" that the Slavs displayed in their encounters deeply moved Bakunin. They gave him the impression of "members of one and the same family, scattered by a terrible fate throughout the whole world," whom the Slav Congress had now reunited after long and arduous separation. "They wept, they laughed, they embraced—and in their tears, in their joy, in their cordial greetings there was no phrasemaking, no falseness, no high-flown bombast. Everything was simple, sincere, sacred." So profoundly was Bakunin seduced by the Slavs that he later confessed that he "was ready to forget almost completely all democratic sympathies tying [him] to Western Europe."[24]

But for the actual operation of the congress, Bakunin had few kind words: "It—just like all other contemporary congresses and political gatherings—was decidedly empty and meaningless."[25] The congress' shortcomings stemmed in particular from the conflicting aspirations of the participating nations. "In a word, everyone was pulling in his own direction and wished to make of the others a steppingstone for his own advancement."[26] Bakunin chastised the organizers for limiting the gathering to Austrian Slavs and thereby excluding the vast majority of Slavs living in the Russian, Prussian, and Ottoman empires. He likened the Austrian Slavs to those Slavs enslaved by Austrian Germans, and their congress to "a congress of German slaves."[27] He emphatically rejected Austro-Slavism, a policy that merely played into the hands of the reactionary Habsburg authorities:

> I know that many of you hope for the support of the Austrian dynasty. It promises you everything now, it flatters you because you are necessary to it; but will it keep its promises. . . ? You will see that the Austrian dynasty not only will forget your services

but will avenge itself upon you for its past shameful weakness, which forced it to humble itself before you and flatter your seditious demands. The history of the Austrian dynasty is richer than others in such examples, and you learned Czechs, you who know so well and in such detail the past misfortunes of your motherland, you should understand better than others that it is not love for the Slavs, or love for Slav independence, or for the Slavic language, or for Slav mores and customs, but only iron necessity that makes it seek your friendship now.[28]

Only the complete destruction of the Austrian empire could pave the way for the liberation and union of all Slavs.

Bakunin also warned those Slavs, especially the Serbs, who in desperation might turn to tsarist Russia for salvation:

No less mistaken are those who, for the restoration of Slav independence, hope for the assistance of the Russian Tsar. The Russian Tsar has concluded a new close alliance with the Austrian dynasty, not for you but against you, not to help you but to return you forcibly . . . to your old subject status, to your old absolute obedience. . . . But now there is no place for you in the womb of the Russian Tsardom. You want life, but deathly silence is there; you demand independence, movement, but mechanical obedience is there. You desire resurrection, elevation, enlightenment, liberation, but death, darkness, and slavish labor are there. Entering the Russia of Emperor Nikolai you would enter the tomb of all national life and of all freedom.[29]

Bakunin conceded that without Russia the Slavs' strength would be limited, but it was senseless to believe in Russian help. For the time being he urged the Slavs "first, to unite outside of Russia" while awaiting that country's early liberation:

Begin your unification in the following manner: proclaim that you Slavs—not Austrian but living on Slav land in the so-called Austrian Empire—have gathered and united in Prague to lay the first foundation of the future free and great federation [federatsiia] of all Slav peoples; and that in expectation that your Slav brothers in the Russian Empire, in the Prussian possessions, and in Turkey will join you—you . . . have concluded among yourselves a strong and indissoluble, defensive and offensive union.[30]

Bakunin's insistence on dismantling the Habsburg state was not shared by most of the congress participants. As we have seen, the Czech liberals, who were strongly supported by the Galician Ukrainian and South Slav delegates, pinned their political aspirations on a revitalized and federally restructured Austria. To thwart German and Magyar nationalist ambitions they willingly allied themselves with the Habsburg court. Even for the Galician Poles, a continuing Austrian tie, at least for the time being, held the best prospect for acquiring greater provincial autonomy. The few days Bakunin spent in Prague scarcely afforded the opportunity for understanding the historical evolution and immediate problems besetting the Austrian Slavs.[31] Bakunin envisioned them essentially as potential supporters for his overriding aims: to destroy Austria and to launch a vast revolutionary campaign in Russia for the overthrow of the tsarist regime.[32]

But Bakunin was disillusioned with the sessions: "Days flowed by and the congress did not move." The Poles, whose section he had joined, were bogged down over procedural and parliamentary formalities and the Ruthene question.[33] Bakunin therefore strongly endorsed the changes in the agenda that Libelt introduced midway in the deliberations. The new program rekindled Bakunin's hopes in the congress and opened broader horizons for his new-found Pan-Slav beliefs. He was appointed to the committee on inter-Slav relations, for which he hurriedly drafted a plan for Slav union. Entitled "The Fundamental Principles of the New Slav Policy," Bakunin's plan was published in fragments and, he maintained, without his knowledge. It first appeared in a Polish newspaper in the aftermath of the June Uprising, and was soon translated into Czech and German.[34]

Bakunin divided his plan into three parts: the first—a kind of preamble of Slav aspirations—bears a remarkable resemblance to passages in Palacký's final version of the European manifesto.[35] Bakunin echoed the pre-March Slav publicists on the heroic future that awaited the Slavs. The time was ripe for the Slavs to forge lasting unity and to assume their rightful place alongside the other "races" in Europe. But the Slavs would not commit the same errors that had plagued other peoples. Having themselves long been victims of oppression, and knowing that it could be equally destructive for the oppressor as for the oppressed, the Slavs would never attempt to impose their will arbitrarily on others. Truth, liberty, and justice would guide their relations with one another and their dealings with other nations. The Slavs rejected the statist orientation of European politics, with its reliance on force and deceitful diplomacy; their new policy was one "of nations, of free and independent peoples." Their strength must lie in unity, for past divisions had led to fratricidal strife and subservience to alien rule. But their ordeal was ending and union was within their grasp; "the hour of deliverance had sounded for the Slavs."

It is the second and third sections of Bakunin's plan, however, that attracted the greatest interest. "The Bases of a Slav Alliance" details the considerable power which will be accorded to the central federative authority. Sovereignty is vested in a Slav council which serves as the highest authority and tribunal. The council alone possesses the power to declare war and conclude agreements with foreign states. The council would arbitrate all disputes arising between individual Slav nations, and its verdicts were binding. Bakunin dwells at length on the sacred duty of each Slav nation toward its brother nations. Failure to aid a brother nation in need, an alliance with a non-Slav power, or even pursuit of an independent policy were deemed treason to all Slavdom.

The last section was devoted to "Internal Regulations" of the member nations. Autonomy was assured in all matters not specifically reserved to the central council, but in accordance with certain inviolable principles: "equality for all, liberty for all, and brotherly love." The Slavs were free in both law and fact; servitude was forever abolished, and only the inequalities ordained by nature would exist. There would be no privileged castes or classes; if the nobility wanted to partake of this new Slav existence, "it must henceforth seek its honor and privilege in its abundant love and in the greatness of its renunciation." Each Slav was free to move about and to settle where he chose within the federation, and he had the right to appeal to the council any injustice at the hands of his own national institutions.

Bakunin's proposal was not a constitutional outline but an exposition of principles to guide the Slavs' future political organization. The national polemics that embroiled the Slavs' deliberations in Prague receive only indirect reference (treated as consequences of Slav disunity that their opponents had fostered to turn the Slavs against one another), in what Bakunin's early biographer, the Ukrainian M.P. Drahomaniv, described as a "utopian, completely idyllic" approach to Slav unity.[36] Yet in the *Confession,* which was unknown at the time of Drahomaniv's writing, Bakunin maintained that the concentration of power in a strong central authority was specifically intended to combat the "selfish and vain pretensions" of the Czechs and the Poles.[37]

Others have pointed out the anti-liberal and potentially coercive features of Bakunin's plan. Benoît-P. Hepner suggests that "despite the anti-statist emphasis of the preamble, it was actually a superstate" that Bakunin wished to create.[38] There is no mention of ways for establishing and operating the federation, nor any suggestion of how to select representatives for the federal council, nor any indication of what form the government would assume. In the *Confession* Bakunin stridently voiced his hostility to representative constitutional government as practiced in parts of Western Europe. He preferred a republic, but of what form he did not elaborate. However, in his remarks on Russia's political future he argued the necessity for a strong dictatorial power that would be devoted to uplifting and educating the masses.[39]

One writer who does not share Drahomaniv's critical assessment of Bakunin's plan is his fellow Ukrainian Ivan Franko. Franko argues that to understand the "New Slav Policy" one must appreciate the emotional impact on Bakunin of the Prague congress. The underlying motif which permeates Bakunin's plan in essentially Christian, not revolutionary: the emphasis is on fellowship and justice, imbued with truth and liberty.[40] The program exudes a newly discovered faith in the great destiny of the Slavs, whom God himself will henceforth lead toward a glorious future. Common adherence to this messianic belief (essentially the application to politics of Kollár's pre-March cultural Pan-Slavism) will suffice to surmount past dissension and enable the Slavs to overcome their enemies.[41]

Bakunin's ideas for Slav federation were not original. Federative schemes were frequently discussed in the Polish exile circles that Bakunin frequented in Paris and Brussels. They held a prominent place in the thinking of the Decembrists and in Kostomariv's program for the clandestine Cyril and Methodius Society. It is the infusion of messianic expectancy, not the specific formulations and principles, that explains the contemporary publicity and attraction of Bakunin's program.

During his brief stay in Prague, Bakunin gathered a band of sympathetic followers into the loosely organized Society of Slav Friends. It was composed mainly of radical Prague students and a few dissident Slav spokesmen.[42] But with the outbreak of the June Uprising the group quickly dissolved. The insurrection took Bakunin, as it did the other congress delegates, by surprise. Its instigators, he maintained, were a few students and the "so-called Czech democrats." They lacked a clear political strategy and their plans were premature and ill-conceived; they had rallied to the banner of insurrection because "rebellions were then generally in vogue."[43]

When the fighting erupted, Bakunin claimed to have tried to dissuade the students from a futile course that would only offer the military an

easy victory.[44] Failing this, Bakunin threw himself into the battle: "However flimsy the prospects he could not remain inactive when revolution
was afoot."[45] By his own account, he armed himself with a rifle and went
from barricade to barricade, encouraging and counseling the leaders in
the rebel headquarters in the Clementinum.[46] Accounts vary, however,
on the degree to which Bakunin actually assumed leadership and command
of the uprising in its last days.[47] Bakunin stayed in Prague until the
insurgents capitulated on June 17, when he managed to escape the net
of Austrian commander Windischgrätz and make his way to Breslau.

v

The example of the German correspondent's astonishment that Palacký
could compose a "liberal" manifesto has been all to readily overlooked in
the outpouring of partisan judgments on the congress, its leaders and its
aims. The majority of participants did agree with the organizers' Austro-
Slav policy, which envisaged the best guarantee of security for the smaller
Danubian Slav nations within a revitalized Austrian state, but very few
were diehard supporters of a reactionary Habsburg order. In the Czecho-
Slovak section both Štúr and Havlíček (purported architects of Austro-
Slavism) openly challenged the legalism of their more cautious co-nationals.

No less can all Poles be viewed as staunch opponents of Austria. Libelt,
the alleged "radical" section chairman, repeatedly urged moderation and
compromise on his more volatile compatriots. And the most significant
contributions to the Austro-Slav imperial petition and the federative plan
were made by the Poles Lubomirski and Helcel. Even Bakunin, his later
rhetorical condemnation of the congress notwithstanding, eagerly contributed to drafting the various pronouncements.

The view that there were clear-cut ideological divisions at the congress
stems largely from the attempts of latter-day writers and historians to
instill order into the apparent confusion of congress activities. Such
forays into facile categorization were initially inspired by the critical
assessments of the congress' opponents. More recently this oversimplifi-
cation has been continued by Marxist authors, who have attempted to
explain the congress as the self-interested action of a nascent Slav (princi-
pally Czech) bourgeoisie in league with feudal-aristocratic interests.[48]
But can Šafařík's revolutionary address at the opening ceremonies (which
was so instrumental in inflaming Slav passions) or the leaders' ready
acceptance of Libelt's new agenda on June 5 be considered as the tactical
measures of a cautious Austro-Slav bourgeoisie?

Had the congress been permitted to run its course, clearer dividing lines would surely have crystallized. But then the gathering might also have lost much of its fascination for later observers. In fact, the paramount place Slav history assigns to the congress stems in no small part from its martyrdom for the cause of Slav unity.

PART 3

THE AFTERMATH

I know of no event of our times that has had more
fateful and damaging consequences for the nation
than this Whitsuntide uprising.

—František Palacký, *Political Testament* (1872)

CHAPTER 8
THE JUNE UPRISING

i

The fighting that erupted on Whitmonday, June 12, took the members of the Slav Congress by surprise and precipitated its premature closing. Essentially it was a spontaneous popular reaction to the provocations of the Austrian military commander in Bohemia, Prince Alfred zu Windisch-grätz.[1] The uprising occurred in an atmosphere of mounting social and national tensions in Prague. Economic disruptions had put scores of craftsmen out of work, and the recent radical victories in Vienna, culminating in the flight of the emperor on May 17, were freshly imprinted on the popular mind. Furthermore, the presence of numerous Slav visitors in the city had sparked patriotic enthusiasm among the Czech populace.

Already in 1848 the relationship between the Slav Congress and the June uprising was the subject of passionate controversy. The Slavs' opponents eagerly traced the outbreak of the fighting to the congress and its members, particularly to alleged radicals in the Polish section. The Slavs denied these charges, contending that the uprising was instigated by their enemies to disrupt the congress and thwart Slav political aspirations.[2] From the outset, the attempts of contemporaries and later historians to assess the blame were hampered by the actions of General Windischgrätz and the Viennese authorities in the aftermath of the uprising.

ii

During the preceding decade, Prague had been transformed from a dormant provincial capital into an expanding urban industrial center.[3] In 1841 steamer transport was introduced on the Vltava, and with the completion that same year of a second bridge spanning the river and connecting the New Town with the industrial suburb of Smíchov, the city rapidly expanded along both banks to the south. Coal from the nearby Kladno fields was brought by rail to power the growing number of steam mills.[4]

The transition from an artisan economy to factory production brought widespread social dislocation. In 1844 day laborers and jobless hand spinners and cotton printers had protested against advancing mechanization.[5] Prague was undergoing a marked change in its ethnic complexion as well, as peasants from surrounding Czech villages flocked to the city to man the new machines.[6] Factory conditions were harsh and living standards among the workers were appallingly low.

The political upheaval in the wake of the March revolution not only emboldened the working classes to voice more forcefully their grievances and demand improved conditions, but also contributed to a slump in production. Supplies of raw materials, American cotton, for example, failed to arrive, credit dried up, and many mills were forced to close.[7] Widespread unemployment and a sharp rise in retail prices brought the workers into the streets again in early May.[8] There were outbreaks of rioting and looting, spurred by an outpouring of anti-Semitic tracts and cartoons that blamed Jewish entrepreneurs and shopkeepers for the economic crisis and the workers' plight.

The city's lower social strata were largely Czech-speaking, while the commercial bourgeoisie was predominantly Germans and German-speaking Jews. The nobility was overwhelmingly German-speaking, although a few aristocrats espoused a Bohemian regional patriotism and supported the Czech cultural revival. A distinct Czech national consciousness, however, was limited to a few middle-class professionals—doctors, lawyers, scholars, and officials—and Prague's student population.

Next to the workers, the students made up the most volatile segment of Prague society. Soon after news of Metternich's fall reached Prague the students drafted a petition demanding sweeping changes in the governance of their institutions. Following the example of their Viennese counterparts, they formed an academic legion, comprising several divisions or cohorts, along the lines of the different faculties. Attired in smart uniforms and sporting arms, the students regarded themselves as staunch defenders of the new constitutional order.[9] The vanguard of the Czech student movement was the Slavia association. Contacts were maintained with the Viennese students, whose repeated successes spurred their Prague counterparts to bolder action.

The main object of the workers' and students' dissatisfaction was Windischgrätz, who resumed command in Prague on May 20, 1848, following an absence of several months.[10] The general was reputed to be a reactionary aristocrat, an ardent proponent of Habsburg absolutism, and a heartless soldier who headed the troops that brutally put down the 1844 workers' rising. As soon as he returned, military activity in the city intensified; patrols were doubled, and at a military review on June 7 the general made pointedly derogatory allusions to the new constitution. He increased the size of the garrison and placed heavy artillery on the Vyšehrad and Petřin heights that dominated the central city.[11]

Popular reaction to these measures was swift.[12] At an open meeting at the St. Wenceslas Baths on June 8, ways to secure Windischgrätz's recall were aired. In the next days the students formulated a series of sweeping and, in the military's eyes, preposterous demands: the immediate surrender of 2000 rifles, 80,000 cartridges, an artillery battery, and the removal of all cannon from strategic points overlooking the city.[13]

Surprisingly, in the midst of this rising tension, both sides appeared together under the same roof. The occasion was a gala Slav ball in the Žofín hall on Saturday, June 10, in honor of the congress delegates. Both Governor Leo Thun and Windischgrätz made an appearance, although the latter stayed only briefly. Despite obvious ill feeling—an observer commented that Windischgrätz's entrance was accompanied by a soft hissing—the general's presence did not mar the festivities.[14]

The following morning the students' mood was less restrained. Having foregone a special Slav Mass in the Týn Church, the students gathered at the university, where they were joined by some radical Prague citizens whose principal spokesman was the young lawyer Karel Sladkovský.[15] A few members of the Slav Congress, notably the Slovak Hurban, were also present. The weather was sweltering, extremely hot and humid for early summer.[16] A delegation headed by Sladkovský conveyed the students' demands personally to Windischgrätz. At military headquarters their reception was chilly. Windischgrätz haughtily maintained that he was responsible only to the emperor and would take all measures necessary to ensure public order. When the delegation returned to the university with the general's reply, shouts of "to the barricades" resounded, and only with difficulty did Sladkovský manage to restore order.[17]

At another meeting later that day at the St. Wenceslas Baths, Sladkovský again opposed a rash violence that might harm the Slav Congress and play into the hands of the military. Instead, plans were laid for a peaceful rally the following day. Weapons were not to be worn.[18] Nevertheless, throughout the day there were sporadic incidents of violence, especially between roaming bands of workers and the city's national guard.

The next morning, Whitmonday, June 12, several thousand protesters, mostly workers and students but including some patriotic citizens and curious onlookers, gathered on the Koňský trh.[19] At the statue of Saint Wenceslas Father Jan Arnold led a Mass in Czech.[20] Following the Mass the crowd, including women and children, dispersed; many headed toward the military headquarters, passing on the way the National Museum, where the congress delegates had just concluded their morning sessions. It appears that the crowd intended only to caterwaul in mock serenade before the general's quarters. But as the marchers neared the military compound they encountered a deputation of conservative German burghers who had just met with Windischgrätz. Scuffling ensued between the crowd and the Germans and with the soldiers who tried to intervene. A few shots were fired and the marchers retreated into the narrow streets and alleyways of the Old Town. Barricades were quickly thrown up as news of the clash spread. The spark had been found to ignite the tension which had been filling Prague for days.

iii

The fighting lasted six days, until June 17, when Windischgrätz dislodged the insurgents by a heavy cannonade from the heights above the city. Fighting with limited arms, and in large measure leaderless, the students and workers, who predominated among the rebels, had held the Austrian grenadiers at bay in close street fighting.[21] Attempts at a mediated settlement by Czech moderates, city councilors, and a deputation from the Austrian cabinet had all been blocked by Windischgrätz's intransigence. After his wife was killed by a stray bullet on the first day of fighting, the general had a personal stake in the battle.[22] Nothing but unconditional surrender would satisfy his desire for vengeance.

When the insurgents capitulated, Windischgrätz put the city under martial law and authorized a military-civilian commission to investigate the causes of the uprising and bring the principal offenders to justice. Both actions were taken on June 18 without the authorization of the Austrian Ministry of War; and the state of siege continued, despite protests in Prague and Vienna, until July 20. The Investigatory Commission (Ausserordentliche gemischte Militär-Gerichts-Untersuchungs-Kommission) was dominated by military judges and, in practice, was simply a tool of Windischgrätz's vindictiveness. The uprising, in the general's view, was clearly the result of a "widespread conspiracy" that the commission must uncover.[23] In the words of one writer, the commission "launched a veritable conspiracy to uncover a conspiracy."[24] While the city remained under martial law the military had unlimited power to search and arrest. Citizens were encouraged to inform against their neighbors.

From the outset the commission directed its attention to two groups: the Prague students and the spokesmen of the Czech national movement. The fact that a number of those most active in the fighting had managed to flee before Windischgrätz's net closed—both Sladkovský and the student leader, J.V. Frič, escaped—in no way inhibited the commission's zeal. The headquarters of Slavia, the Czech student association, was raided and its papers seized, including plans of the locations and concentrations of the city's military fortifications and supplies. Largely based on testimony provided by the polytechnic student Maximilian Maux, the commission charged that the plans were drafted by Frič for the purpose of preparing the uprising.[25] In his memoirs, Frič, while admitting the existence of such plans, insisted that the measures adopted by Slavia were only defensive.[26]

The commission also investigated charges that a number of radical Viennese students had met in secret in Prague on the eve of the uprising, hoping to duplicate in Prague their recent victories in Vienna. The view that Viennese students had deliberately provoked hostilities in order to break up the Slav Congress was also advanced by several moderate Czech leaders.[27]

While the investigation of the students uncovered, in the eyes of the commissioners, ample evidence of aggressive measures against the military authorities, it failed to round out Windischgrätz's case for an organized conspiracy committed to the destruction of the Austrian state. To justify this allegation the commission turned its attention to the Czech political leaders and the affairs of the Slav Congress.

Even prior to the uprising the congress delegates had been subjected to harassment from local authorities. On June 11, while the congress was in session, Prince Josef von Lobkowitz, on his own authority as head of the predominantly German Prague National Guard, had summarily ordered the visiting delegates, especially Poles and South Slavs, to leave the city.[28] The next day, June 12, shortly after the initial clash at military headquarters, a detachment of soldiers stormed the Czech National Museum on the pretext that shots had been fired from an upstairs window. When they entered the building they found only the librarian, Václav Hanka, and no evidence of shooting. Nevertheless, the military used this occasion to search the museum.[29] A similar incident occurred at the nearby Blue Star Inn, where many foreign delegates were staying. Again charging that shots had been fired, the hotel and its occupants were searched.[30]

On June 13 many of the visiting delegates were rounded up and expelled from the city. A number of Poles, including Prince Sapieha, Jędrzej Moraczewski, and Karol Malisz, were put aboard a steamer for Dresden. In his memoirs Sapieha described their passing another steamer headed toward Prague filled with German students from Leipzig who hoped to arrive in time to fight the Slavs.[31] Other delegates, including Jerzy Lubomirski, whom the military had arrested, and the South Slavs Subotić, Grujić, and Stamatović, were placed on a train for Olomouc.[32] Despite orders to leave the city, a few delegates told Palacký they were willing to remain if he, as congress president, believed the meetings could continue.[33] Still others, already forced to leave the city, repeatedly inquired the likelihood of reconvening the congress.[34] However, with Prague under military control there was no chance that any delegates would be permitted to return. Eventually, on June 28, the Czech leaders issued an announcement that the congress was indefinitely postponed.[35]

On June 21 Windischgrätz had ordered the Prague municipal police to keep close watch on the activities of František Palacký;[36] Pavel Josef Šafařík was also under surveillance.[37] Toward a third prominent Czech political figure the commission showed fewer scruples: on the basis of an anonymous denunciation, Karel Havlíček's lodgings were searched on July 3 and his arrest followed several days later. His personal papers were seized and the soldiers turned upside down the offices of his Czech daily, *Národní Nowiny*, in search of incriminating evidence.[38] News of Havlíček's arrest spread quickly and created a stir among the Czechs in Bohemia. Taking place on the eve of elections to the Imperial Parliament— Havlíček was returned from five separate voting districts while in jail— the incident became a source of embarrassment to the Austrian ministry, which now confronted a Slav majority in parliament.[39]

Particularly damaging to the Czechs, however, was an anonymous pamphlet that began circulating in Bohemia in late June, *Die Hochverräther, welche für 7 Millionen Rubel Oesterreich an Kaiser von Russland verkaufen wollten*, a copy of which was forwarded conveniently to the Investigatory Commission on July 6. Its author charged that a plot had been carefully laid to betray Austria from within while Russian soldiers approached the border. It singled out the Bohemian nobles Baron Drahotín Villani, Count Jiří Buquoi, and Count Vojtěch Deym as the chief conspirators, and alleged that Villani had corresponded with the Russians and had already received 7 million rubles. Their goal was purportedly to turn the Austrian Slavs against the Germans and Magyars and later to unite with Russia. Buquoi would head a provisional government until the Russians arrived. The Czech fanatic Petr Faster had drawn up a list of rich Germans and Jews who would be massacred on a second Bartholomew's Night, which was planned for June 15. Fortunately, the pamphlet concluded, the leaders had been arrested in time—Buquoi, Deym, Villani, and Faster had been seized by Windischgrätz's soldiers—and with the compromising correspondence.[40]

iv

Reliable news on the uprising was slow in reaching the outside. The earliest reports, carried by frightened citizens who fled the city at the outbreak of fighting, were sketchy and exaggerated. Wild rumors of Slav atrocities against the Prague Germans abounded in neighboring Dresden. One "eyewitness" account in the *Deutscher Volksfreund* on June 17 reported that Prague Germans were being tortured; the Czechs were dragging wounded soldiers from their hospital beds and had hacked off the hands of a German student and left him to fend for himself.[41]

The initial accounts in the Viennese Pan-German press characterized the fighting as a national conflict between fanatical ultra-Czechs and Bohemian Germans. Windischgrätz was grudgingly hailed as the savior of German interests.[42] From Leipzig, *Die Grenzboten* showered praise on the general for his handling of the Czech "terrorists": "Windischgrätz is an aristocrat, but truly in the best sense of the word. If only there were some men of such caliber among the democrats!"[43] Not until more reports drifted in did the Viennese democrats perceive the broader implications of the clash in Prague. *Der Freimüthige*, which on June 16 had described the Czechs as "unsere Todfeinde" ("our deadly enemies") who must be answered by the sword, reported on the following day that "the national question has receded into the background; Germans and Czechs are fighting as one against Windischgrätz."[44] *Der Volksfreund*, which at first had expressed gratitude to Windischgrätz, now described his measures in Prague as "the acts of a barbarian."[45] The Viennese liberals were not prepared to whitewash the obstinate Slavs, but the question now on their minds was: "If this could happen in Prague, what about Vienna?"[46]

News of the fighting in Prague was delayed in reaching Frankfurt. There, as elsewhere in the German lands, the initial reaction was to view events as a national struggle between Slavs and Germans. In a session on June 20, several delegates again clamored for the immediate dispatch of Prussian, Saxon, and Bavarian armies to aid their beleaguered German compatriots in Prague. Ignaz Kuranda, just arrived from Prague, opposed such futile action. The conflict in Prague, he pointed out, was not national; only a small group of fanatical Czechs and proletarians had risen against the military, and Windischgrätz had no need of reinforcements. The Austrian authorities, he insisted, must be made to protect German interests in Bohemia. The matter was again referred to the Austro-Slav Committee to formulate an appropriate response to the Prague developments.[47] On July 1 the committee reported on two proposals. The first denounced the aggressive Pan-Slav designs to mold Austria into a "great Slav empire." The Austrian ministry was enjoined to undertake immediate steps to assure elections to Frankfurt from the "Germano-Slav land." The second proposal reiterated the earlier demand that a German military force be dispatched to Bohemia.[48] In the ensuing debate, the Viennese representative Berger tried to redirect attention beyond the national question. "The time may soon come," he warned, "when both [nationalities] will have to join against a third, more dangerous power." Berger had in mind, of course, the reactionary court camarilla, the only group that really gained from Windischgrätz's victory in Prague.[49]

But when put to a vote, both recommendations were overwhelmingly endorsed. However, the pace of events had outstripped whatever relevance these measures might have possessed. By July 1 Windischgrätz completely dominated the situation in Bohemia; the Habsburgs had no intention of inviting German intervention in their affairs; and later, when assistance was sought, Austria would turn to tsarist Russia. Moreover, elections in Austria were already under way for the Imperial Parliament in Vienna, which would overshadow the transactions in Frankfurt.

Only the most radical wing of the German left treated the June uprising sympathetically and rejected the nationalist outburst that had dominated the German press. As early as June 17 Friedrich Engels, in the *Neue Rheinische Zeitung,* wrote a dispassionate and remarkably accurate account of developments in Prague. As revolutionaries the Czechs were to be applauded: "The insinuations in the German papers that the Czechs were serving the reactionaries, the aristocracy, and the Russians were utter lies."[50] The Democratic Club in Breslau, headed by Marx's erstwhile collaborator Ruge, considered issuing a manifesto of support to the Prague insurgents, but the matter was tabled "until it could be determined for a fact that the Slavs were democrats"![51]

v

The Investigatory Commission did not immediately delve into the affairs of the Slav Congress. Although the congress received much publicity in the Slav as well as the German press, its specific deliberations and final pronouncements were not known to the public at large. Only the opening ceremonies on June 2 had been covered extensively in the press. Following the publication in the Czech newspaper *Pokrok* of the protocol of the Czecho-Slovak section meeting of June 3, the congress leaders decided to withhold specific reports until the congress had concluded its deliberations. Due to the uprising, the European manifesto and the petition to the emperor were not published until early July.

Eventually, on June 28, the commission approached Governor Thun to secure the congress files. Thun, in turn, addressed requests to Palacký and Šafařík as the leading congress officers still in Prague to submit all pertinent papers and documents. On June 30 Šafařik forwarded the printed congress pronouncements, and several days later he relinquished a number of the handwritten protocols.[52] Palacký, who was anxious to join his ailing wife in the country, sent a lengthy note to Thun in which he defended the congress and denied any part in the uprising.[53] Privately, however, the congress leaders showed more concern over the uses to which the documents might be put by the commissioners. In a note to Palacký on July 3, Šafařik expressed reluctance at turning over the handwritten protocols and hoped that it might be feasible to make certain corrections before releasing the papers.[54]

Thun duly turned over the materials he received to the Investigatory Commission on July 8.[55] Personally, Thun did not share the commission's suspicion that the congress was directly linked to the uprising. In late July, shortly after his dismissal as governor, he submitted to the new Austrian Interior Minister, Baron Anton Doblhoff, his own report on the Slav Congress. From a reading of the documents, Thun was convinced that the congress had "no other intention than to achieve a cordial understanding and close union of all the Austrian Slavs under the Habsburg scepter in order to secure the full public recognition and status for their nationality that the Germans and Magyars now enjoyed." Such gatherings were no danger to the state as long as they limited themselves to the enhancement of national well-being and did not presume to have any legislative or administrative authority.[56] But Thun's influence in the aftermath of the Prague debacle had so diminished that his belated defense of the congress and its Czech leadership had little effect on either Windischgrätz or the Austrian cabinet. When the authorities in Vienna did eventually move to moderate Windischgrätz's witch-hunt, they acted out of political opportunism and not from sympathy for Slav national pride.

vi

Despite the abundance of denunciatory letters and pamphlets, as well as the large number of suspects under arrest, the commission's case for a widespread conspiracy was not progressing. The interrogations of the more prominent captives had failed to turn up sufficiently damaging evidence.[57] But in mid-July the floundering efforts of the commission took a dramatically fortunate turn when testimony was obtained to link the uprising and the Slav Congress to a vast conspiracy of Slavs. The source of this sensational testimony was the young law student from Slovakia, Marcel Turánsky. Although he had been questioned on June 27 and July

6, Turánsky did not begin his tale of conspiracy until his third interrogation on July 15. On that date he determined to make a "full confession" and "place himself at the mercy of Austrian justice."[58]

In 1847, while studying in Prešov (Eperjes) in northern Hungary, Turánsky had become acquainted with several Polish émigrés. Gradually they took him into their confidence. The Poles were in secret contact with a number of prominent Slavs, including František Palacký. Their common goal was the creation of a "great Slavic Empire" comprising Croatia, Slavonia, Serbia, the Czech crownlands, Northern Hungary, and Galicia. In this new constellation of nations the Hungarian kingdom would cease to exist. The conspirators were still disagreed on whether their new empire would become a republic or a kingdom.[59] But they had been corresponding, employing invisible ink, with radical circles in France.

Their plan was not to go into effect until the year 1850, when simultaneous revolts were to break out in four key locations: Zagreb, Prague, Kraków, and in the area of Bratislava. But when the February Revolution erupted in France, they decided to advance the timetable. Arrangements were made to coordinate outbreaks in the above cities which would also coincide with peasant disturbances in Slovakia and Galicia. As to the names of the conspirators, Turánsky claimed only partial knowledge. The leaders in Bratislava were the Slovaks L'udovít Štúr and J.M. Hurban; in Prague, he felt sure, the organization was headed by "a certain Palacký." He knew of letters Palacký had written to the ringleaders in Prešov, but he had not read them.[60]

As to his own role, Turánsky claimed he had been ordered on April 21 to the Galician town of Nowy Sącz (Sandez), where "an attack by a hundred Polish émigrés on the region's banks was planned." There Turánsky was to meet the Pole Karol Zielonka and together they were to determine the sentiments of the peasants in the area around Kraków. He failed to meet his contact, however. From there Turánksy journeyed to Lvov, where he presumably met with the Galician Pole Karol Malisz. It was Malisz who suggested that he attend the forthcoming Slav Congress in Prague and urged him to "carry a weapon" as "the outbreak would soon be starting there."[61] Turánsky arrived in Prague on May 30 in the company of Malisz and several other Poles and found lodging at the Blue Star Inn.

The general tenor of expression at the Slav Congress was hostility toward the government, Windischgrätz, and the military. Turánsky claimed he was a member of the Polish-Ukrainian section, although there is no record of his belonging to any section or committee of the congress.

Quite likely he passed the time in the company of other students, particularly Poles, who had come to Prague but failed to gain congress
membership. In addition to the scheduled sessions, Turánsky reported that
a number of secret meetings were held in which the Poles Karol Libelt,
Jerzy Lubomirski, and other congress delegates were active. The purpose
of these meetings, in Turánsky's opinion, was surely to lay preparations
for an armed insurrection "shortly after Whitsuntide." This testimony
conveniently dovetailed with the charges in the anonymous pamphlet
that the commissioners had received earlier.

In the days following his initial disclosures, Turánsky was questioned
repeatedly on details of his story. The common pattern of interrogation
was for the investigators to mention a name and for Turánsky to volunteer
some incriminating information on that individual's activities. Turánsky
was also "permitted" to confront the most important prisoners for the
purpose of identification. In this manner the commission's prize captives
were easily linked to the growing conspiracy. Among the congress delegates, Turánsky noted that their discussions often turned to the subject
of barricades. In his hotel, where many Polish delegates were staying,
weapons had been collected in anticipation of the uprising. Turánsky also
reported that even before June 12 members of the Czech militia, Svornost,
had been sent into the surrounding villages to drum up support for the
impending uprising. Turánsky had not learned the ultimate aim of the
uprising, however; but judging from the talk of the instigators it certainly
amounted to "the separation of Bohemia from the Austrian state."[62]

Contemporary observers and later historians have posited an array of
conflicting explanations for Turánsky's disclosures. They agree only that
Turánsky was not what he claimed to be: an authority on a conspiracy
by Slavs to destroy Austria. Little evidence, however, has been uncovered
to sustain the view that Turánsky was a Magyar agent sent to Prague to
disrupt the Slav Congress and sabotage the Slavs' political aspirations.[63]
The Czech priest Jan Arnold, who was imprisoned with Turánsky in the
St. George Monastery, recalled that fellow prisoners cautioned him about
"a young Magyar from Prešov," who was reported to be an "informer."[64]
Earlier, when Turánsky had arrived in Lvov in late April and presented
himself to the Polish Rada Narodowa there, he requested a detailed report
on the views of the Galician Poles which he intended to send to Lajos
Kossuth.[65] The charge was also raised that it was in fact Turánsky who
first exhorted the demonstrators to "serenade" Windischgrätz at military
headquarters on June 12.[66] But at best such evidence is highly conjectural
and circumstantial.

The Magyars would have unquestionably welcomed any setback to the Austrian Slavs,[67] but would they have entrusted so vital and dangerous a task to a nineteen-year-old student? Furthermore, Turánsky was not ethnically a Magyar. His father, who died early, came from a Slovak family in Liptovský Svätý Mikuláš. His mother, who raised him, was a Galician Pole. More plausible is the view that Turánsky was simply an adventurous youth who had associated with Polish revolutionaries while a student in Prešov, and who journeyed to Prague in search of excitement.

The individuals Turánsky named in Prešov were indeed associated with the Prešov section of the radical, émigré Centralizacja. From Slovakia, a center of revolutionary activity in the pre-March years, the Polish émigrés hoped to stir up insurrection in Western Galicia.[68] Turánsky is known to have associated in 1847 with the Pole Karol Zielonka, at the time actually an Austrian police informer with the code name "Ritter," and the radical Slovak Janko Francisci-Rimavský.[69] Turánksy's linking the democratic Polish *emigracja* to Palacký in Prague, however, was pure fantasy.

During his short stay in Prague, Turánsky displayed a pronounced exhibitionist tendency. The idea of becoming a star witness, rather than languishing anonymously in a military prison, coupled with a possible hint of reward from his questioners if he cooperated,[70] might well have contributed to his desire to make "a full confession." This would help explain the curious fact that he waited until his third hearing before unfolding his story. His testimony suggested a clever blend of minor facts and large-scale fabrication as he related precisely what the investigators most wished to hear.

The circumstances leading to Turánsky's arrest provide further indication of a desire for attention and recognition. Following the uprising he reportedly sought the company of soldiers and boasted of how he had started the shooting from the Blue Star Inn on June 12.[71] Eventually his behavior attracted the attention of a Captain Müller, who went in search of him. At the Blue Star Inn he learned that Turánsky had left the hotel on June 17 without paying his bill. Turánsky was finally arrested on June 27 when Müller found him staying at another hotel in one of the most expensive rooms.[72]

vii

Turánsky's testimony had breathed new life into the faltering investigations. Although much of his story was a boastful and malicious fabrication, the commissioners chose to believe it. Interrogations of other witnesses were stepped up; yet when these failed to yield the slightest corroboration for a conspiracy, the commission continued to give complete credence to Turánsky's version. Immediately following

Turánsky's initial disclosures, the commissioners had forwarded part of his testimony to the Hungarian Palatine, Archduke Stephen, requesting that the individuals mentioned in Prešov be investigated. The archduke forwarded the inquiry to the Hungarian Interior Ministry, which in turn dispatched its own investigators to Prešov. They failed, however, to turn up any of the alleged conspirators.[73]

The Czech historian Zdeněk Tobolka has suggested that the Investigatory Commission and Windischgrätz found so much of Turánsky's monolithic view of the Slav movement acceptable because they themselves were so poorly informed on the divergent aspirations of the Slav peoples in the wake of the March Revolution.[74] In this respect they shared the ill-informed judgment of the German critics of the Slav Congress.

A detailed account of Turánsky's testimony first became public in a report which Windischgrätz issued on August 2, 1848, regarding the causes and goals of the June uprising.[75] The occasion for its disclosure at that time was the turning over of the investigation to the Prague criminal courts, which fell under the authority of the Austrian Ministry of Justice. Windischgrätz wanted his views clearly on record, since the subsequent investigation would be largely out of his hands. He gave full support to Turánsky's story and singled out the Polish section at the congress as a particular source of treasonous activities. The names of the chief conspirators were known to the authorities, but in order not to prejudice the further investigation Windischgrätz conveniently refrained from citing them.

Windischgrätz's charges provoked an immediate outcry among the Slavs.[76] From Vienna, where they were both deputies to the Imperial Parliament, Palacký and Lubomirski issued a joint denial of the general's allegations and challenged him to make public the supposedly incriminating documents.[77] In Prague protest meetings were called, and on August 24 a group of Czech lawyers addressed a formal complaint to the parliament.[78] However contrived Windischgrätz's charges might have been, they repeatedly placed the Slavs on the defensive. For his own part, Windischgrätz was under no compulsion to answer for his actions, especially as the investigation was no longer under his direction.

Turánsky's case was handled more discretely in the civilian courts; no new disclosures were forthcoming, but Turánsky apparently stuck to his story.[79] From Vienna, Justice Minister Alexander Bach now viewed the continued investigation as embarrassing to his government and pressed for its early liquidation.[80] The task of preparing an evaluation of the Turánsky case fell to a clerk of the Prague court, J. Roob. His lengthy report, though never made public, reflected the civilian investigation's judgment on Turánsky and, indirectly, the relationship of the Slav

Congress to the uprising.[81] Roob concluded that, although some form of confrontation with the military was undoubtedly "planned and prepared," it hardly anticipated the violence which ensued. Despite Turánsky's testimony, which Roob did not specifically reject, doubt remained regarding the actual purpose of the uprising. As for the congress, Roob noted that, whereas certain individuals attending may have entertained or even expressed treasonous views and their remarks could have been misconstrued, the congress as a whole, judging from its pronouncements, protocols, and the subsequent declarations by its leaders, had no such character. It was by no means certain that the Slavs who had gathered in Prague sought to undermine the integrity of the Austrian state. Had Roob's report seen the light of day it would have pleased neither Windischgrätz nor the Slavs.

The matter of the Investigatory Commission was not allowed to die following the amnesty of the remaining political prisoners on September 14, 1848, and the release of the last prisoner, Antonín Špaček, in December.[82] On January 24, 1849, the Czech deputy to the Imperial Parliament (then meeting in Kroměříž), Dr. Klaudi, demanded that Justice Minister Bach make available the commission's papers. Bach waited to reply until March, when the fate of the parliament was already sealed and the Slav deputies were no longer needed to bolster the government's policies. Offering no documentary evidence, he merely read into the record an earlier summary of Turánsky's testimony to the Investigatory Commission which the Bohemian Appellate Judge Franz Scharfen had prepared.[83] His report echoed Windischgrätz's claim that the uprising issued from a well-established conspiracy that was tied to the Slav Congress. Bach's duplicity incensed the Czech deputies, but the government simply ignored their protests when the parliament was dissolved.[84]

Nor could the Slavs demand to confront their accuser. On October 27, 1848, the Prague criminal court authorized Turánsky's release and ordered the same Captain Müller who had arrested the youth to accompany him to the Hungarian frontier.[85] In later years Turánsky married a Polish heiress, purchased property in Slovakia, and assumed the position of a gentleman farmer. Occasionally he crossed the frontier into Russian Poland to visit his wife's relatives and, according to the testimony of one later acquaintance, became "favorably disposed to the Slav cause."[86] But, by all accounts, he scrupulously avoided active political involvement. In short, Turánsky disappeared from the public eye as suddenly as he had emerged in the summer of 1848.

For his part, Turánsky in later life stubbornly refused to discuss his role in the events of 1848. When questioned in 1875, following the publication of an article in the Czech periodical *Světozor,* which alluded to his involvement in the June uprising, Turánsky simply smiled.[87] As late as 1900 he was still living, his silence unbroken. Whether his silence was prompted by embarrassment over youthful indiscretions or whether it was a lasting tribute to his Magyar employers of a half-century before remains unanswered.

CHAPTER 9
EPILOGUE

i

The premature closing of the Slav Congress and the precipitate departure of many delegates was a crushing blow to its supporters. This disappointment was no more dramatically apparent than in the reaction of Šafařík, who equated his grief with Jeremiah's lament over the destruction of the Temple in Jerusalem. Never again, Šafařík was convinced, would such a display of fraternal Slavdom be repeated.[1] For its critics, the brutal victory of the reactionary court faction in Prague made mockery of the noble phrases and aims embodied in the congress' manifestos. The "yoke of oppression," whose collapse the Slavs had applauded, once again reigned in the heart of Central Europe. To be sure, Slav spokesmen continued to acclaim the congress as a historical milestone and to strive for a common Slav policy. Most notable in this vein were the efforts of the Slovanská lípa society to continue the work begun at the congress. Chapters were founded in Lvov and Zagreb, and on October 2, 1848, the parent Prague chapter began publication of a newspaper, Lípa slovanská, to report on the chapters' activities and to serve as a forum for perpetuating inter-Slav exchange.[2]

But the dominant tone in the Slavs' writings during the ensuing months was pessimism and recrimination. The triumph of absolutism, first in Prague and later in Vienna, Kroměříž, and Pest, only intensified the bitterness born of disappointment. Why had democratic hopes failed to take hold? Had the Slavs' adherence to Austria, as their critics charged, foredoomed their lofty aspirations? And were the Slavs irrevocably split politically and nationally following the Prague débâcle, as Anton Springer later maintained?[3] These were some of the questions which evoked heated polemical exchanges among the defeated Forty-Eighters.

František Palacký to the end of his life remained convinced that the Slavs' enemies had provoked the uprising to disrupt the congress and compromise the newly formed Bohemian provincial government.[4] As congress president and architect of the European Manifesto, Palacký maintained that the Prague Slavs had remained faithful to their Austro-Slav program.[5] Palacký's assurances of the congress' loyalty were challenged by Count Leo Thun who, in his account of events in Bohemia in 1848-49, condemned the Czech national party for failing to break with such critics of Austria as Štúr and Hurban, and for allowing "Libelt and other Polish archenemies of Austria" to turn the congress on a negative course.[6]

Whereas conservatives like Thun chided Palacký and the Czech national leadership for yielding the congress into the hands of the radical Poles, the latter denounced Palacký as a tool of the "Germanized nobility" and an enemy of Poland. For Jędrzej Moraczewski, "there was neither patriotism nor a burning commitment to liberty in Palacký; his habits and way of thinking were more German than Slav."[7] However, Palacký's most vocal critic among the Slavs was the itinerant Russian revolutionary Mikhail Bakunin. In his *Confession*, Bakunin accused the "semiofficial, half Slav, and half governmental" Czech party of seeking a dominant role in a Slav Austria. The Habsburg capital would move to Prague and the Czech language would reign not only in Bohemia and Moravia but in Slovakia and Galicia. If the Poles objected, they would be threatened with another Ukrainian jacquerie.[8]

Bakunin's indictment of the Czechs found a clear echo in the writings of the German socialist Friedrich Engels. When the Czecho-Slovaks and South Slavs lent active support to the Habsburgs against radical Vienna and Pest, Marx and Engels, who earlier had applauded the "democratic" Prague uprising, turned their full anger against the "Slavonian *dilettanti*," whose "anti-historical movement . . . intended nothing less than to subjugate the civilized West under the barbarian East, the town under the country, trade, manufactures, intelligence under the primitive agriculture of Slavonian serfs." Their "chief champion, . . . Professor Palacký, [was] himself nothing but a learned German run mad, who even now [could not] speak the Tschechian language correctly and without foreign accent." Engels accused the Czech and Croatian "Pan-Slavists [of] betraying the revolutionary cause for the shadow of nationality" which played directly into Russian hands. The Slav Congress, he contended, "would have proved a decided failure even without the interference of the Austrian military." Engels also reiterated the charge that the Slavs were "obliged to express themselves in the hated German language." But the supreme irony of the congress was that "Galician lancers, Croatian and Slovak grenadiers, and Bohemian gunners and cuirassiers, . . . the real Slavonic Congress, . . . in less than twenty-four hours drove the founders of an imaginary Slavonic supremacy out of town, and dispersed them to the winds."[9]

Nowhere was the disappointment with the Slavs' failures in 1848-49 more tragically reflected than in L'udovít Štúr, who had labored relentlessly in the spring of 1848 to spread the congress idea and promote closer understanding among the Slavs. After the congress, Štúr journeyed to Zagreb, where he plunged into the armed struggle of the South Slavs against the Magyars.[10] And later he led his own Slovaks against the Magyars. The deception and ingratitude of Bach's neo-absolutist regime was a bitter setback for Štúr. Forbidden to travel and unable to find suitable employment, he retired to the Slovak village of Modrá and devoted his few remaining years to literary and historical studies.

The intervening time led Štúr to reexamine his activities in 1848-49 and to renounce the Austro-Slav program that he had earlier supported. In his political testament, the posthumously published *Das Slawenthum und die Welt der Zukunft (Slavdom and the World of the Future)*, he accused the Czechs—as had Bakunin, Engels, and the Polish radicals before him—of seeking to establish hegemony over the Austrian Slavs under the apparent leadership of the "knowledgeable and sedate but unimaginative and shortsighted Bohemian historiographer Palacký," but actually guided by "Bohemian aristocrats, Catholic priests, and their venal servants." Štúr now attributed the congress call exclusively to the Czechs, who had hurriedly organized the gathering and maneuvered to impose their program on all the participating Slavs. In Štúr's judgment, the experience of 1848 had shown the utter bankruptcy of the idea of Slav federation in a German-ruled Austria. The sole viable course of action for the oppressed West and South Slavs was a union with tsarist Russia.[11] Quite understandably the Russian organizers of the next international gathering of Slavs, the 1867 Moscow Ethnographic Exhibition, chose Štúr's work to distribute to the participants.[12]

ii

The disparaging and recriminatory assessments that were subsequently leveled at the congress and its Czech leadership should not lead one to a hasty judgment of failure. Why the congress did not fully succeed in achieving its ambitious aims of reconciling past differences among the Slavs and of fashioning a program for mutual defense must be viewed in the light of centuries of widely differing cultural, social, and historical development, as well as the political and national turbulence in which the March Revolution embroiled Central Europe. Neither the Germans nor the Italians, each possessing a common national heritage and a more mature political consciousness than the Slavs, were able to overcome in 1848-49 a particularism spawned by centuries of divisive political aspirations and regional identities.

At its inception the congress idea stood as an attempt by the smaller Slav nations of East Central Europe to respond to the threat to their national well-being which they perceived in German and Magyar nationalist policies. The preparatory phase had made the congress planners acutely aware of the conflicting interests of the Slavs themselves, most notably in the attitude of the Poles. Underscoring these differing opinions was the scarcely veiled attempt of the Czech organizers to guide the congress in a loyalist Austro-Slav direction.

The arrival of the colorful Slav guests in Prague and the festive congress opening witnessed a fervid efflorescence of Slav sentimentality and euphoria, which certainly added to the already mounting political and social tensions in the city and may have contributed to the disaffection of several conservative Bohemian aristocrats. The early deliberations soon indicated the unsuitability of the original congress program. Agreement was reached on a more realistic agenda, which both afforded the participating Slav nations an opportunity to air their national concerns in a common petition and moved the congress beyond its initial reactive and defensive posture. In addition to the several manifestos, a notable achievement of the gathering, although it was never effectively implemented, was the national agreement between the Galician Poles and Ukrainians.

Despite claims by some contemporary observers and later historians, there was no radical swing to the left, no Polish "coup," nor any insurmountable barriers—the Polish-Magyar affinity notwithstanding—to reaching agreement at the congress. Though few participants left Prague converted to the views of others, most took away a deeper understanding of the concerns and aspirations of their fellow Slavs. The congress afforded not only an occasion to renew old acquaintances and form new ties, but provided valuable experience in parliamentary deliberations, which several delegates would apply in the Imperial Parliament.

That the congress was unable to continue its activities did not stem from any disinterest of the participants, but was rooted in the rapidly altered political balance in Austria following Windischgrätz's triumph in Prague and Radetzky's June victories in Italy. But at the time the congress convened, there had been widespread belief that Austria faced immediate collapse. The choice then before the Slavs in Prague was to fashion a revitalized political base within Austria or risk absorption by the partitioning Germans, Magyars, and Russians. It was in this atmosphere that the Slavs raised the difficult issue of federally restructuring the Habsburg state. For some Slavs the Austrian tie was an iron necessity; for most it was the only viable and available expedient; and for a very few it was wholly untenable.

As the first attempt to bring together representatives of the scattered Slav peoples, the congress was the culmination of an initial phase of national awakening and heralded the transformation of the previously cultural concept of a common Slavdom into political expression. The extensive press coverage of the congress caused many Europeans for the first time to take serious notice of the Danubian Slavs, who heretofore had perhaps seemed to be exotic tribes on the fringe of civilization. Likewise, German and Magyar nationalists who anxiously followed the events in Prague could no longer blithely pursue their paternalistic mission to raise the cultural level of the primitive Slavs. Nor was it any longer possible to dismiss the Danubian Slavs as mere tools of tsarist machinations. In common forum they had demanded the same national and political recognition that Germans and Magyars believed only they were ready and due to receive.

No less significantly, the congress' deliberations and manifestos foreshadowed programs which would be advocated over the next three-quarters of a century for the political reorganization of the Danubian basin. The ambiguous legacy of the congress was its affirmation of the Slavs' shared heritage and affinities, and at the same time the assertion of the primacy of nationality—the *sine qua non* in the political thought of the Slavs and their Central European neighbors to this day—as the natural basis for the formation of state entities.

NOTES
CHAPTER 1

1. Šafařík studied in Jena between 1815 and 1817, Kollár from 1817 to 1819. See Othmar Feyl, "Die führende Stellung der Ungarländer in der internationalen Geistesgeschichte der Universität Jena," *Wissenschaftliche Zeitschrift der Friedrich-Schiller-Universität Jena*, III (1953-54), 427-431.

2. See esp. Matthias Murko, *Deutsche Einflüsse auf die Anfänge der böhmischen Romantik* (Graz, 1897), pp. 127-134, 192 ff. Kollár left a record of his experience in Jena in *Pamäti z mladších rokov života* (Bratislava, 1972). The passages on Jena and the Wartburg festival are in German translation in Murko, pp. 293-365.

3. The first three cantos were published in Buda in 1824. The completed poem is in volume 1 of *Spisy Jana Kollára*, 4 vols. (Prague, 1862-64).

4. From "Prelude," trans. Alfred French, in *Anthology of Czech Poetry* (Ann Arbor, 1973), pp. 170-171.

5. The work is best known in its German edition of 1837: *Ueber die literarische Wechselseitigkeit zwischen den verschiedenen Stämmen und Mundarten der slawischen Nation*. The several versions of the treatise are in Kollár, *Rozpravy o slovanské vzájemnosti*, ed. Miloš Weingart (Prague, 1929).

6. *Ibid.*, pp. 37, 39, 45, 135-137.

7. *Ibid.*, pp. 153-163. Šafařík had made many of these very suggestions privately as much as a decade earlier. See Albert Pražák, "The Slovak Sources of Kollár's Pan-Slavism," *Slavonic and East European Review*, VI, No. 18 (March 1928), 582.

8. "Jan Kollár 1793-1852," *Slavonic and East European Review*, XXXI, No. 76 (December 1952), 89-90. Cf. Arne Novák, "Politické myšlensky v Kollárově spise 'O literární vzájemnosti mezi kmeny a nářečími slovanskými,'" *Slavia*, III (1924-25), 65-74.

9. J.G. Herder, *Outlines of a Philosophy of the History of Man*, trans. T. Churchill (1800; rpt. New York: Bergman, 1966), Book XVI, chap. 4, pp. 482-484. On Herder's influence on the Slavs, see esp. Holm Sundhaussen, *Der Einfluss der Herderschen Ideen auf die Nationalbildung bei den Völkern der Habsburger Monarchie* (Munich, 1973), pp. 50-54; Konrad Bittner, "J.G. Herders 'Ideen zur Philosophie der Geschichte der Menschheit' und ihre Auswirkungen bei den slavischen Hauptstämmen," *Germanoslavica*, III (1933), 453-480; and Murko, *Deutsche Einflüsse*, pp. 216-235, who maintains that Kollár in effect versified Herder's entire "Slav Chapter" in *Slávy dcera*.

10. The most authoritative study on Šafařík is Karel Paul, *Pavel Josef Šafařík: Život a dílo* (Prague, 1961). A recent biography with extensive excerpts from his writings is Jan Novotný, *Pavel Josef Šafařík* (Prague, 1971).

11. See Sundhaussen, *Einfluss der Herderschen Ideen*, pp. 117-118.

12. Reprint of 3rd ed. (1849), (Prague, 1955).

13. Letter to K.J. Erben, August 5, 1842, in Murko, *Deutsche Einflüsse*, pp. 179-180.

14. See John Erickson, *Panslavism* (London, 1964), p. 7.

15. *Rozpravy o slovanské vzájemnosti*, p. 63.

16. Since the last years of the eighteenth century, Austrian authorities had increasingly restricted attendance at German universities by Habsburg subjects; finally in 1820, all permission was withdrawn. See Sundhausen, *Einfluss der Herderschen Ideen*, pp. 112-113n.

17. Dobrovský's address is reproduced in Flora Kleinschnitzová, "Josefa Dobrovského řeč 'Über die Ergebenheit und Anhänglichkeit der slawischen Völker an das Erzhaus Östreich' z r. 1791," *Listy filologické*, XLV (1917), 96-104. For a recent assessment of Dobrovský's contribution to the development of Austro-Slavism, see esp. Zdeněk Šimeček, "Slavista J. Dobrovský a austroslavismus let 1791-1809," *Slovanský přehled*, LVII (1971), 177-190.

18. Linhart entitled his work *Versuch einer Geschichte von Krain und den übrigen südlichen Slaven Österreichs*. The passage in question from the introduction to vol. II reads: "Dass aber unter den Völkern der österreichischen Monarchie die Slaven an Zahl und Macht die überlegendsten sind, dass, wenn es in der Staatskunde üblich wäre die Summe der vereinten Kräfte, worauf die Majestät dieses Staates ruht, von der grössten homogenen Kraft zu benennen, Österreich eben so eigentlich als Russland, ein slavischer Staat heissen musste, darauf, glaube ich, ist man noch zu wenig aufmerksam gewesen." In Václav Žáček, "K dějinám austroslavismu rakouských Slovanů," *Slovanské historické studie*, VII (1968), 131n.

19. In *Barth. Kopitars Kleinere Schriften*, ed. F. Miklosich, I (Vienna, 1857), 60. See also Stanislaus Hafner, "Das austro-slawische kulturpolitische Konzept in der ersten Hälfte des 19. Jahrhunderts," *Österreichische Osthefte*, V (1963), 435ff.

20. "Patriotische Phantasien eines Slaven," in *Kopitars Kleinere Schriften*, I, 61-70.

21. See esp. Eduard Winter, "Wien als Mittelpunkt der Slawistik und der Einbruch des romantischen nationalen Denkens im Vormärz," *Wissenschaftliche Zeitschrift der Humboldt-Universität zu Berlin*, Gesellschafts- und Sprachwissenschaftliche Reihe, XVII, No. 2 (1968), 209-212.

22. See Eduard Winter, "Eine grundlegende Urkunde des Austroslawismus," *Zeitschrift für Slawistik*, III (1958), 107-124, where Kopitar's letter of April 7, 1827, to Metternich urging Austria's active pursuit and exploitation of these Slav literary relics is reproduced. Cf. Stanislaus Hafner, "B. Kopitar und die slawischen Handschriften der Athosklöster," *Südostforschungen*, XVIII (1959), 89-122.

23. Cf. Arthur Haas, "Metternich and the Slavs," *Austrian History Yearbook*, IV-V (1968-69), 120-149.

24. The contribution of the *matica* movement to the pre-March Slav awakening is examined in Stanley B. Kimball, *The Austro-Slav Revival: A Study of Nineteenth-Century Literary Foundations*, Transactions of the American Philosophical Society, NS, LXIII, Part 4 (Philadelphia, 1973).

25. Quoted in Hans Koch, "Slavdom and Slavism in the Polish National Consciousness, 1794-1848," in *Eastern Germany*, II: *History*, ed. Goettingen Research Committee (Würzburg, 1963), 223.

26. "Myśli o równowadze politycznej w Europie," cited *ibid.*, p. 239. Cf. Zofia Klarnerówna, *Słowianofilstwo w literaturze polskiej lat 1800 do 1848* (Warsaw, 1926), pp. 57-62.

27. Cited in Wacław Lednicki, "Poland and the Slavophil Idea," *Slavonic and East European Review*, VII, No. 19 (June 1928), 135-137. See also Hans Kohn, *Pan-Slavism: Its History and Ideology*, rev. ed. (New York, 1960), pp. 32-33.

28. Lednicki, "Poland and the Slavophil Idea," pp. 137-138.

29. Citing English text in *Konrad Wallenrod and Other Writings of Adam Mickiewicz*, ed. G.R. Noyes (Berkeley, 1925), p. 143.

30. Marceli Handelsman, "La politique slave de la Pologne aux XVIIIe et XIXe siècles," *Le Monde slave*, NS, XIII, No. 4 (December 1936), 440.

31. A notable exception, to be sure, was the Polish lexicographer Samuel Bogumił Linde (1771-1847), who, in a preface to his pioneering six-volume *Słownik języka polskiego* (Dictionary of the Polish Language) (1807-14), called for the creation of "one general Slavic literary language." See Koch, "Slavdom and Slavism in the Polish National Consciousness," pp. 229-230.

32. See Paul, *Šafařík*, pp. 47-74; and Václav Žáček *et al.*, *Češi a Jihoslované v minulosti* (Prague, 1975), pp. 236 ff.

33. Cited in Wayne S. Vucinich, "Croatian Illyrism: Its Background and Genesis," in Stanley B. Winters and Joseph Held, eds., *Intellectual and Social Developments in the Habsburg Empire from Maria Theresa to World War I: Essays Dedicated to Robert A. Kann* (Boulder, 1975), p. 83, which discusses the principal Serbo-Croatian literature on Illyrism. Cf. the important contribution by a leading contemporary Croatian historian: Jaroslav Šidak, "Der Illyrismus-Ideen und Probleme," in *L'udovít Štúr und die slawische Wechselseitigkeit*, ed. L. Holotík (Bratislava, 1969), pp. 61-89; and the recent study in English on Gaj: Elinor M. Despalatović, *Ljudevit Gaj and the Illyrian Movement* (Boulder, 1975). Kollár's influence on the South Slavs is examined in Krešimir Georgijević, "Kollárova ideja slovenske uzajamnosti kod Hrvata i Srba"; and in Julius Heidenreich, "Kollár a 'nařeči illyrské,'" in J. Horák, ed., *Slovanská vzájemnost 1836-1936* (Prague, 1938), pp. 63-125. See also Žáček, *Češi a Jihoslované v minulosti*, pp. 255 ff.

34. Gaj's newspaper appeared under several titles between 1835 and 1848: *Novine Hervatske* (1835-36), *Ilirske Narodne Novine* (1836-43), *Narodne Novine* (1843-44), and *Novine Dalmatinsko-Hervatsko-Slavonske* (1844-48). The poems, historical essays, and literary articles appearing in *Danica* (*Danica Ilirska* between 1836 and 1843) made it the more significant of the two periodicals.

35. See Philip E. Mosley, "A Pan-Slavist Memorandum of Liudevit Gaj in 1838," *American Historical Review*, XL (1935), 704-716.

36. On the transition from Kollár's Pan-Slavism to Štúr's "Slovakism," see L. Haraksim, "Od Kollárova slovanství k slovenství (1835-1848)," in *Slovanství v národním životě Čechů a Slováků*, ed. V. Šťastný (Prague, 1968), pp. 158-167. A succinct discussion of the national question in Hungary and the Slovak awakening to 1848 is in Daniel Rapant, *Slovenské povstanie roku 1848-49*, 5 vols in 13 (Turčiansky Svätý Martin & Bratislava, 1937-72), I, i, 84-177. Two recent syntheses on the Slovak rebirth are Jozef Butvin, *Slovenské národnozjednocovacie hnutie* (1780-1848) (Bratislava, 1965); and Ludwig von Gogolák, *Beiträge zur Geschichte des slowakischen Volkes*, II: *Die slowakische nationale Frage in der Reformepoche Ungarns (1790-1848)* (Munich, 1969). See also the stimulating essay in English by Peter Brock: *The Slovak National Awakening* (Toronto, 1976).

37. Facsimile reprint of all issues (1845-1848): Bratislava: Slovenské vydavateľstvo politickej literatúry, 1956.

38. *Hlasowé o potřebě jednoty spisowného jazyka pro Čechy, Morawany a Slowáky* (Prague, 1846). On the language conflict, see esp. Thomas G. Pešek, "The 'Czechoslovak' Question on the Eve of the 1848 Revolution," in Peter Brock and H. Gordon Skilling, eds., *The Czech Renascence of the Nineteenth Century* (Toronto, 1970), pp. 131-145.

39. On the impact of the November 1830 uprising on the Czechs, see Vladimír Hostička, "Polské povstání 1830-1831 a jeho vliv na českou společnost," in *Slovanství v národním životě Čechů a Slováků*, pp. 122-133; and Václav Žáček, *Čechové a Poláci roku 1848* (Prague, 1947-48), I, 85-118.

40. *Über den gegenwärtigen Stand der böhmischen Literatur und ihre Bedeudung* (Prague, 1842), esp. pp. 69-90. Thun's "feudal Austro-Slavism" is critically examined in Miloslav Novák, "Austroslavismus, příspěvek k jeho pojetí v době předbřeznové," *Sborník archivních prací*, VI (1956), 26-50.

41. The memorandum, entitled "Über die Beziehungen des Wiederauflebens der böhmischen Sprache zu der österreichischen Regierung," has not survived. The text is reconstructed from a contemporary police report, *ibid.*, pp. 38-42.

42. *Die Stellung der Slowaken in Ungarn* (Prague, 1843).

43. Differences between the cautious Bohemian nobility (represented by Leo Thun and his cousin, J.M. Thun) and the more assertive nationally minded Czechs (in the person of Jakub Malý) over the intent and meaning of Austro-Slavism sharpened by the mid-forties. This formative phase of political Austro-Slavism is examined in Novák, "Austroslavismus," pp. 42 ff.; Žáček, "K dějinám austroslavismu," pp. 132-144; Jan Heidler, *Čechy a Rakousko v politických brožurách předbřeznových* (Prague, 1920), esp. pp. 127-148; Jaroslav Vávra, "Poměr česko-ruský v době předbřeznové," *Československá rusistika*, II (1957), 454-466; and Vladimír Hostička, "Vznik českého austroslavismu a jeho vztah k obrozenskému slovanství," *Slovanský přehled*, LIV (1968), 225-232.

44. See esp. Heidler, *Čechy a Rakousko*, pp. 143-145, who compares the widely varying figures advanced at this time. The first population statistic based on nationality, compiled in 1851 (admittedly at a time of renewed German centrist activity), indicated just how exaggerated had been the Slavs' claims. In 1851 they comprised less than half (48.6%) of the monarchy's population (excluding the non-Slav Vlachs).

45. In 1846 Havlíček recorded his impressions of his three-year stay in Poland and Russia in a series of articles in *Pražské Nowiny*, entitled "Slovan a Čech" (The Slav and the Czech). They and his polemical exchange with Jakub Malý are reprinted in Havlíček, *Politické spisy*, ed. Zdeněk V. Tobolka, 3 vols. in 5 (Prague, 1900-03), I, 28-102. Cf. Josef Kočí, "Karel Havlíček a počátky austroslavismu," *Slovanský přehled*, LVII (1971), 191-201.

46. Citing English version in Hans Kohn, ed., *The Mind of Russia* (New York, 1962), pp. 84-85, 87, 90.

47. Henryk Batowski, *Przyjaciele Słowianie: Szkice historyczne z życia Mickiewicza* (Warsaw, 1956), pp. 85-105; and Žáček, *Čechové a Poláci 1848*, I, 273-288.

48. Václav Žáček, "Česko-polská diskuse o austroslavismu r. 1842-1843," *Slavia*, XVII (1963), 227-239.

49. A recent study of the 1846 *rabacja* (slaughter) is Arnon Gill, *Die Polnische Revolution 1846* (Munich & Vienna, 1974). Postwar Polish literature on 1846 is examined in Thomas W. Simons, "The Peasant Revolt of 1846 in Galicia: Recent Polish Historiography," *Slavic Review*, XXX (1971), 795-817.

50. *Lettre d'un gentilhomme polonais sur les massacres de Gallicie adressée au Prince de Metternich* (Paris, 1846).
51. P.A. Zaionchkovskii, *Kirillo-Mefodievskoe obshchestvo* (Moscow, 1959). See also Frank Fadner, *Seventy Years of Pan-Slavism in Russia, Karazin to Danilevskii, 1800-1870* (Washington, 1962), pp. 124-146.
52. Isaiah Berlin, "Russia and 1848," *Slavonic and East European Review*, XXVI, No. 67 (April 1948), 345.
53. Cited in Erickson, *Panslavism*, p. 13.

CHAPTER 2

1. The most comprehensive study of the March Revolution in the Habsburg lands is J.A. Helfert, *Geschichte der österreichischen Revolution im Zusammenhange mit der mitteleuropäischen Bewegung der Jahre 1848-1849* (Freiburg im Breisgau & Vienna, 1907-09), I. See also Anton Springer, *Geschichte Oesterreichs seit dem Wiener Frieden 1809* (Leipzig, 1865-67), II, 135 ff.; and Josef Redlich, *Das österreichische Staats- und Reichproblem* (Leipzig, 1920-26), I, i, 89 ff.
2. The major modern treatment of the revolution in Hungary is Gy. Spira, *A magyar forradalom 1848-49-ben* (Budapest, 1959).
3. See Fran Zwitter, *Les problèmes nationaux dans la monarchie des Habsbourg* (Belgrade, 1960), p. 63. After the Hungarians' defeat in 1849, Magyar nationalist historians propagated the thesis that Croat, Serb, and Slovak disgruntlement was nurtured by the court to combat Magyar separatism in 1848.
4. See Ferdo Šišić, "Kako je Jelačić postao banom," *Jugoslavenska njiva*, VII, No. 2 (1923), 169-183; and Gunther E. Rothenberg, "Jelačić, the Croatian Military Border, and the Intervention against Hungary in 1848," *Austrian History Yearbook*, I (1965), 50-51.
5. Wacław Felczak, *Węgierska polityka narodowościowa przed wybuchem powstania 1848 roku* (Wrocław, 1964), pp. 75ff.
6. No. 48, cited *ibid.*, p. 70.
7. Hrvoje Jurčić, "Das ungarisch-kroatische Verhältnis im Spiegel des Sprachenstreites 1790-1848," *Ungarn-Jahrbuch*, III (1971), 85. See also Ferdo Šišić, "Hrvati i Madžari uoči sukoba 1848," *Jugoslavenska njiva*, VII, No. 2 (1923), 409-419, 453-462.
8. Cf. J[aroslav] Š[ida]k, "Josip Jelačić," *Enciklopedija Jugoslavije* (Zagreb, 1955-), IV, 478-480; and Wayne S. Vucinich, "Jelačić and the Frontier in Modern History," *Austrian History Yearbook*, I (1965), 68-72.
9. Rothenberg, "Jelačić and the Intervention against Hungary in 1848," pp. 52-53.
10. *Grada za istoriju srpskog pokreta u Vojvodini 1848-1849:* Series I, book 1: *Mart-Juni 1848* (Belgrade, 1952), pp. 5-6.
11. Felczak, *Węgierska polityka narodowościowa*, p. 84.
12. *Ibid.*, pp. 84-85; and *Grada,* pp. 45-48.
13. Several versions of this colorful exchange have been offered. The various wordings are relayed in József Thim, *A magyarországi 1848-49-iki szerb fölkelés története* (Budapest, 1930-40), I, 38-39, n. 3.
14. Cf. G. Mérei, "Über die Möglichkeiten eines Zusammenschlusses der in Ungarn lebenden Völker in den Jahren 1848-49," *Acta Historica Academiae Scientiarum*

Hungaricae, XV, Nos. 3-4 (1969), 258 ff., who faults the Magyars' shortsightedness in strengthening the hand of the nationalities' conservative leaders who were inclined to do Vienna's bidding.

15. See Felczak, *Węgierska polityka narodowościowa,* pp. 85-86.

16. Text in Thim, *A magyarországi 1848-49-iki szerb fölkelés története,* II, 206-213.

17. Charles Jelavich, "The Croatian Problem in the Habsburg Empire in the Nineteenth Century," *Austrian History Yearbook,* III, part 2 (1967), 93-94.

18. See S. Kapper, *Die serbische Bewegung in Südungarn* (Berlin, 1851), pp. 72-89.

19. The Slovaks' weakness was poignantly acknowledged by L'udovít Štúr in an article of March 31 in his newspaper *Slovenskje Národňje Novini,* No. 274, pp. 1093-1094.

20. As early as March 22, however, Kollár urged privately that the Slovaks present their demands to the Hungarian authorities. To Ján Seberíni, in Daniel Rapant, *Slovenské povstanie roku 1848-49* (Turčiansky Svätý Martin & Bratislava, 1937-72), I, ii, 47-49.

21. See *Slovenskje Národňje Novini,* April 4, 1848, No. 275, p. 1100; and Rapant, *Slovenské povstanie,* I, ii, 52-55, 59-61, 73-80.

22. See *ibid.,* I, i, 221.

23. Rapant, "Slovak Politics in 1848-49," *Slavonic and East European Review,* XXVII, No. 68 (December 1948), 83. The petition was nevertheless published several days later in *Slovenskje Národňje Novini,* together with a proposal for an all-Slovak petition (May 2, 1848, No. 282, pp. 1125-1127).

24. The Mikuláš demands are in Rapant, *Slovenské povstanie,* I, ii, 202-205, and discussed at length, *ibid.,* I, i, 291-313.

25. Magyar fears were poignantly reflected in notations that Count Széchenyi made in his diary: "Ich ging mit der Impression nach Haus, dass uns die Slaven vernichten werden! Sie hassen uns. . ." (April 12); "Wir Ungarn sing weg! Slaven fressen uns. Kosacken allein eroben das Land!" (May 10 and 19). In Felczak, *Węgierska polityka narodowościowa,* p. 97.

26. See Stefan Kieniewicz, ed., *Rok 1848 w Polsce: Wybór źródeł* (Wrocław, 1948), pp. 234-251.

27. In the nineteenth century the name "Ruthenes" (Uk. Rusyny) was applied to and used by the East Slav, Uniate populace in Austrian Galicia. The anglicized version derives from the Latin name for the inhabitants of old Rus'. The name was also used to designate Ukrainians and Belorussians in the Polish-Lithuanian Commonwealth. The name "Ukrainian" did not gain wide acceptance in Austria until shortly before World War I.

28. German text of demands in Alfred Fischel, ed., *Materialien zur Sprachenfrage in Österreich* (Brno, 1902), pp. 283-285; Polish text in Kieniewicz, *Rok 1848,* pp. 199-202. The scene with Stadion is depicted in Władysław Zawadzki, *Dziennikarstwo w Galicji w roku 1848* (Lvov, 1878), reprinted in *Pamiętniki życia literackiego w Galicji,* ed. A. Knot (Kraków, 1961), pp. 195 ff.

29. One of the delegates, the Lvov lawyer, Floryan Ziemiałkowski, kept a diary of the journey. *Pamiętniki* (Kraków, 1904), II, 40-52.

30. German text of April 6 petition in Fischel, *Materialien zur Sprachenfrage,* pp. 287-291; Polish in Kieniewicz, *Rok 1848,* pp. 224-231.

31. Pillersdorff's reply of May 19, 1848, in the official *Gazeta Lwowska*, June 9, 1848, No. 68 (Dodatek); excerpts in Fischel, *Materialien zur Sprachenfrage*, pp. 291-292.

32. German text of Ruthenian petition in Fischel, *Materialien zur Sprachenfrage*, Doc. 74, pp. 284-286; Ukrainian text in *Zoria Halytska*, May 23, 1848, No. 2, pp. 7-8. For a discussion of Polish-Ukrainian relations in this period, see esp. V.O. Borys, "Deiaki pytannia pol'sko-ukrains'kykh vidnosyn pid chas revoliutsii 1848 r. v Halychyni," *Ukrains'ke slov'ianoznavstvo*, VI (1972), 74-87; and Jan Kozik, *Między reakcją a rewolucją: Studia z dziejów ukraińskiego ruchu narodowego w Galicji w latach 1848-1849* (Kraków, 1975), pp. 184-212.

33. See *Rada Narodowa*, April 19, May 9, 10, and 11, 1848, Nos. 1, 15, 16 and 17, pp. 2-3, 55-56, 59-60, and 63.

34. No. 39, pp. 161-162.

35. Some authors attribute this initiative to Pillersdorff instead. See C.A. Macartney, *The Habsburg Empire 1790-1918* (New York, 1969), p. 368n.

36. Cited in Peter Burian, *Die Nationalitäten in Cisleithanien und das Wahlrecht der Märzrevolution 1848/49* (Graz & Cologne, 1962), p. 105.

37. See Kozik, *Między reakcją a rewolucją*, p. 34n.

38. Uniate Metropolitan Levyts'kyi to Bishop Iakhymovych, May 1, 1848, and Iakhymovych to Levyts'kyi, May 7, 1848, in Kyrylo Studyns'kyi, ed., "Materialy do istorii kul'turnoho zhyttia v Halychyni 1795-1857," *Ukrains'ko-rus'kyi arkhiv*, XIII-XIV (1920), 312-316.

39. Cf. Peter Brock, "Ivan Vahylevych (1811-1866) and the Ukrainian National Identity," *Canadian Slavonic Papers*, XIV, No. 2 (1972), 153-190; and N.M.Pashaeva, "Otrazhenie natsional'nykh i sotsial'nykh protivorechii v Vostochnoi Galichine v 1848 g. v listovkakh Russkago Sobora," *Slavianskoe vozrozhdenie: Sbornik statei i materialov* (Moscow, 1966), pp. 48-62.

40. See Mierosławski's recollections, in Kieniewicz, *Rok 1848*, pp. 16-22.

41. See Lewis Namier, *1848: The Revolution of the Intellectuals* (London, 1946), pp. 57-65.

42. Text in Kieniewicz, *Rok 1848*, pp. 26-28.

43. Stefan Kieniewicz, *Społeczeństwo polskie w powstaniu poznańskiem 1848 roku* (Warsaw, 1935), pp. 108-109; and Józef Feldman, *Sprawa polska w roku 1848* (Kraków, 1933), p. 157.

44. Cited in Namier, *1848*, p. 59.

45. *Ibid.*, pp. 72-73.

46. Text of the Jarosławiec agreement in Kieniewicz, *Rok 1848*, pp. 84-86.

47. On the Willisen mission, see Namier, *1848*, pp. 73-77; Feldman, *Sprawa polska 1848*, pp. 158 ff.; and Kieniewicz, *Społeczeństwo polskie w powstaniu poznańskiem*, pp. 171 ff.

48. Namier, *1848*, pp. 66-71, 78-91; Frank Eyck, *The Frankfurt Parliament 1848-1849* (New York, 1968), pp. 49-50, 57-58; Jan Kucharzewski, "The Polish Cause in the Frankfort Parliament of 1848," *Bulletin of the Polish Institute of Arts and Sciences in America*, I, No. 1 (October 1942), 42-73; and Roy Pascal, "The Frankfort Parliament, 1848, and the *Drang nach Osten,*" *Journal of Modern History*, XVIII, No. 2 (June 1946), 108-122.

49. Cited in Namier, *1848*, p. 65.

50. See Bernard Piotrowski, "Delegacja wielopolska na Zjeździe Słowiańskim w Pradze (1848 roku)," *Zeszyty Naukowe Uniwersytetu im. Adama Mickiewicza w*

Poznaniu, No. 47, *Historia,* No. 6 (1964), 109-113.

51. The name was adopted by the radicals after the appearance of an article on Irish politics by Karel Havlíček in *Pražské Nowiny* in June 1847, although Havlíček himself was not a member. See Karel Slavíček, *Tajná politická společnost Český Repeal 1848* (Prague, 1947), pp. 73 ff.

52. The Czech and German text of Brauner's proposal appeared in *Bohemia,* March 18, 1848, extra edition; the Czech text is reprinted in Jan M. Černý, ed., *Boj za právo: Sborník aktů politických u věcech státu a národa českého od roku 1848* (Prague, 1893), pp. 12-17. For a comparison of Brauner's version with the more radical Repeal draft, see Stanley Z. Pech, *The Czech Revolution of 1848* (Chapel Hill, 1969), pp. 50-53.

53. Pech, *Czech Revolution of 1848,* p. 62; Czech text in Černý, *Boj za právo,* pp. 3-6; German in Fischel, *Materialien zur Sprachenfrage,* pp. 48-50.

54. Zdeněk Tobolka, *Politické dějiny československého národa od r. 1848 až do dnešní doby* (Prague, 1932-37), I, 41-42. German text in Alfred Fischel, ed., *Das österreichische Sprachenrecht: Eine Quellensammlung* (Brno, 1901), pp. 61-63.

55. Czech text of second petition, dated March 29, in Černý, *Boj za právo,* pp. 58-59; German in Fischel, *Materialien zur Sprachenfrage,* pp. 51-52.

56. See Tobolka, *Politické dějiny,* I, 43.

57. Czech text of April 8 Cabinet Rescript in Černý, *Boj za právo,* pp. 101-104; German in Fischel, *Das österreichische Sprachenrecht,* pp. 63-66.

58. Pech, *Czech Revolution of 1848,* p. 73.

59. The protest was dated April 9, but drafted prior to the government's reply to the Czechs. German text in Fischel, *Materialien zur Sprachenfrage,* pp. 58-59; Czech in Robert Maršan, *Čechové a Němci r. 1848 a boj o Frankfurt* (Prague, 1898), pp. 48-49. Cf. Anon., "Die Revolution von 1848/1849 und die Sudetendeutschen," *Archiv für Politik und Geschichte,* VII (1926), 437.

60. Palacký's letter of April 11 was widely reprinted in the Czech and German press: in Czech, *Radhost* (Prague, 1871-73), III, 10-17; in German, *Gedenkblätter* (Prague, 1874), pp. 149-155, editions of Palacký's writings. English translation is in *Slavonic and East European Review,* XXVI, No. 67 (April 1948), 303-308. For a recent assessment of the letter's importance, see Pech, *Czech Revolution of 1848,* pp. 80-85.

61. *Ibid.,* pp. 79-80, 89.

62. Kuranda's report to the Commttee of Fifty on May 3, 1848, in F. Jucho, ed., *Verhandlungen des Deutschen Parlaments* (Frankfurt a/M, 1848), II, 291.

63. Czech protocol of meeting in Černý, *Boj za právo,* pp. 160-170.

64. Kuranda's report in Jucho, *Verhandlungen,* II, 296.

65. Pech, *Czech Revolution of 1848,* p. 88.

66. Burian, *Nationalitäten in Cisleithanien,* pp. 119-120.

67. On Slovene resistance to Frankfurt, see Josip Apih, *Slovenci in 1848 leto* (Ljubljana, 1888), pp. 90 ff.

68. Full text in Fischel, *Materialien zur Sprachenfrage,* pp. 331-332, which erroneously dates the address April 1. An abridged English version, in Robert A. Kann, *The Multinational Empire: Nationalism and National Reform in the Habsburg Monarchy 1848-1918* (New York, 1950), I, 299-300, also misdates the address. The Graz Slovenija society was not founded until April 16. Cf. Apih, *Slovenci in 1848 leto,* p. 88.

69. Burian, *Nationalitäten in Cisleithanien,* p. 139.
70. *1848,* p. 101.

CHAPTER 3

1. Václav Žáček, ed., *Slovanský sjezd v Praze roku 1848: Sbírka dokumentů* (Prague, 1958), pp. 15-16*n.* See also Georg Plaschka, "Zur Einberufung des Slaven-kongresses 1848," *Archiv für österreichische Geschichte,* CXXV (1966), 199; *Jahr-bücher für slawische Literatur, Kunst und Wissenschaft* (Leipzig), No. 11 (1848), pp. 107-108; and *Wčela* (Prague), February 15 and 18, 1848, Nos. 13, 14, pp. 51, 54-55. According to a contemporary estimate, about 80,000 Slavs lived in Vienna.

2. Croat representatives arrived on March 31, as did the Galician Poles; the second Czech deputation came on April 1; Serb and Slovak representatives had been in Vienna for several days.

3. See *Národní Nowiny* (Prague), April 9, 1848, No. 5, p. 17; *Týdenník* (Brno), April 13, 1848, No. 15, pp. 116-117; and a report by Viennese police in Daniel Rapant, *Slovenské povstanie roku 1848-49* (Turčiansky Svätý Martin & Bratislava, 1937-72), V, i, 3-5, where the date of this meeting is confirmed. On the Sperl encounters, see also John Erickson, "The Preparatory Committee of the Slav Congress, April-May 1848," in Peter Brock and H. Gordon Skilling, eds., *The Czech Renascence of the Nineteenth Century* (Toronto, 1970), pp. 178-179.

4. *Týdenník,* April 13, 1848, No. 15, pp. 116-117.

5. The Czech writer Dr. Cyril Kampelík reported this conversation with Štúr in a letter to his family in Prague, April 2, 1848. Printed in *Pražské Nowiny,* April 16, 1848, No. 31, supplement. See also Jan Novotný, "Příspěvek k vzájemným vzta-hům Čechů a Slováků v první etapě revoluce roku 1848," *Historický časopis,* XI (1963), 373-374, who cautions against accepting Kampelík's version.

6. *Der grosse Peter,* April 9, 1848, No. 1, in Žáček, *Slovanský sjezd,* p. 18.

7. "Ked' treba, ospravedlníme sa" (Bratislava), April 18, 1848, No. 279, pp. 1113-1114.

8. Rapant, *Slovenské povstanie,* V, i, 4.

9. See Václav Čejchan, "Ke vzniku myšlenky slovanského sjezdu roku 1848," *Slovanský přehled,* XX (1928), 403-404.

10. See Floryan Ziemiałkowski, *Pamiętniki* (Kraków, 1904), II, 30-31, 54-55; Josef Václav Frič, *Paměti* (Prague, 1875-77), II, 361-385, *passim;* and Václav Žáček, *Čechové a Poláci roku 1848* (Prague, 1947-48), II, 37-38.

11. Ziemiałkowski, *Pamiętniki,* II, 54. Ziemiałkowski had taken an active part in pre-March Polish conspiratorial activities against Austria. By June his demo-cratic, pro-German, Magyarophile convictions would take him to Frankfurt as a mem-ber of the Polish delegation.

12. *Ibid.,* p. 55.

13. *Ibid.,* pp. 69-70.

14. *Ibid.,* p. 56. Ziemiałkowski could not comprehend how any Pole could foster contacts with the Czechs "in view of the loathing which every Pole had for the Czechs." *Ibid.,* p. 30.

15. Žáček, *Čechové a Poláci 1848,* II, 39.

16. *Pamiętniki,* II, 69.

17. Žáček, *Čechové a Poláci 1848*, II, 41. On his own initiative, Prince Lubomirski met with Magyar leaders in nearby Bratislava shortly before April 14. However, the discussions broke down due to Kossuth's unwillingness to talk with such an outspoken Slavophile.

18. "Kakva tréba da bude u obće politika naša" (Zagreb), No. 37, p. 145.

19. The Czech historian Václav Žáček has suggested that Kukuljević's emphasis on the German threat to the Slavs was specifically intended to attract Czech and Polish support for his proposal. *Čechové a Poláci 1848*, II, 53-54.

20. *Národní Nowiny* (May 7, 1848, No. 28, p. 11) reported that a price had been placed on Štúr's head: "The Magyars are offering 200 ducats to whomever kills Štúr." Actually, Hungarian Interior Minister B. Szemere issued an order for his arrest on May 12. Similar orders were given on May 22 for the Slovak J.M. Hurban and on June 1 for another Slovak, M.M. Hodža. See Wacław Felczak, *Węgierska polityka narodowościowa przed wybuchem powstania 1848 roku* (Wrocław, 1964), p. 101.

21. Frič, *Paměti*, III, 26-27. In his memoirs the Czech student leader J.V. Frič claimed principal responsibility for encouraging Štúr to come to Prague and for arranging his welcome. See also Jan Novotný, *Češi a Slováci za národního obrození a do vzniku československého státu* (Prague, 1968), pp. 142ff.

22. This was the work *Hlasowé o potřebě jednoty spisowného jazyka pro Čechy, Morawu a Slowáky*. See Frič, *Paměti*, III, 27; and *Národní Nowiny*, April 25, 1848, No. 17, p. 68. Vilém Dušan Lambl, writing in *Národní Nowiny*, April 27, 1848 (No. 19, p. 76), drew attention to the fact that Štúr's newspaper *Slovenskje Národňje Novini*, as well as the Slovak literary society Tatrín had adopted Czech orthography for written Slovak.

23. Frič, *Paměti*, III, 21, 27-28. Jan Novotný maintains that Havlíček was the most important figure in opening doors for Štúr in Prague. He argued that it was Havlíček who introduced Štúr to the Czech liberals who often gathered at the Měšt'-anská beseda and also placed his newspaper *Národní Nowiny* at Štúr's disposal. "Příspěvek k vzájemným vztahům," pp. 379-380; and *Češi a Slováci*, pp. 147-148. *Národní Nowiny* did in fact devote much attention to Štúr's activities in Prague in late April (Nos. 17, 19, 23, 25, pp. 68, 76, 92, 97), and published a lengthy piece by him on the West and South Slavs. "Pohled na hýbaní zapadních a jižních Slovanů," May 2, 1848, No. 23, pp. 89-90.

24. *Korrespondence a zápisky Frant. Ladislava Čelakovského*, Vol. III: ed. F. Bílý (Prague, 1915), 578.

25. *Paměti*, III, 28.

26. Czech translation in *Pokroková revue*, I (1905), 200-201. See also Moraczewski's account of his démarche in his *Opis pierwszego Zjazdu słowiańskiego* (Poznań, 1848), p. 8; and "Pamiętnik Jędrzeja Moraczewskiego," in *Wizerunki polityczne dziejów państwa polskiego* (Leipzig, 1865), IV, 138.

27. *Opis*, p. 8. However, at the first organizational meeting of the congress planners on April 30, J.P. Jordan alluded to Poznanian interest in a congress of Slavs. See minutes in H. Traub, "O přípravách k Slovanskému sjezdu v Praze r. 1848," *Časopis Musea království českého*, XCII (1918), 249. Moraczewski's claim is supported by a press account of the reception following the congress opening on June 2 (see below, chap. v) at which "Brauner brachte einen Toast auf den polnischen Literaten Moraczewski aus, der den Czechen zuerst den Gedanken zur

Einberufung einer allgemeinen slawischen Versammlung gegeben." *Allgemeine Oder-Zeitung* (Breslau), June 7, 1848, No. 131, Erste Beilage.

28. Thun's letter of June 19, 1848, to Prince Josef von Lobkowitz, in Václav Chaloupecký, "Hrabě Josef Matyáš Thun a Slovanský sjezd v Praze r. 1848," *Český časopis historický*, XIX (1913), 89. On this meeting, see chap. ii.

29. Nos. 21, 22, pp. 81, 86.

30. Quoted in Zdeněk V. Tobolka, *Slovanský sjezd v Praze roku 1848* (Prague, 1901), pp. 50-51.

31. The Czech historian, Zdeněk V. Tobolka, writing at the turn of the century, maintained that "the Slav Congress was a Czech enterprise. . . . The Czechs undertook the realization of the congress idea, and therefore the congress belongs to them alone." *Slovanský sjezd*, pp. 49-50. The Slovak publicist Jozef Škultéty argued that the initiative lay primarily with Štúr and the Slovaks, whose situation in the monarchy was even more desperate than that of the Croats. "Slovanský sjazd v Prahe roku 1848," *Slovenské pohl'ady*, XLIV (1928), 461. The Pole Jędrzej Moraczewski, as noted above, claimed the initiative for himself.

32. Jan Petr Jordan, *Aktenmässiger Bericht über die Verhandlungen des ersten Slavenkongresses in Prag* (Prague, 1848), pp. 10-11. See also *Zpráwa o sjezdu slowanském* (Prague, 1848), pp. 1-2.

33. Minutes in Traub, "O přípravách," p. 249.

34. April 30, 1848, in Žáček, *Slovanský sjezd*, pp. 60-61.

35. Minutes in Traub, "O přípravách," pp. 249-250. Those selected with the number of votes each received were K.V. Zap (20), Baron Drahotín Villani (17), Václav Štulc (17), F.L. Rieger (16), Václav Hanka (16), Baron Neuberg (16), Witalis Grzybowski (16), Count Vojtěch Deym (15), Palacký (15), Vocel (15), K.J. Erben (15), and J.P. Jordan (14). As alternates: František Brauner (13), K.B. Štorch (13), Havlíček (13), and Jan Slavík (13). Five Prague burghers, whose task was to plan the local arrangements, were added: Martin Brabec, K.H. Caspar [Kašpar], F.L. Jaroš, Pavel Mnouček, and Jan Rypota. During the meeting these Bohemian nobles were added: Baron Hildeprandt, Count Bedřich Rummerskirch, Count Hanuš Kolovrat-Krakovský, and Count Kristian Waldstein.

36. Erickson, "Preparatory Committee," pp. 180-181.

37. Minutes in Traub, "O přípravách," p. 250. Cf. Tobolka, *Slovanský sjezd*, pp. 53-54; and Władysław T. Wisłocki, *Kongres słowiański w r. 1848 i sprawa polska* (Lvov, 1927), p. 25.

38. To Neuberg, May 2, 1848, in Žáček, *Slovanský sjezd*, pp. 61-62.

39. Štúr's version was published nevertheless in the Leipzig *Deutsche Allgemeine Zeitung*, May 5, 1848, No. 126, pp. 1618-1619; and in the Poznań *Gazeta Polska*, May 13, 1848, No. 43, p. 161, thus adding to the confusion. His original draft, with the ending crossed out and the new wording added, is in ANM, SS-1848. It is reprinted in L'udovít Štúr, *K přátelům, k bratrům* (Prague, 1956), p. 269. Štúr initially proposed May 21 for the congress opening; this was later changed to May 31.

40. The official version, dated May 1, 1848, was first published in *Národní Nowiny*, May 5, 1848, No. 26, p. 103. Additional signatures were added on May 7, 1848, No. 28, p. 109; and May 12, 1848, No. 32, p. 125.

41. Protocol in Traub, "O přípravách," p. 251.

42. To Neuberg, May 4, 1848, in Žáček, *Slovanský sjezd*, p. 67 Cf. my "Did the Slavs Speak German at Their First Congress?" *Slavic Review*, XXXIII, No. 3 (September 1974), 515-521.

43. Minutes in Traub, "O přípravách," p. 251. Thun later noted that when he was first asked to be chairman he hesitated due to his weak knowledge of Czech. He insisted that he had been assured that the congress would be a gathering of only loyal Austrian Slavs. See Thun to von Lobkowitz, June 19, 1848, in Chaloupecký, "Thun a slovanský sjezd," p. 89.

44. May 3, 1848, in Žáček, Slovanský sjezd, pp. 62-63.

45. Ibid., pp. 65-66.

46. Protocol and minutes of May 5, 1848, in Traub, "O přípravách," pp. 252-253. Cf. Chaloupecký, "Thun a slovanský sjezd," pp. 89-90.

47. Palacký's draft in German and the final copy are in ANM, SS-1848.

48. Dated May 5, 1848, it first appeared in the Constitutionelles Blatt aus Böhmen (Prague), May 6, 1848, No. 31; and thereafter in the Wiener Zeitung, May 9, 1848, No. 129, p. 620. The signatures of the two Poles, Malisz and Grzybowski, as well as Štúr's, were noticeably absent from the Erklärung, a discrepancy which the Wiener Zeitung (May 13, 1848, No. 133, p. 637) readily pointed out.

49. In Žáček, Slovanský sjezd, pp. 70-71. Šafařík eventually returned to Prague on May 18.

50. Neuberg's call was published in German (Ein Wort zur Verständniss über Slawenversammlung in Prag) and in Czech (Záležitostí Slowanského kongresu). Copies are in SÚA, ST 1848, fasc. 7/76; and ANM, SS-1848. The German text is in H. Traub, "Zum Slavenkongresse in Prag im J. 1848," Union (Prague), September 25, 1913, No. 264.

51. May 8, 1848, in Žáček, Slovanský sjezd, pp. 74-75.

52. To Neuberg, May 8, 1848; to Zap, May 9, 1848; to Neuberg, May 10, 1848; and to Neuberg, May 14, 1848. Ibid., pp. 76-83. The last reference was to the rioting of unemployed workers on May 1 and 2 against the Prague backers and Jewish merchants.

53. To Neuberg, ibid., pp. 81-82.

54. See Šafařík to Neuberg, May 4, 1848, ibid., pp. 67-69. Šafařík noted: "Wir werden überall als Verräter, als Russen oder Russomannen angeklagt und verdächtigt." See also his letters to Palacký, May 6, 1848, and to Neuberg, May 8, 1848, ibid., pp. 73-74, 76-78.

55. May 13, 1848, in Čeněk Zíbrt, "Pobyt P.J. Šafaříka v Berlíně r. 1841 a ve Vídni r. 1848 i 1851 v novém světle dopisů choti Julii," Osvěta, XXXIX (1909), 620-621.

56. "Panslavismus vor der Thür," May 9, 1848, No. 41, pp. 616-617.

57. "Das lustige alte Wien," May 8, 10, and 12, 1848, Nos. 18, 20, 22.

58. See Wiener Schnellpost, May 13/14 and 20/21, 1848, Nos. 12/13, 19/20, pp. 45-46, 78-79; and Der Freimüthige, May 11 and 13, 1848, Nos. 35, 37, pp. 142-143, 152.

59. Protocol of Minister-Rath meeting, in Žáček, Slovanský sjezd, p. 174.

60. Ibid., pp. 175-176.

61. Ibid., pp. 176-177.

62. See Friedrich Prinz, Prag und Wien 1848 (Munich, 1968), pp. 42-45.

63. See Die Constitution, May 24, 1848, No. 52, p. 703; "Ein slavisches Balkensteigen," Der Volksfreund, May 20, 1848, No. 23, p. 95; Josef Kopp, "Der Slavismus, seine Ansprüche und Absichten," Wiener Schnellpost, May 17 and 18, 1848, Nos. 16-17, pp. 63, 66-68; ibid., May 26, No. 25, p. 99; and Wiener Zeitschrift für Recht, Wahrheit, Fortschritt, Kunst, Literatur, Theater, Mode, und geselliges Leben, May 29, 1848, No. 108, p. 429. Almost alone among the Viennese newspapers, the Wiener

Abendzeitung, edited by Ludwig August Frankl, treated the congress plans sympathetically. See "Böhmische Zustände," May 29, 1848, No. 53, pp. 217-218. The conservative *Wiener Zeitung* and the quasi-governmental *Constitutionelle Donau-Zeitung* showed more moderation than the liberal and radical press in discussing the congress.

64. On the policy of the Batthyány government toward the Slavs in the spring of 1848, see Wacław Felczak, *Węgierska polityka narodowościowa,* chap. iv.

65. Instructions of Hungarian Minister-President, Count Lajos Batthyány, to his envoy in Vienna, Prince Pál Eszterházy, in Rapant, *Slovenské povstanie,* I, ii, 225-226.

66. Protocol of Minister-Rath meeting, in Žáček, *Slovanský sjezd,* pp. 177-178.

67. L. Szalay, *Diplomatische Aktenstücke zur Beleuchtung der Ungarischen Gesandtschaft in Deutschland* (Zürich, 1849), p. 7.

68. Hungarian Interior Minister B. Szemere to L. Szalay, May 24, 1848, in Rapant, *Slovenské povstanie,* I, ii, 247-248.

69. No. 113, p. 1219. The greatest interest in the congress was in Prussian Silesia, Saxony, and Bavaria. See also Augsburg *Allgemeine Zeitung,* June 4, 1848, No. 156, p. 2485.

70. At the outbreak of the March Revolution the journal was appearing with an edition of over 4,000 copies. See Gerda Koberg, *"Die Grenzboten* 1842-1848 und ihr Verhältnis zu Böhmen," Diss. Deutsche Universität, Prague, 1938, pp. 117-133; and Francis L. Loewenheim, "German Liberalism and the Czech Renascence: Ignaz Kuranda, *Die Grenzboten,* and Developments in Bohemia, 1845-49," in Brock and Skilling, *The Czech Renascence,* pp. 146-172.

71. "Aus Prag," *Die Grenzboten,* 1848, semester 1, pt. 2, pp. 277-278; "Böhmische Vorrede zum Slavenkongress in Prag," *ibid.,* pp. 317-320; and "Eingaben an den Panslavenreichstag zu Prag," *ibid.,* pp. 379-382.

72. *Ibid.,* p. 385.

CHAPTER 4

1. See Václav Žáček, ed., *Slovanský sjezd v Praze roku 1848: Sbírka dokumentů* (Prague, 1958), pp. 44-45.

2. Protocol in H. Traub, "O přípravách k Slovanskému sjezdu v Praze r. 1848," *Časopis Musea království českého,* XVII (1918), 252.

3. Actually neither list was signed. The first was clearly in Hanka's handwriting. See original in ANM, SS-1848. The second list has commonly been attributed to committee secretary Zap.

4. Minutes in Traub, "O přípravách," pp. 254-255. Vocel and Rieger supported the proposal; the possibility of inviting Rumanians and Italians was also raised.

5. Cf. Władysław T. Wisłocki, *Kongres słowiański w r. 1848 i sprawa polska* (Lvov, 1927), pp. 32, 38, who maintains that Prince Lubomirski and the other Poles had signed the congress announcement with the understanding that Magyars would also be invited. This opinion was echoed at a meeting of the Polish Rada Narodowa on May 25. Protocol in AGAD, fond. 269, p. 133; and Žáček, *Slovanský sjezd,* p. 106.

6. Copies or acknowledgments are preserved of Zap's letters to the editors Jan Oheral (Brno *Týdenník*), Ljudevit Gaj (Zagreb *Novine Dalmatinsko-Hervatsko-*

Slavonske), Ante Kuzmanić (Zadar *Zora Dalmatinska),* Theodor Pavlović (Pest *Sveobšte Jugoslavenske i serbske narodne novine),* and A. Szukiewicz (Kraków *Jutrzenka).* See Žáček, *Slovanský sjezd,* pp. 45, 69, 154-155.

7. *Jutrzenka,* May 17, 1848, No. 41, p. 169.

8. Žáček, *Slovanský sjezd,* p. 46.

9. *Ibid.,* pp. 155-156.

10. Čeněk Zíbrt, "Život a činnost P.J. Šafaříka ve světle dopisů synovi Janovi (1834-1859)," *Časopis Musea království českého,* LXXIV (1910), 104.

11. See Kollár to Jan Sebrini, May 12, 1848, in Žáček, *Slovanský sjezd,* p. 95.

12. The Polish historian Władysław Wisłocki notes that the following sentence was added to the announcements sent to foreign Slavs: "Do not be misled that the announcement reads only to Austrian Slavs. In our present surroundings we could not have acted otherwise, but we urge that you especially be represented in large numbers at our congress." *Kongres słowiański,* pp. 26-27.

congress." *Kongres słowiański,* pp. 26-27.

13. For a list of the delegates selected, see Žáček, *Slovanský sjezd,* p. 94.

14. "Stanowy Slowanské Lípy," in ANM, LS. See also Václav Žáček, "České a jihoslovanské Slovanské lípy v roce 1848," *Literární archiv,* VI (1971), 195-239.

15. Ohéral to Zap, May 8, 1848, in Žáček, *Slovanský sjezd,* p. 70.

16. Olomouc Slovanská lípa to Preparatory Committee, May 28, 1848, *ibid.,* pp. 89-90.

17. Mikšíček's authorization and instructions, *ibid.,* p. 91.	See also Václav Schulz, "Průkaz vyslance lidu moravského, sběratele pohadek M. Mikšíčka, k Sjezdu Slovanskému v Praze r. 1848," *Český lid,* VII (1898), 383-384; and Václav Žáček, "Moravský účastník svatodušních bouří 1848: Příspěvek k životu a působení Matěje Mikšíčka," *Časopis Matice moravské,* LVII (1933), 191-192, 209-210.

18. See Josef Macůrek, *Rok 1848 a Morava* (Brno, 1948), pp. 63-69. When the diet convened on May 31, the Czech-speaking representatives held a slim one-vote margin over their German counterparts.

19. *Korrespondence a zápisky Frant. Ladislava Čelakovského.* Vol. III: ed. F. Bílý (Prague, 1915), 588-589. See also his letter to J.V. Plánek, May 15, 1848, *ibid.,* pp. 585-587.

20. See Kollár to Palacký, June 1, 1848, quoted in Zdeněk V. Tobolka, *Slovanský sjezd v Praze roku 1848* (Prague, 1901), p. 98.

21. See Adolf Černý, "Dr. Jan Petr Jordan," *Zlatá Praha,* VIII (1891), 438. Cf. Peter Brock, "J.P. Jordan's Role in the National Awakening of the Lusatian Serbs," *Canadian Slavonic Papers,* X (1968), 335-336.

22. See his "Die Lausitzer Serben und die Slavenversammlung," *Slavische Central- blätter,* June 5, 1848, No. 10, p. 37.

23. *Bohemia* (Prague), May 26, 1848, No. 84; and H. Tourtzer, *Louis Stúr et l'idée de l'indépendance slovaque* (Paris, 1913), p. 196.

24. *Novine Dalmatinsko-Hervatsko-Slavonske,* May 13, 1848, No. 47, p. 189. Prica replaced Djoro Kontić who was originally selected; Vraz was added to the delegation later. Neither Gaj nor Kukuljević-Sakcinski attended.

25. József Thim, *A Magyarországi 1848-49-iki szerb fölkelés története* (Buda- pest, 1930-1940), III, Doc. 105, 206-209; and Jovan Subotić, "Zápisky dra subotiće, účastníka slovanského sjezdu," *Naše doba,* X (1902-1903), 887. The delegation also included Mate Topalović, Djordje Stojaković, and Jovan Subotić.

26. See Jan Nevole to Palacký, May 22, 1848, in Žáček, *Slovanský sjezd,* p. 173.

136 NOTES

The two delegates, Lazar Arsenijević and Jovan Marinović, members of the Serbian senate, attended as guests and were not officially enrolled as participants.

27. The Graz "Slovenija" was headed by a Moravian, J. Dragoni-Křenovský. His letters to Prague are in *Národní Nowiny*, May 13, 1848, No. 33, pp. 130-131; and Žáček, *Slovanský sjezd*, p. 160. On the Slovene reaction to the congress preparations, see also Josip Apih, *Slovenci in 1848 leto* (Ljubljana, 1888), pp. 118 ff.; and Fran Petrè, "Zahteva po 'Kraljevini Sloveniji' 1. 1848 v praškich dokumentih," *Glasnik Muzejskega društva za Slovenijo*, XXI (1940), 38-59.

28. See Žáček, *Slovanský sjezd*, pp. 157-158. On Slovene interest for the congress in Ljubljana, Klagenfurt, as well as Oroslav Caf's activities in Fram in Southern Styria, see *ibid.*, pp. 158-159, 161-165.

29. *Ibid.*, pp. 166-168.

30. Minutes in Traub, "O přípravách," pp. 319-321.

31. See Václav Žáček, *Čechové a Poláci roku 1848* (Prague, 1947-1948), II, 62-63. Cf. Wisłocki, *Kongres słowiański*, pp. 41-42.

32. Žáček, *Slovanský sjezd*, pp. 80-81.

33. *Ibid.*, pp. 84-85.

34. No. 32, pp. 125-126. Also reprinted in Havlíček's collected political writings as "The Austrian Government and the Poles." *Politické spisy*, ed. Z.V. Tobolka (Prague, 1900-1903), II, i, 30-35. See also M. Frančić, *Sprawa polska w publicystyce Karola Hawliczka-Borowskiego* (Kraków, 1948), pp. 31-34.

35. "Czesi i ich dążenia," No. 42, pp. 173-174.

36. Minutes in Traub, "O přípravach," pp. 321-323. The recent victory of the radicals in Vienna and the ensuing flight of the emperor and royal family dominated the discussion and no congress business was transacted.

37. Helcel to Palacký, May 13, 1848, in Žáček, *Slovanský sjezd*, pp. 114-115; and Leon Sapieha, *Wspomnienia z lat od 1803 do 1863 r.*, ed. B. Pawłowski (Lvov and Warsaw, n.d.), pp. 225-226.

38. "Odezwa do Polaków," in Wisłocki, *Kongres słowiański*, pp. 162-163. For a caustic commentary on Grzybowski's presumptuous advice to his countrymen, see *Dziennik Mód Paryskich* (Lvov), June 3, 1848, No. 23, p. 187.

39. Surprisingly, Grzybowski had received more votes in the Preparatory Committee elections than either Palacký, Vocel, or Havlíček. He obviously had succeeded in attaching himself to Czech intellectual circles, but when the congress convened he disappeared into the background.

40. Floryan Ziemiałkowski, *Pamiętniki* (Kraków, 1904), II, 127, 131.

41. Wisłocki, *Kongres słowiański*, pp. 157-159. Among the signatories was Karol Libelt who would later chair the Polish-Ukrainian section. On the Wrocław gathering, see Marian Tyrowicz, *Polski kongres polityczny w Wrocławiu 1848 r.* (Kraków, 1946). Cf. John Erickson, "The Preparatory Committee of the Slav Congress, April-May 1848," in Peter Brock and H. Gordon Skilling, eds., *The Czech Renascence of the Nineteenth Century* (Toronto, 1970), pp. 186-187, 195, who notes "the significant absence of any support [in the Wrocław manifesto] for the (Prague) Congress by the Cracow Poles."

42. See *Postęp* (Lvov), May 13, 1848, No. 12, p. 46.

43. Protocols of Rada Narodowa meetings in AGAD, fond. 269. Excerpts in Žáček, *Slovanský sjezd*, pp. 104-106. On the Rada's deliberations, see also Aleksander Batowski, *Diariusz wypadków 1848 roku*, ed. Marian Tyrowicz (Wrocław, 1974), pp. 190, 195, 199-200, 205-206, 215-216; and Žáček, *Čechové a Poláci 1848*, II, 82-87.

44. Instructions of May 25, 1848, to the delegate Jan Dobrzánski, in Wisłocki, *Kongres słowiański,* pp. 159-162.

45. Lubomirski to Rada chairman Seweryn Smarzewski, May 25, 1848, in Žáček, *Slovanský sjezd,* pp. 113-114.

46. See Henryk Grajewski, *Komitet Emigracji Polskiej z 1848 roku* (Łódź, 1960).

47. May 16, 1848, in Žáček, *Slovanský sjezd,* pp. 129-130.

48. Protocol of May 25, 1848, meeting, *ibid.,* pp. 130-131.

49. Letter to Jakubowski, May 26, 1848, *ibid.,* pp. 131-132.

50. Minutes of June 15, 1848, meeting, *ibid.,* pp. 133-134.

51. Lelewel's letter of May 30, 1848, *ibid.,* pp. 135-136.

52. May 25, 1848, *ibid.,* pp. 121-123. See also Adam Lewak, "Dozór polski w Genewie w r. 1848," *Kwartalnik historyczny,* XXXIII (1919), 45-60.

53. See Czartoryski to Walewski, late May and early June 1848, in Žáček, *Slovanský sjezd,* pp. 118-120. On Czartoryski's activities in 1848, see Marceli Handelsman, *Adam Czartoryski* (Warsaw, 1948-1950), II; M. Kukiel, *Czartoryski and European Unity 1770-1861* (Princeton, 1955), chap. xviii; and M.K. Dziewanowski, "1848 and the Hotel Lambert," *Slavonic and East European Review,* XXVI, No. 67 (April 1948), 361-373.

54. Walewski to Czartoryski, May 27, 1848, in Žáček, *Slovanský sjezd,* pp. 117-118.

55. Unnamed spokesman for legionaries to Czartoryski, May 30, 1848, *ibid.,* pp. 137-138.

56. See Handelsman, *Czartoryski,* II, 277. Czartoryski mentioned his intention to visit Prague in a note to Prince Sapieha on June 3, cited in Žáček, *Čechové a Poláci 1848,* II, 105.

57. Žáček, *Slovanský sjezd,* pp. 126-128.

58. *Zoria Halytska,* 1848, Nos. 8 and 9, pp. 32, 37; and Holovna Rada Rus'ka to Preparatory Committee, May 21, 1848, in Žáček, *Slovanský sjezd,* pp. 146-147. On the Ukrainian response to the congress, see also Ivan Sozans'kyi, "Do istorii uchasty halyts'kykh Rusyniv u slovians'kim kongresi v Prazi 1848 r.," *Zapysky Naukovoho Tovarystva imeny Shevchenka,* LXXII (1906), 112-121; Ivan Bryk, "Slavians'kyi zizd u Prazi 1848 r. i ukrains'ka sprava," *Zapysky Naukovoho Tovarystva imeny Shevchenka,* CXXIX (1920), 141-217; M. Danilák, "Ukrajinci a slovanský zjazd v Prahe roku 1848," *Slovanské štúdie,* X (1968), 5-28; Oleksii Zaklyns'kyi, *Zapysky prokha starykh bohorodchan,* 2nd ed. (Toronto, 1960), p. 45; and Jan Kozik, *Między reakcją a rewolucją: Studia z dziejów ukraińskiego ruchu narodowego w Galicji w latach 1848-1849* (Kraków, 1975), pp. 56 ff.

59. May 21, 1848, in Žáček, *Slovanský sjezd,* pp. 148-149. See also Jachim to Palacký, and Čeněk Vrba to the Moravian F.M. Klácel, both of the same date, *ibid.,* pp. 147-150. On Czech-Ukrainian cooperation in this period, see esp. Vladimír Hostička, *Spolupráce Čechů a haličských Ukrajinců v letech 1848-1849* (Prague, 1965).

60. See Wisłocki, *Kongres słowiański,* pp. 37-38.

61. "In allem dem entgegen, was von der Polen ausgehen und beantragt werden wird." J.A. Helfert, "Graf Leo Thun, III: Slaven-Congress," *Österreichisches Jahrbuch,* XX (1896), 182.

62. Žáček, *Slovanksý sjezd,* p. 143. Holovats'kyi informed Zap of Virskyi's selection on May 19, 1848, in K. Studyns'kyi, *Korespondentsiia Iakova Holovats'koho v litakh 1835-49* (Lvov, 1909), pp. 244-245. The Ukrainian historian Ivan

Bryk suggests that Virskyi withdrew because of Polish threats. "Slavians'kyi zizd i ukrains'ka sprava," p. 184. A more plausible explanation is that the Holovna Rada Rus'ka discouraged this independent initiative from the more liberal provincial Uniate clergy.
        63. See V.A. Frantsev, "Priglashenie russkikh na slavianski s"ezd,"v Prage," *Golos minuvshago*, II:5 (1914), 238-240.
        64. Quoted in Frank Fadner, *Seventy Years of Pan-Slavism in Russia, Karazin to Danilevskii, 1800-1870* (Washington, 1962), p. 147.
        65. May 10 (22), 1848, to Paskevich, in A.P. Shcherbatov, *General-fel'dmarshal kniaz' Paskevich, ego zhizn' i deiatel'nost'* (St. Petersburg, 1888-1904), VI, 223.
        66. Frantsev, "Priglashenie russkikh," p. 240.
        67. On the participation of the Russians Bakunin and the Orthodox priest Miloradov, see below, chaps. v and vii.
        68. Quoted in Nicholas Riasanovsky, *Nicholas I and Official Nationality in Russia 1825-1855* (Berkeley & Los Angeles, 1959), p. 164.
        69. See E. Andics, *Das Bündnis Habsburg-Romanow: Vorgeschichte der zaristischen Intervention in Ungarn im Jahre 1849* (Budapest, 1963), pp. 83-84.
        70. "Slavischer Volkstag in Prag," No. 34, p. 137.

CHAPTER 5

        1. Protocol in Václav Žáček, ed., *Slovanský sjezd v Praze roku 1848: Sbírka dokumentů* (Prague, 1958), p. 47. This is the only clear estimate of the congress' anticipated duration.
        2. *Slavische Centralblätter*, May 31, 1848, No. 7, p. 25. The newspaper cited "an ardent patriot, B. v. N.," who had met the costs "out of his own pocket." Count J.M. Thun claimed that he contributed over 500 florins. See Thun to Lobkowitz, June 19, 1848, in Václav Chaloupecký, "Hrabě Josef Matyáš Thun a slovanský sjezd v Praze r. 1848," *Český časopis historický*, XIX (1913), 90.
        3. Jordan's recommendations, subsequently adopted as the congress "Rules of Procedure," were published in *Národní Nowiny*, May 30, 1848 (No. 46, pp. 182-183), and as a broadsheet in several languages. They are reprinted in Czech in *Zpráwa o sjezdu slowanském* (Prague, 1848), pp. 20-24; and in Polish in Žáček, *Slovanský sjezd*, pp. 218-220.
        4. Minutes of Preparatory Committee, May 24, 1848, in H. Traub, O přípravách k Slowanskému sjezdu v Praze r. 1848," *Časopis Musea království českého*, XCII (1918), 323-324. Cf. J.P. Jordan, *Aktenmässiger Bericht über die Verhandlungen des ersten Slavenkongresses in Prag* (Prague, 1848), pp. 22-23.
        5. In April 1848 Zach broke off his formal service to the Polish prince, expressing dissatisfaction with Belgrade, where little transpired. He did not, however, completely sever ties with Czartoryski, to whom he continued to send reports. Czartoryski, for his part, was quite unwilling to lose such a valuable agent and hoped that Zach might be induced to transfer to the more active Zagreb post. See Václav Žáček, *Čechové a Poláci roku 1848* (Prague, 1947-48), II, 107-108.
        6. A Czech version of the agenda, "Program předmětů, o nichž se na slowanském sjezdu rokowati má," appeared in *Národní Nowiny*, June 2, 1848 (No. 49, pp. 194-195); and Polish, German and Serbo-Croat translations were made available for the

delegates. The Polish version is in Władysław T. Wisłocki, *Kongres słowiański w r. 1848 i sprawa polska* (Lvov, 1927), pp. 175-181.

7. See Žáček, *Čechové a Poláci 1848*, II, 72-73.

8. Minutes of Preparatory Committee, May 27, 1848, in Traub, "O přípravách," pp. 324-326.

9. See *Kwěty*, May 27, 1848, No. 63, p. 270.

10. No. 46, p. 184. The newspaper estimated that 159 participants would be arriving on the Vienna train; those coming from Poland boarded the train at the Moravian town of Přerov.

11. *Národní Nowiny*, May 31, 1848, No. 47, p. 188; and *Kwěty*, June 1, 1848, No. 65, p. 277. Accounts of the delegates' arrival were also carried in *Pražský Posel*, 1848, No. 15, pp. 114-115; *Swatowáclawské Poselstwí*, June 1, 1848, No. 1, p. 4; *Constitutionelle Prager Zeitung*, June 1, 1848, No. 86, p. 1590; *Pražský Wečerní List*, June 1, 1848, No. 1, pp. 1-2; and *Gazeta Narodowa* (Lvov), June 6, 1848, No. 35, pp. 136-137.

12. *Gazeta Polska* (Poznań), June 10, 1848, No. 66, p. 257. See also *Illyrisches Blatt* (Ljubljana), June 20, 1848, No. 50, p. 200; and *Allgemeine Oder-Zeitung* (Breslau), June 7, 1848, No. 131, Erste Beilage.

13. *Constitutionelles Blatt aus Böhmen*, June 2, 1848, No. 54.

14. "Bilder aus Frankfurt—Auf der Fahrt zum Parlamente," *Kölnische Zeitung*, July 16, 1848, No. 198. See also B. Nikolajevskij, "Prag in den Tagen des Slavenkongresses 1848," *Germanoslavica*, I (1931-32), 300-312.

15. June 18, 1848, No. 166, p. 1322. See also *Allgemeine Oder-Zeitung*, June 4, 1848, No. 129, Erste Beilage.

16. June 4, 1848, No. 156, p. 2485.

17. The instructions were printed in Polish, Czech, Ukrainian, and Serbo-Croat. Copy in SÚA, ST 1848, fasc. 7, No. 92. They were also published in *Národní Nowiny*, June 1, 1848, No. 48, p. 192.

18. Protocol of Polish section meeting in Wisłocki, *Kongres słowiański*, pp. 48-49. Zap stipulated that only Austrian Poles had the right to vote on admission to the section. Other Polish "guests" could nevertheless be members of the section and participate in its activities. However, there was no objection to their voting on congress business, once admitted to the section. See *Gazeta Narodowa* (June 10, 1848, No. 39, p. 153), which maintained that a minimum age of 24 was stipulated for admittance.

19. Wisłocki, *Kongres słowiański*, p. 49. See also Bakunin's version in his *Confession* (English trans. by Robert C. Howes: *The "Confession" of Mikhail Bakunin* [Ithaca, 1977], p. 73).

20. *Michael Bakunin* (New York, 1961), p. 163.

21. *Bohemia*, June 1, 1848, No. 87.

22. Václav Čejchan, "M. Bakunin v Praze roku 1848," *Český časopis historický*, XXXVIII (1932), 564-569.

23. See Václav Čejchan, *Bakunin v Čechách: Příspěvek k revolučnímu hnutí českému v letech 1848-49* (Prague, 1928), pp. 20-21.

24. Protocol in Wisłocki, *Kongres słowiański*, pp. 51-52.

25. See esp. Antoni Helcel to Margrave Alexander Wielopolski, June 1, 1848, in Žáček, *Slovanský sjezd*, pp. 211-212.

26. See J. Karásek, "Karel Libelt, účastník Slovanského sjezdu," *Moravská Orlice* (Brno), June 7, 1908, No. 131.

27. Wisłocki, *Kongres słowiański*, pp. 53-55. The list was undoubtedly of later date, for it also included names of delegates who reached Prague after May 31.

28. *Ibid.*, pp. 56-61. However, the appointment of Bakunin, who met neither requirement, to the South Slav section would indicate that these stipulations were not strictly followed.

29. Protocol in Žáček, *Slovanský sjezd*, pp. 200-202.

30. Letter, *ibid.*, p. 205.

31. Only the original name register for the Czecho-Slovak section has been preserved, which contains the signatures of all members in the order of their admission. In ANM, SS-1848.

32. Pp. 7, 57-66.

33. *Slovanský sjezd v Praze 1848: Sbírka dokumentů*. Part 1 [all printed] (Prague, 1952), pp. 311-343. In a later edition, Žáček revised this figure to 68 "unofficial participants, guests, observers, and witnesses," for a total of 385 names. *Slovanský sjezd*, pp. 544-561.

34. See testimony of Baron Jan Neuberg before the Investigatory Commission, July 25, 1848, in SÚA, KV, fasc. 11/21. Portions are reprinted in Žáček, *Slovanský sjezd*, pp. 212-213. That the Lvov Rada Narodowa purposely discouraged independent Polish representation in Prague is evident in Celarski's letter of May 29 to the Rada president: "In Rzeszów [a Galician town en route to Prague] they wanted to send representatives to Prague, but they desisted when informed by me that this was not the will of the Central Rada Narowoda." AGAD, f. 277.

35. A group of fourteen students, only one of whom was an official participant, submitted a petition to the Polish section on June 1 which urged the delegates not to compromise the spirit of freedom or become instruments of reaction. The Polish students rejected the notion that the congress was merely an Austro-Slav gathering. Wisłocki, *Kongres słowiański*, pp. 169-171.

36. Celarski to Rada Narodowa, June 2, 1848, in Žáček, *Slovanský sjezd*, p. 239.

37. *Ibid.*; and "Kongres słowiański i rewolucya w Pradze," *Gazeta Narodowa*, June 21, 1848, No. 47, p. 186. See also Wisłocki, *Kongres słowiański*, p. 62.

38. J.A. Helfert, "Graf Leo Thun, III: Slaven-Congress," *Österreichisches Jahrbuch*, XX (1896), 190.

39. Josef Jireček suggests that the presidency was first earmarked for Šafařík, whose "extensive knowledge of all Slav idioms" uniquely qualified him for the position. He reportedly declined and the choice then fell to Palacký. "Paul Joseph Šafařík: Ein biographisches Denkmal," *Österreichische revue*, XIII (1865), 45.

40. F.J. Schopf, *Wahre und ausführliche Darstellung der am 11. März... begonnenen Volks-Bewegung und der hierauf gefolgten Ereignisse* (Leitmeritz, 1848), V, 9-10; and *Constitutionelle Prager Zeitung*, June 2, 1848, No. 87, pp. 1613-1614. Štúr's late arrival in Prague likely explains why he did not figure prominently among the congress officers.

41. *Národní Nowiny*, June 6, 1848, No. 52, pp. 205-206. On the day's events, see also *Pražský Wečerni List*, June 2, 1848, No. 2, pp. 6-7; *Slavische Centralblätter*, June 4, 1848, No. 9, pp. 34-35; Jordan, *Aktenmässiger Bericht*, pp. 24-25; and Schopf, *Wahre und ausführliche Darstellung*, V, 11-14.

42. No. 16, p. 122.

43. June 3, 1848, No. 55. See also Anton Springer, *Geschichte Oesterreichs seit dem Wiener Frieden 1809* (Leipzig, 1863-65), II, 333. Alone among Czech

newspapers, *Swatowáclawské Poselstwí* (June 6, 1848, No. 2, p. 8) reported that the procession was greeted enthusiastically by the Prague citizenry.

44. Jan M. Černý, *Slovanský sjezd v Praze roku 1848* (Prague, 1888), p. 15, who cites Josef Jireček as his source.

45. To Lobkowitz, June 19, 1848, in Chaloupecký, "Thun a slovanský sjezd," pp. 90-91.

46. May 26, 1848, in Žáček, *Slovanský sjezd,* pp. 86-87.

47. *Národní Nowiny,* June 4, 1848, No. 51, p. 201; and *Zpráwa o sjezdu slowanském,* pp. 32-34.

48. *Národní Nowiny,* June 6, 1848, No. 52, p. 206; and Władysław T. Wisłocki, *Jerzy Lubomirski 1817-1872* (Lvov, 1928), p. 63n, where a different version of Lubomirski's remarks is printed. Lubomirski's aristocratic bearing impressed observers at the meeting: "A slender smallish figure, in simple but elegant dark national attire: pale-complexioned with flashing eyes and an aquiline nose above a black, pointed moustache." *Bohemia,* June 4, 1848, No. 89.

49. *Kwěty,* June 6, 1848, No. 68, p. 290; and *Národní Nowiny,* June 7, 1848, No. 53, p. 210.

50. See *Národní Nowiny,* June 7 and 8, 1848, Nos. 53, 54, pp. 210, 213; and Jordan, *Aktenmässiger Bericht,* pp. 26-27. Jordan suggested that Hodža's speech left perhaps the deepest impression.

51. *Národní Nowiny,* June 3, 1848, No. 50, p. 197; and *Kwěty,* June 3, 1848, No. 66, p. 279.

52. Frič, *Paměti* (Prague, 1875-77), III, 158; and Jireček, "Paul Joseph Šafařik," p. 45.

53. Cited in Helfert, "Slaven-Congress," p. 248.

54. Quoted in Jan Kabelík, ed., *Korrespondence a zápisky Jana Helceleta* (Brno, 1910), p. 36.

55. See *Jutrzenka* (Kraków), June 9, 1848, No. 60, p. 249; *Národní Nowiny,* June 8, 1848, No. 54, p. 214; and Celarski to Rada Narodowa, June 2, 1848, in Žáček, *Slovanský sjezd,* p. 240.

56. "Das kleine Treiben in Prag ," *Wiener Abendzeitung,* June 3, 1848, No. 57, pp. 237-238; *Oesterreichisch deutsche Zeitung,* June 6, 1848, p. 187; and "Der eröffnete slavische Congress," *Allgemeine Oesterreichische Zeitung,* June 8, 1848, No. 159 [NS No. 69], p. 763; and *Wahrheit,* June 6, 1848, No. 3, p. 12.

57. June 8, 1848, p. 1266.

58. *Wanderer,* June 7, 1848, No. 136; *Wiener Tageblatt für alle Stände,* June 8, 1848, No. 3; and *Gerad'aus,* June 3, 1848, No. 20.

59. June 25, 1848, p. 483.

60. See Springer, *Geschichte Oesterreichs,* II, 334; and Matthias Murko, *Deutsche Einflüsse auf die Anfänge der Böhmischen Romantik* (Graz, 1897), p. 287. Cf. my "Did the Slavs Speak German at Their First Congress?" *Slavic Review,* XXXIII, No. 3 (September 1974), 515-521.

61. *Stenographischer Bericht über die Verhandlungen der deutschen constituirenden Nationalversammlung zu Frankfurt a.M.,* ed. Franz Wigard (Frankfurt a.M., 1848-49), I, 237-243. See also Zdeněk V. Tobolka, "Česká otázka v jednáních frankfurtského parlamentu roku 1848," *Časopis Matice moravské,* XXX (1906), 223-224; O. Weber, "Die Prager Revolution von 1848 und das Frankfurter Parlament," *Festschrift des Vereins für Geschichte der Deutschen in Böhmen* (Prague,

1902), p. 173; and Roy Pascal, "The Frankfurt Parliament, 1848, and the *Drang nach Osten,"Journal of Modern History*, XVIII (1946), 110-112.
  62. *The Czech Revolution of 1848* (Chapel Hill, 1969), pp, 130-131.

CHAPTER 6

  1. Protocol in Václav Žáček, ed., *Slovanský sjezd v Praze roku 1848: Sbírka dokumentů* (Prague, 1958), pp. 247-256.
  2. See Jan Novotný, *Češi a Slováci za národního obrození a do vzniku československého státu* (Prague, 1968), p. 151.
  3. Václav Žáček, *Čechové a Poláci roku 1848* (Prague, 1947-48), II, 143. Cf. Josef Václav Frič, *Paměti* (Prague, 1885-87), III, 161-162, who blames Palacký for the disagreements. Actually Palacký took no part in the June 3 discussions.
  4. The South Slav request was forwarded to the other sections on June 3. Copy to Czecho-Slovaks in Žáček, *Slovanský sjezd*, pp. 261-262.
  5. József Thim, *A Magyarországi 1848-49-iki szerb fölkelés története* (Budapest, 1930-40), II, 278-283.
  6. Protocols in Žáček, *Slovanský sjezd*, pp. 259-260, 262-263. Unlike the protocols of the other sections which relate the views of individual speakers, the South Slav documents provide only a bare outline of the section's deliberations.
  7. See Otakar Odložilík, review of *Slavenska Renesansa 1780-1848*, by Milan Prelog, in *Časopis Matice moravské*, LI (1927), 338-339.
  8. Žáček, *Slovanský sjezd*, p. 256.
  9. Protocols in Władysław T. Wisłocki, *Kongres słowiański w r. 1848 i sprawa polska* (Lvov, 1927), pp. 67-73, 75-84.
  10. For a list of those selected to both committees, see *ibid.*, pp. 72-73.
  11. The Czecho-Slovak section agreed to support only the first part of the South Slav request. At Štúr's urging, the section elected not to intervene at the court in the matter of Jelačič's legal status vis-à-vis the Hungarian ministry.
  12. Chojecki to an unidentified party, June 4, 1848, in Julius Glücklich, "Dopis Poláka ze Slovanského sjezdu 1848," *Časopis Matice moravské*, XLIX (1925), 417-421.
  13. The Prague press estimated the attendance at close to 10,000. On the Mass, see *Slavische Centralblätter*, June 5, 1848, No. 10, p. 40; *Kwěty*, June 6, 1848, No. 68, pp. 289-290; *Pražský posel*, 1848, Nos. 17, 18, pp. 132-133, 142; and *Národní Nowiny*, June 6, 1848, No. 52, p. 208.
  14. Protocol in Žáček, *Slovanský sjezd*, pp. 284-289.
  15. It was agreed later in the meeting that the deputation would not be sent immediately.
  16. Before adjourning, the Plenary Committee appointed the first committee to draft the European manifesto. The Diplomatic Committee's members included Jordan, Klácel, Vocel, Praus, Siemieński, Libelt, Kušljan, Zach, and Moraczewski. Palacký, as president of the congress, was chairman.
  17. *1848: The Revolution of the Intellectuals* (London, 1946), p. 112.
  18. Cf. Žáček, *Čechové a Poláci 1848*, II, 148-151.
  19. Czech text in *Zpráwa o sjezdu slowanském* (Prague, 1848), pp. 34-37. Two handwritten drafts are preserved in ANM, SS-1848, č. 20: a Czech version appended to the section protocol of June 6; and an undated Polish version, later published

in Wisłocki, *Kongres słowiański,* pp. 188-190. The slight differences in theseversions are compared in Zdeněk V. Tobolka, *Slovanský sjezd v Praze roku 1848* (Prague, 1901), p. 130.

20. Jan Helcelet to J.I. Hanuš, June 7, 1848, in Jan Kabelík, ed., *Korrespondence a zápisky Jana Helceleta* (Brno, 1910), p. 38.

21. Protocol in Žáček, *Slovanský sjezd,* pp. 291-294.

22. Protocol, *ibid.,* pp. 295-304. Many delegates were still confused over the new program, so Šafařík again was obliged to clarify the new procedures.

23. Protocol of June 6 meeting in Wisłocki, *Kongres słowiański* pp. 103-108.

24. *Ibid.,* pp. 92-95. Pogłodowski's action left the committee divided 3 to 3 between the Ukrainians who favored partition and the "Polish" Ruthenes who opposed any division of the province.

25. "Žądania Rusinów w Galicji," *ibid.,* pp. 191-193.

26. See *ibid.,* pp. 112-113. The agreement passed the entire section on June 8 with only two negative notes. Several writers attribute the quick settlement of the national question to the mediation of the Czech congress leaders, especially Zap, Šafařík, and Palacký, though there is no specific evidence of their intervention. See Jędrzej Moraczewski, *Opis pierwszego Zjazdu słowiańskiego* (Poznań, 1848), p. 30. Cf. the contrasting opinions in Wisłocki, *Kongres słowiański,* pp. 109-110; and Ivan Bryk, "Slavians'kyi zizd u Prazi 1848 r. i ukrains'ka sprava," *Zapysky Naukovoho Tovarystva imeny Shevchenka,* CXXIX (1920), 203-206.

27. The Rada Narodowa, meeting on June 16 and 17, assigned the issue of the Prague agreement to its executive committee (whose action, if any, is not known); already in an address of June 9 the Holovna Rada had called specifically for the partition of Galicia into Polish and Ukrainian provinces. Jan Kozik, *Między reakcją a rewolucją: Studia z dziejów ukraińskiego ruchu narodowego w Galicji w latach 1848-1849* (Kraków, 1975), p. 77.

28. Wisłocki, *Kongres słowiański,* p. 113; and Bryk, "Slavians'kyi zizd iukrains'-ka sprava," pp. 213-214. For the Czech historian Žáček, "the Polish-Ukrainian agreement was the most realistic accomplishment of the congress." *Čechové a Poláci 1848,* II, 186. Cf. Kozik, *Między reakcją a rewolucją,* pp. 73-78.

29. See protocol of June 7 meeting in Wisłocki, *Kongres słowiański,* pp. 113-119.

30. South Slav section protocols of June 5-7, 1848, in Žáček, *Slovanský sjezd,* pp. 304-307.

31. Protocol, *ibid.,* pp. 315-319.

32. On the Slovak position and Štúr's political posture at the congress, see esp. Karol Goláň's articles: "Príspevok k vývoju slovenskej politickej myšlienky," *Historica Slovaca,* I-II (1940-41), 270-275; and "Štúrove reči na Slovanskom sjazdu roku 1848," *Slovenské pohľady,* LII (1936), 417-429. Goláň attributes Štúr's radicalism at the June 3 meeting to his harrowing experiences in Slovakia at the end of May and to the influence of Bakunin at the beginning of the congress; he ascribes Štúr's re-embracing the Mikuláš position (May 10 Slovak demands) on June 7 to the "guiding influence" of Šafařík.

33. Text of Tyl's play is in Zdeněk Tobolka and Václav Žáček, eds. *Slovanský sjezd v Praze 1848: Sbírka dokumentů,* part 1 (Prague, 1952), pp. 498-501. See also the comments on the performance by Matěj Mikšíček to a friend in Brno, *ibid.,* p. 501; and Seweryn Celarski to Rada Narodowa, June 9, 1848, in Žáček, *Slovanský sjezd,* p. 345.

34. June 25, 1848, p. 483.

35. Protocol of June 8, 1848, in Žáček, *Slovanský sjezd*, pp. 319-322. Šafařík employed the word *konfederace*. Usually the Czech congress documents use the terms *spolčení* or *spolek*, which can be translated variously as "union," "association," "league," or "confederation." The Polish documents generally speak of *federacja, sojusz*, and *federacyny sojusz*.

36. Protocol of June 8, 1848, in Wisłocki, *Kongres słowiański*, pp. 121-125.

37. June 9, 1848, in Žáček, *Slovanský sjezd*, pp. 344-345.

38. Protocol in Wisłocki, *Kongres słowiański*, pp. 126-136.

39. Celarski to Rada Narodowa, June 8, 1848, in Žáček, *Slovanský sjezd*, p. 343.

40. See E. Grim, ed., "Pamiętniki Pawła Stalmacha," in *Paweł Stalmach: Jego życie i działalność w świetle prawdy* (Cieszyn, 1910), p. 212.

41. See Žáček, *Čechové a Poláci 1848*, II, 187 ff.; and Franciszek Popiołek, "1848 in Silesia, II: The Duchy of Teschen," *Slavonic and East European Review*, XXVI, No. 67 (April 1948), 384-389. Klucki sent a message to the Preparatory Committee identifying Stalmach and Kotula, as well as a Dr. Plucar (a Czech) and a Świerkiewicz, as delegates from Silesia. In Wisłocki, *Kongres słowiański*, pp. 193-194. On reaction in Silesia to the congress, see also J.L. Mikoláš, "Slezsko a slovanský sjezd v Praze roku 1848," *Věstník Matice opavské*, XXXIII-XXXIV (1927-28), 22-28; and Václav Čepelák, "Opavsko a slovanský sjezd 1848," *Věstník Matice opavské*, XXXVI (1931), 15-25.

42. "Dlatego Śląsk, ile jest słowiański, łączyć się chce do Polski," in Wisłocki, *Kongres słowiański*, pp. 194-196.

43. In his memoirs Stalmach later maintained that "the Czechs agreed at the time to the joining of the Teschen principality to Galicia on the basis of common nationality." Grim, "Pamiętniki Stalmacha," pp. 213-214.

44. "Żądania Ślązaków," in Wislocki, *Kongres słowiański*, pp. 196-197.

45. The most detailed description of this last meeting is in J.P. Jordan, *Aktenmässiger Bericht über die Verhandlungen des ersten Slavenkongresses in Prag* (Prague, 1848), pp. 49-50.

46. On June 16, during a short-lived truce in the street fighting, several members tried to reconvene the congress with the few delegates still free and in Prague. When fighting broke out again that evening, this final attempt was abandoned. See *Zpráva o sjezdu slowanském*, p. 14.

CHAPTER 7

1. J.P. Jordan, *Aktenmässiger Bericht über die Verhandlungen des ersten Slavenkongresses in Prag* (Prague, 1848), p. 34; and Libelt to Palacký, June 9, 1848, in Václav Žáček, ed., *Slovanský sjezd v Praze roku 1848: Sbírka dokumentů* (Prague, 1958), p. 361n. All the preserved drafts, as well as Palacký's final version, were prepared in German.

2. Citations from English text: "Manifesto of the First Slavonic Congress to the Nations of Europe," trans. William Beardmore, *Slavonic and East European Review*, XXVI, No. 67 (April 1948), 309-313. The manifesto was published as a broadsheet in both Czech and German following the June Uprising (copies in SÚA, ST 1848, č. 7, No. 101), and appeared contemporaneously in Polish, Slovene, Serb, as well as in German and Czech newspapers.

3. The manifesto also cited British refusal "to recognise the Irishman as an equal," though no reference was made to Russia's treatment of its neighbors.

4. Author's translation.

5. Of the three partitioning powers, only Prussia was singled out by name.

6. "The Achievements of the Slavonic Congress," *Slavonic and East European Review*, XXVI, No. 67 (April 1948), 330-334.

7. *Geschichte Oesterreichs seit dem Wiener Frieden 1809* (Leipzig, 1863-65), II, 336-339.

8. *The Czech Revolution of 1848* (Chapel Hill, 1969), pp. 133-134.

9. The German nationalist newspaper, *Wiener Schnellpost*, June 17, 1848 (No. 47, pp. 189-191), charged that "Russian gold" and "Russian enticers" (*Lockpfeifen*) were covering Bohemia and the South Slav lands. Similarly, Kossuth's newspaper, *Kossúth Hirlapja* (July 14, 1848, No. 12, p. 51), in commenting on the manifesto, asked if the Slavs will ever cease their "incessant flirtation with Muscovite might." On the russophobia of Viennese liberals, see R. John Rath, *The Viennese Revolution of 1848* (Austin, 1957), pp. 253-255.

10. See Otakar Odložilík, "The Slavic Congress of 1848," *Polish Review*, IV, No. 4 (1959), 11.

11. "Prag und der neue Panslavismus II," semester 1, part 2, pp. 438-439.

12. Libelt's draft in Žáček, *Slovanský sjezd*, pp. 361-365.

13. Pech, *Czech Revolution of 1848*, p. 135.

14. Zach's draft in Žáček, *Slovanský sjezd*, pp. 365-368. Recommendations were also offered by Šafařík and Bakunin. See *ibid.*, pp. 368-369; and for Bakunin's views, see below, pp. 96ff.

15. On Helcel's role, see an unsigned and undated outline in Polish of "Material for the Manifesto to the Emperor," in ANM, SS-1848. See also *Zpráwa o sjezdu slowanském* (Prague, 1848), p. 12; and Václav Žáček, *Čechové a Poláci roku 1848* (Prague, 1947-48), II, 161.

16. *Aktenmässiger Bericht*, p. 39. See also Josef Václav Frič, *Paměti* (Prague, 1885-87), III, 178; and Šafařík to Palacký, July 3, 1848, in Žáček, *Slovanský sjezd*, pp. 485-486.

17. *Národní Nowiny*, July 11, 1848, No. 74, pp. 291-293; *Prager Zeitung*, July 13, 1848, No. 11. Copies of the broadsheets are in ANM, SS-1848; and SÚA, ST 1848, č. 7, No. 102. The Czech text also appeared in *Zpráwa o sjezdu slowanském*, pp. 42-49. The "official" German text is reprinted in Žáček, *Slovanský sjezd*, pp. 370-375.

18. An anonymous draft of the Slovene demands preserved among the congress documents made no reference either to a separate Slovene kingdom or to a Slovene university, and, in essence, echoed the more moderate demands of the Slovaks in urging national equality in administration and education. The source of the more radical formulation in the final version is not known. For a comparison with Slovene demands made earlier in April 1848, see Robert A. Kann, *The Multinational Empire: Nationalism and National Reform in the Habsburg Monarchy 1848-1918* (1950; rpt. New York, 1964), pp. 299-300.

19. *Zpráwa o sjezdu slowanském*, p. 12.

20. The document was uncovered among Lubomirski's papers by Władysław T. Wisłocki and first published in his *Kongres słowiański w r. 1848 i sprawa polska* (Lvov, 1927), pp. 142-144, 210-215. Václav Žáček located a second, more complete, though unsigned, copy among Palacký's papers, which he produces in his

collection of congress documents: *Slovanský sjezd*, pp. 379-383. Elsewhere Žáček argued that the plan was drafted primarily by Antoni Helcel, who possessed the best legal mind at the congress. Due to Helcel's illness during the final days of the congress, the draft was not readied for discussion in time. *Čechové a Poláci 1848*, II, 164.

21. See Otakar Odložilík, "A Czech Plan for a Danubian Federation—1848," *Journal of Central European Affairs*, I, No. 3 (October 1941), 253-274.

22. Bakunin's *Confession (Ispoved')* was unearthed following the February 1917 revolution in the secret files of the tsarist Third Section. It was first published in its entirety in 1921 by V. Polonskii (*Ispoved' i pis'mo Aleksandru II*) and reissued in a more authoritative, annotated version in Vol. I of Polonskii's *Materialy dlia biografii M. Bakunina*, 3 vols. (Moscow-Petrograd/Leningrad, 1923-33), Doc. 32, pp. 95-248. English trans. by Robert C. Howes: *The "Confession" of Mikhail Bakunin* (Ithaca, 1977). Although an invaluable source on Bakunin's activities in 1848, the *Confession* must be treated with caution; it was written from memory, three years after the events and conversations described.

23. The most useful studies of Bakunin's Pan-Slav activities in Prague in May and June 1848 are Benoît-P. Hepner, *Bakounine et le panslavisme révolutionnaire* (Paris, 1950), pp. 236 ff.; Václav Čejchan, *Bakunin v Čechách: Příspěvek k revolučnímu hnutí českému v letech 1848-1849* (Prague, 1928); and B.A. Evreinov, "Bakunin i slavianskii s"ezd 1848 goda v Prage," *Zapiski Russkago Nauchnago Instituta v Belgrade*, XIII (1936), 131-160.

24. *"Confession" of Mikhail Bakunin*, pp. 67-68.

25. *Ibid.*, p. 69.

26. *Ibid.*, p. 72.

27. *Ibid.*, p. 74.

28. *Ibid.*, pp. 74-75.

29. *Ibid.*, pp. 75-76.

30. *Ibid.*, p. 76.

31. The contrasting views of Bakunin and the Czech liberals are examined in Václav L. Beneš, "Bakunin and Palacký's Concept of Austroslavism," *Indiana Slavic Studies*, II (1958), 79-111.

32. *"Confession" of Mikhail Bakunin*, p. 77.

33. *Ibid.*, p. 73.

34. Although written in French, Bakunin's plan was first published in Polish in the Lwów *Dziennik Narodowy*, August 31 and September 5, 1848 (Nos. 132, 136, pp. 554-555, 568). This Polish text is reproduced in Žáček, *Slovanský sjezd*, pp. 383-386. A Czech version appeared in the Prague newspaper *Wčela*, September 15, 1848 (No. 75), and a German version in Jan Petr Jordan's *Jahrbücher für slawische Literatur, Kunst und Wissenschaft* (Leipzig), September 30, 1848 (No. 49), pp. 257-260. Bakunin's plan first appeared in Russian in the Russian edition of Bakunin's correspondence with Herzen and Ogarev: *Pis'ma M.A. Bakunina k A. I. Gertsenu i N. P. Ogarevu*, ed. M.P. Dragomanov (Geneva, 1896), pp. 364-368. In 1912 the Ukrainian writer Ivan Franko uncovered and published Bakunin's original French draft, which had come into the possession of the Ukrainian congress delegate Ivan Borysykevych ("Osnovy novoi slavians'koi polityky Bakunina," *Zapysky Naukovoho Tovarystva im. Shevchenka*, CVI [1912], 155-165). An English version of Bakunin's proposal may be found in my "Bakunin's Plan for Slav Federation, 1848," *Canadian-American Slavic Studies*, VIII (1974), 107-115.

35. It is commonly believed that Bakunin actually put two separate proposals before the congress: his federative scheme and his suggestions (assumed lost) for the European Manifesto which Karol Libelt mentioned in a letter of June 9, 1848, to congress president František Palacký that accompanied his own suggestions: "I enclose. . . a similar [project] by Bakunin in French" (Žáček, *Slovanský sjezd*, p. 361n). In all likelihood these are the same document. In the *Confession* Bakunin refers to only one proposal that he presented to the congress. Moreover, when Libelt's new agenda was unveiled in the Polish section on June 7, Bakunin emphatically voiced his opposition to issuing separate manifestos to the European nations and the Slavs. He recommended issuing "a simple declaration of principles" (Protocol in Wisłocki, *Kongres słowiański*, p. 116).

36. Introduction to *Michail Bakunins Sozial-politischer Briefwechsel mit Alexander Iw. Herzen und Ogarjow* (Stuttgart, 1895), p. liv.

37. *"Confession" of Mikhail Bakunin*, p. 77.

38. *Bakounine et le panslavisme révolutionnaire*, p. 256.

39. *"Confession" of Mikhail Bakunin*, pp. 90-91.

40. Franko, "Osnovy novoi slavians'koi polityky Bakunina," pp. 164-165; Dragomanov, *Bakunins Sozial-politischer Briefwechsel*, p. liv.

41. Cf. Evreinov, "Bakunin i slavianskii s"ezd," pp. 148-149; Frank Wollman, *Slavismy a antislavismy za jaro národů* (Prague, 1968), pp. 219-221.

42. *"Confession" of Mikhail Bakunin*, p. 95. One prominent congress participant with whom Bakunin established close ties was the Slovak L'udovít Štúr. Cf. Tatjana Ivantyšynová, "L'udovít Štúr a Michail Bakunin v revolúcii 1848-1849," *Zborník Filozofickej Fakulty Univerzity Komenského—Historica*, XXI (1970), 9-25, who overemphasizes the community of beliefs shared by Štúr and Bakunin.

43. *"Confession" of Mikhail Bakunin*, pp. 95-96.

44. *Ibid.*, p. 96.

45. E.H. Carr, *Michael Bakunin* (New York, 1961), p. 169.

46. *"Confession" of Mikhail Bakunin*, p. 96. J. Šesták, in his memoirs, reported a conversation that Bakunin supposedly had with Mayor Vaňka during the uprising: "Herr Bürgermeister, was ist das für eine Revolution, keine Ordnung, keine Organization. Jeder macht, was er will!" Quoted in Zdeněk V. Tobolka, *Slovanský sjezd v Praze roku 1848* (Prague, 1901), p. 186n.

47. Cf. Anna Bajerová, *Svatodušní bouře v Praze r. 1848 ve světle soudního vyšetřování* (Plzeň, 1920), pp. 163-164.

48. See esp. John Erickson, "Recent Soviet and Marxist Writings: 1848 in Central and Eastern Europe," *Journal of Central European Affairs*, XVII, No. 2 (July 1957), 119-126. Such attempts have been most apparent in the writings of the Soviet historian I.I. Udal'tsov. His work *Ocherki iz istorii natsionalno-politicheskoi borby v Chekhii v 1848 godu* (Moscow, 1951) contains a lengthy section on the congress. German and Czech translations of his work also appeared.

CHAPTER 8

1. The most extensive treatment of the June Uprising is Anna Bajerová, *Svatodušní bouře v Praze r. 1848 ve světle soudního Vyšetřování* (Plzeň, 1920). The literature on the uprising is surveyed in Stanley Z. Pech, "The June Uprising in

Prague in 1848," *East European Quarterly*, I, No. 4 (January 1968), 341-370. See also David Ward, "Windischgrätz and the Bohemian Revolt, 1848," *History Today*, XIX (1969), 625-633.

2. The controversy was waged energetically in the contemporary press. See the Slavs' defense in "Události pražské v tydnu po sv. Duchu 1848," *Národní Nowiny*, June 24 and 25, 1848, Nos. 57, 59/60, pp. 225-229, 233-234; *ibid.*, July 4, 1848, No. 67, p. 265; "Die Prager Revolte und ihre Nachwehen für das Slaventhum," *Slavische Centralblätter*, July 7, 1848, No. 29, pp. 113-114; and "Kongres słowiański i rewolucya we Pradze," *Gazeta Narodowa* (Lvov), June 21, 26, and July 1, 1848, Nos. 47, 50, 54, pp. 186, 198, 216. From the German nationalist side, see "Die Prager Pfingsten" and "Die böhmische Verschwörung," *Die Grenzboten*, 1848, semester 1, part 2, pp. 488-492, 524-527.

3. By 1848 the city comprised about 150,000 inhabitants, including the new industrial suburbs. See Antonín Boháč, *Hlavní město Praha: Studie o obyvatelstvu* (Prague, 1923), p. 13.

4. See Josef Janáček, ed., *Dějiny Prahy* (Prague, 1964), pp. 427-430. In 1845 Prague was linked by rail with Vienna.

5. See Eberhard Wolfgramm, "Der böhmische Vormärz, im besonderen die böhmischen Arbeiterunruhen des Jahres 1844 in ihren sozialen und politischen Zusammenhängen," in *Aus 500 Jahre deutsch-tschechoslowakischer Geschichte*, ed. K. Obermann and J. Polišenský (Berlin, 1958), pp. 179 ff.

6. See Ludmila Kárníková, *Vývoj obyvatelstva v českých zemích* (Prague, 1965), pp. 104-108.

7. See Zdeněk V. Tobolka, *Počátky dělnického hnutí v Čechách*, 2nd ed. (Prague, 1923), pp. 31 ff. See also the demands of the textile printers on May 24, 1848, in M. Novotný, ed., *Letáky z roku 1848* (Prague, 1948), pp. 128-130.

8. See *Kwěty* (Prague), May 2 and 4, 1848, Nos. 53, 54, pp. 230, 234.

9. See Stanley Z. Pech, *The Czech Revolution of 1848* (Chapel Hill, 1969), pp. 309 ff.

10. On Windischgrätz' return, see *ibid.*, pp. 140-141; and Paul Müller, *Feldmarschall Fürst Windischgrätz: Revolution und Gegenrevolution in Österreich* (Vienna & Leipzig, 1934), pp. 102-113.

11. See *Constitutionelles Blatt aus Böhmen*, June 9, 1848, No. 60 (Beilage); F.J. Schopf, *Wahre und ausführliche Darstellung der am 11. März 1848 . . . begonnenen Volks-Bewegung . . .*(Leitmeritz, 1848), V, 81-82; and Josef Václav Frič, *Paměti* (Prague, 1885-87), III, 208-209.

12. The events leading up to the clash on June 12 are carefully examined in Bajerová, *Svatodušní bouře*, pp. 38 ff.

13. A facsimile of the demands, known as the "red posters" because of the ink used, is in Karel Kazbunda, *České hnutí roku 1848* (Prague, 1929), facing p. 248.

14. Schopf, *Wahre und ausführliche Darstellung*, V, 32. See also Frič, *Paměti*, III, 173-175.

15. Sladkovský had studied law in Vienna before returning to Prague in March 1848 and plunging into radical politics among the city's workers. See Josef Matoušek, *Karel Sladkovský a český radikalism za revoluce a reakce* (Prague, 1929), pp. 9-37.

16. The Moravian delegate, Matěj Mikšíček, likened the sultry weather to the torrid political situation. But he also noted that the Prague burghers, as was their custom on Sundays, were prominading in their finest attire and giving little

apparent thought to the political turmoil. A couple of days earlier the *Národní Nowiny* had voiced the forewarning: "We have quiet now, but the quiet that precedes a storm" (June 9, 1848, No. 55, p. 217).

17. See Bajerová, *Svatodušní bouře*, pp. 41-49.

18. *Ibid.*, pp. 49-51. See also Frič, *Paměti*, III, 194-195. The Slovak Hodža reported that the radicals gave their solemn word that as long as the Slav Congress continued in session they would not initiate any violence. Letter to his wife, June 19, 1848, in Václav Žáček, ed., *Slovanský sjezd v Praze roku 1848: Sbírka dokumentů* (Prague, 1958), p. 398.

19. The events of June 12 are most exhaustively related in Bajerová, *Svatodušní bouře*, pp. 54-127. See also J.A. Helfert, *Der Prager Juni-Aufstand 1848* (Prague, 1897), pp. 12-75. The most reliable of the contemporary accounts, in addition to the newspaper reports cited in n. 2, are Ferdinand Kopp, *Die Ereignisse der Pfingstwoche des Jahres 1848 in Prag und in dessen nächster Umgebung* (Prague, 1848), pp. 40 ff.; H. Cocles, *Die Prager Pfingstwoche* (Prague, 1848), pp. 8 ff; Schopf, *Wahre und ausführliche Darstellung*, VI.

20. Arnold had recently worked among the poorer Czech students in Prague. His brother, Emanuel Arnold, was a leader of the Czech radicals and a close associate of Sladkovský. When asked to lead the Mass, Arnold had assumed it would be similar to the Slav Masses on June 4 and 11; but when he stopped at the National Museum early in the morning of June 12, he learned that the Mass had no connection with the congress. See A. Rezek, "Zápisky faráře Jana Arnolda r. 1848 a o době reakční," *Sborník historický*, III (1885), 350-351.

21. According to contemporary hospital statistics, most of the insurgents' casualties were workers and students. See J. Halla, "Die Opfer der Prager Pfingsten," *Vierteljahrschrift für die praktische Heilkunde*, V, No. 4 (1848), 141-154.

22. She was shot while standing near an open second-floor window in the military headquarters. The circumstances gave rise to various theories—blaming the insurgent students as well as the military—though investigation failed to reveal the guilty party. The incident is examined in Anna Bajerová, *Z české revoluce 1848* (Prague, 1919), pp. 44-57.

23. He expressed this view as early as June 17 in a letter to Emperor Ferdinand, in Kazbunda, *České hnutí 1848*, pp. 404-410. On the establishment and operations of the commission, see Otakar Odložilík, "Vyšetřovací komise z roku 1848 a jejich registratura," *Sborník Archivu ministerstva vnitra Republiky česko-slovenské*, II (1929), 1-90.

24. Pech, *Czech Revolution of 1848*, p. 158.

25. See *Prager Zeitung*, August 4, 1848, No. 30; and Ernst, *Die Prager Juni-Ereignisse in der Pfingstwoche des Jahres 1848* (Vienna, 1849), pp. 60-63, and following p. 73.

26. *Paměti*, III, 122-124. See also Bajerová, *Svatodušní bouře*, pp. 239-241, 397-398, and following p. 413, where copies of the purported plans are reproduced. Václav Čejchan, who examined the surviving protocols of Slavia's military section, supports Frič's claim that the students did not deliberately plan a hostile confrontation with the military. "Přípravy k svatodušním bouřím v Praze roku 1848?" *Zprávy Vojenského archivu a musea RČS*, V (1929), 61-72.

27. See Baron Neuberg's testimony of July 25, 1848, before the Investigatory Commission, in SÚA, KV, fasc. 11/21. See also Palacký to Leo Thun, July 3, 1848, in Palacký, *Gedenkblätter* (Prague, 1874), pp. 167-169. According to a contemporary

press report, most of the Viennese students had left Prague before the uprising. *Constitutionelles Blatt aus Böhmen*, June 6, 1848, No. 57. Interestingly, at the same time the Viennese press noted the presence of numerous radical Prague students in their city. *Wiener Schnellpost*, June 8, 1848, No. 38, p. 149; and *Wiener Zeitschrift für Recht, Wahrheit* . . . , June 10, 1848, Nos. 117/118, p. 472.

28. *Zpráwa o sjezdu slowanském* (Prague, 1848), p. 14; and Frič, *Pamĕti*, III, 176-177. They were accorded until the afternoon of June 13 to comply with the order.

29. See Kopp, *Ereignisse der Pfingstwoche*, pp. 60-62; Cocles, *Prager Pfingstwoche*, pp. 14-17; and Bajerová, *Svatodušní bouře*, pp. 66-68. The congress delegates had already left the building.

30. Carl Malisz, *Der Slaven-Kongress und die neusten Ereignisse in Prag* (Mannheim, 1848), pp. 16-17; and Bajerová, *Svatodušní bouře*, p. 115.

31. Leon Sapieha, *Wspomnienia* (Lvov & Warsaw, n.d.), pp. 230-232.

32. See Jan Petr Jordan, *Aktenmässiger Bericht über die Verhandlungen des ersten Slavenkongresses in Prag* (Prague, 1848), p. 39; and Jovan Subotić, "Zápisky dra Subotiće, učastníka slovanského sjezdu," *Naše doba*, X (1902-03), 890.

33. See Praus and Helcel to Palacký, June 13, 1848, in Žáček, *Slovanský sjezd*, pp. 421-422.

34. The Poles Sawczyński and Stabkowski to Palacký, June 14 (Olomouc); Sapieha, Krainski, and Potocki to Palacký, June 14 (Saxon border town of Bad Schandau); Lubomirski to Palacký, June 15 (Bohumín); Zaleski to Palacký, June 19 (Kolín); and Lubomirski to Šafařík, June 23 (Dresden), *ibid.*, pp. 422-426.

35. *Kwĕty*, No. 73, p. 307.

36. Otakar Odložilík, "Pokus o soudní vyšetřování Fr. Palackého r. 1848," *Národní Osvobození* (Prague), May 26, 1926, No. 143.

37. SÚA, KV, fasc. 260.

38. See Bajerová, *Svatodušní bouře*, pp. 293-312. Havlíček's arrest on July 7 followed the appearance in *Národní Nowiny* of an article praising the attempts of rural Czech militia to join in defending Prague against the Austrian soldiers.

39. See Havlíček to F.L. Krajník, July 12, 1848, in Ladislav Quis, ed., *Korrespondence Karla Havlíčka* (Prague, 1903), pp. 767-768.

40. SÚA, KV, fasc. 11/7. See also R. Maršan, *Čechové a Nĕmci r. 1848 a boj o Frankfurt* (Prague, 1898), pp. 166-173.

41. Cited in *Národní Nowiny*, June 27, 1848, No. 61, p. 243.

42. "Das Prager Blutbad," *Der Freimüthige*, June 16, 1848, No. 62, p. 256; "Die Schauereignisse in Prag," *Der Volksfreund*, June 15, 1848, No. 34, p. 137; and "Die grosse panslavistische Verschwörung," *ibid.*, June 18, 1848, No. 37, pp. 148-149.

43. "Die Prager Pfingsten," 1848, semester 1, part 2, p. 491.

44. "Neuestes aus Prag," June 17, 1848, No. 63, pp. 258-259; and "Die Plane der Camarilla beginnen zu reifen," June 18, 1848, Nos. 64/65, p. 265.

45. "Die Bluttage in Prag und ihre Ruckwirkung auf Wien," June 23, 1848, No. 42, pp. 169-170.

46. See "Heute mir, morgan dir, oder die Beschiessung von Prag," *Gerad'aus*, June 20, 1848, No. 33.

47. *Stenographischer Bericht über die Verhandlungen der deutschen constituirenden Nationalversammlung zu Frankfurt a.M.*, ed. Franz Wigard (Frankfurt a.M., 1848-49), I, 618-622.

48. *Ibid.,* pp. 661-662. A minority report, drafted by Arnold Ruge, argued that military be dispatched only if requested by the Austrian authorities. *Ibid.,* p. 663.

49. *Ibid.,* p. 674. See also Friedrich Prinz, "Die Sudetendeutschen im Frankfurter Parlament," in *Zwischen Frankfurt und Prag* (Munich, 1963), p. 120.

50. June 18 and 25, 1848, Nos. 18 and 25. The anti-Slav outburst was also rejected in the democratic *Allgemeine Oder-Zeitung,* June 18, 1848, No. 140, Erste Beilage.

51. Meetings of June 27 and July 5 reported in *Breslauer Zeitung,* June 28, 1848, No. 148, pp. 1649-1650; and Ruge's *Die Reform,* July 7, 1848, No. 91, p. 744.

52. The documents accompanied his letters to Thun of June 30 and July 4, Žáček, *Slovanský sjezd,* pp. 484-485 and 486-487.

53. July 3, 1848, in Palacký, *Gedenkblätter,* pp. 167-169.

54. Žáček, *Slovanský sjezd,* pp. 485-486. Šafařík did in fact make certain alterations in the documentation before turning it over to Thun.

55. Thun's letter in SÚA, KV, fasc. 3. The commission was not in a position to use the documents immediately. Several of the protocols were barely legible, and translations of the Polish and Serbo-Croat materials had to be prepared.

56. Žáček, *Slovanský sjezd,* pp. 488-490.

57. These included Baron Villani, leader of the Czech militia, Svornost, who had been arrested on June 16 and questioned repeatedly throughout July; Count Deym, who had guided the St. Wenceslas Committee and the Bohemian National Committee; Count Buquoi; Faster; Dr. Václav Frič, father of the student leader J.V. Frič; and Jan Arnold.

58. The original protocols of Turánsky's testimony, indicating the dates on which questioning took place, are in SÚA, KV, fasc. 52/2. A second, clearer copy, though lacking his final testimony of August 19, 1848, is *ibid.,* fasc. 294/9. Portions of Turánsky's testimony are in Žáček, *Slovanský sjezd,* pp. 454-459. A slightly different version, which was prepared by the commission for the Hungarian authorities, is in Daniel Rapant, *Slovenské povstanie roku 1848-49* (Turčiansky Svätý Martin & Bratislava, 1937-72), I, ii, 342-344.

59. In the version sent to Hungary a sentence was added here to the effect that if their plans went awry they would endeavor to deliver the Slav nations "into the hands of Russia." *Ibid.,* p. 343.

60. Palacký later rejected this claim as pure fabrication. *Politisches Vermächtniss,* p. 12.

61. Turánsky actually brought along a rifle, two pistols, and a saber. See Bajerová, *Svatodušní bouře,* p. 246.

62. Testimony of July 17, 19, and 20, 1848, in SÚA, KV, fasc. 52/2.

63. This view was first raised in *Národní Nowiny* on July 29, 1848, No. 91, p. 360, and later supported by Palacký, who pointed to an anti-Slav article by the Hungarian correspondent of the Augsburg *Allgemeine Zeitung,* which appeared on June 29, 1848, No. 181, p. 2885; that is, before Turánsky had commenced his story, which conspicuously dovetailed with Turánsky's later testimony. Their common source, in Palacký's opinion, could be found in Pest.

64. Rezek, "Zápisky Arnolda," p. 353.

65. Protocol of Rada Narodowa, April 28, 1848, AGAD, fond. 269. His request was turned down by the Rada because he was not acting in an official capacity. Cf. Václav Žáček, *Čechové a Poláci roku 1848* (Prague, 1947-48), II, 42.

66. Frič, *Paměti*, III, 201. In his brochure *Der Slowak* which appeared in 1848, the Slovak Michal Miloslav Hodža dramatically claimed: "Die verruchte Hand eines Magyaren (ich habe ihn gesehen) that den ersten Schuss auf die Soldaten."

67. The Magyars applauded Windischgrätz's suppression of the Prague uprising and cooperated enthusiastically in the subsequent investigation. See Wacław Felczak, *Węgierska polityka narodowościowa przed wybuchem powstania 1848 roku* (Wrocław, 1964), pp. 113-115.

68. See Rapant, *Slovenské povstanie*, I, i, 342-346.

69. See Milan Hodža, *Československý rozkol* (Turčiansky Svätý Martin, 1920), pp. 390 ff.; and Václav Žáček, *Z revolučných a politických pol'sko-slovenských stykov v dobe predmarcovej* (Bratislava, 1966), pp. 182-190. The Czecho-Slovak historian Albert Pražák claimed that Turánsky had based his disclosures in Prague on a pamphlet which Francisci wrote in 1847. "The Slavonic Congress of 1848 and the Slovaks," *Slavonic and East European Review*, VII, No. 19 (June 1928), 157. The revolutionary pamphlet, *Zrkadlo pre l'ud slovenský* (A Mirror for the Slovak People), with which Turánsky was undoubtedly familiar, exhorted the Slovaks to throw off their alien Magyar and German masters, but made no mention of any organized group which was devoted to realizing this task.

70. A fellow prisoner, Karel Sabina, himself later a police spy, who apparently gained Turánsky's confidence, reported Turánsky's claim that he would not be in jail for long, as Windischgrätz would soon make him a lieutenant in the Hussars. See Rezek, "Zápisky Arnolda," p. 353.

71. See Bajerová, *Svatodušní bouře*, pp. 115n, 246. Little was learned of Turánsky's actions during the uprising itself.

72. Müller's report in SÚA, KV, fasc. 52/1. Turánsky claimed to be awaiting funds from home.

73. See Rapant, *Slovenské povstanie*, I, ii, 342-345, 368.

74. *Slovanský sjezd v Praze roku 1848* (Prague, 1901), pp. 194-196.

75. *Prager Zeitung*, August 4, 1848, No. 30. The thrust of Turánsky's testimony had already leaked out; see *Národní Nowiny*, July 29, 1848, No. 91, p. 360.

76. "Offizielle Kundmachung über die Slaven-Verschwörung," *Slavische Centralblätter*, August 6, 8, and 9, 1848, Nos. 57, 59-60, pp. 225-227, 233-235, 237-240. See also, "Die Prager Juni-Ereignisse und ihre Ursachen," *Bohemia*, August 8-11, 1848, Nos. 137-140; and "Alfred Fürst Windischgrätz und die weitverzweigte Verschwörung," *Constitutionelle Allgemeine Zeitung von Böhmen*, August 5-10, 1848, Nos. 23-28, pp. 161, 165, 171, 175, 179, 183.

77. Their statement of August 10 was printed in *Wiener Zeitung*, August 19, 1848, No. 227, p. 66. Palacký did not learn that he was cited as a chief conspirator by Turánsky until the following spring.

78. Jan M. Černý, ed., *Boj za právo: Sborník aktů politických u věcech státu a národa českého od roku 1848* (Prague, 1893), pp. 366-375.

79. Turánsky was interrogated only once more—on August 19.

80. See Odložilík, "Vyšetřovací komise," pp. 50 ff.; and Bajerová, *Svatodušní bouře*, pp. 343-373.

81. SÚA, KV, fasc. 52/39. The report was dated October 13, 1848. Portions are printed in Žáček, *Slovanský sjezd*, pp. 475-483.

82. See Odložilík, "Vyšetřovací komise," pp. 69ff.; and Bajerová, *Svatodušní bouře*, pp. 366-367n. Only the purported instigators of the uprising were to remain in custody. The amnesty was proclaimed by Bach and not directly by the emperor.

83. *Verhandlungen des österreichischen Reichstages nach der stenographischen Aufnahme* (Vienna, 1848-49), V, 342-345. Scharfen had briefly headed the criminal investigation. His report, "Actenmässige Darstellung der Prager Juni-Ereignisse v[om] J[ahre] 1848," had been prepared prior to the more moderate findings of Roob. See also Lajos Steier, *A tót nemzetiségi kérdés 1848-49-ben* (Budapest, 1937), II, 69-78, where a major portion of this report is reproduced.

84. The Czech protest was presented by Brauner on March 6, 1849, the final day of the Reichstag session. See *Verhandlungen des österreichischen Reichstages,* V, 380-381; and a Czech version in Černý, *Boj za právo*, pp. 553-555.

85. The court's instruction to Müller in SÚA, KV, fasc. 52. See also Odložilík, "Vyšetřovací komise," pp. 77-78. Turánsky's release was recommended by Roob in his report of October 13, as no further corroborative evidence could be reasonably expected. and there was insufficient evidence to charge Turánsky with treason for his part in the uprising. *Ibid.,* fasc. 52/39.

86. J[úlius] B[otto], "Z listin slovenského národovca," *Slovenské pohl'ady,* XXI (1901), 82. This testimony came from Michal Bakulíni, himself a veteran of 1848-49, who became acquainted with Turánsky in the late 1860's.

87. Jozef Škultéty, "Slovanský sjazd v Prahe roku 1848," *Slovenské pohl'ady,* XXI (1901), 669.

CHAPTER 9

1. Testimony of Jan Palacký, cited in Zdeněk V. Tobolka, *Slovanský sjezd v Praze roku 1848* (Prague, 1901), p. 165. Shortly thereafter Šafařík resigned the presidency of the Prague Slovanská lípa and withdrew from political activity.

2. See Václav Žáček, "České a jihoslovanské Slovanské lípy v roce 1848," *Literární archiv,* VI (1971), 195-239.

3. *Geschichte Oesterreichs seit dem Wiener Frieden 1809* (Leipzig, 1863-65), II, 349.

4. *Politisches Vermächtniss* (Prague, 1872), pp. 9-14.

5. See his "Nothgedrungene Erklärung," *Prager Zeitung,* January 26, 1849, reprinted in Palacký, *Gedenkblätter* (Prague, 1874), pp. 181-184.

6. *Betrachtungen über die Zeitverhältnisse, insbesondere im Hinblicke auf Böhmen* (Prague, 1849), pp. 96-97. Possibly Thun now blamed the Czech liberals and the congress for the personal political setbacks to him in Bohemia after the June Uprising. Cf. above, Thun's views on the congress in July 1848, p. 110.

7. From Moraczewski's manuscript "O kongresie słowiańskim w Pradze, zebranym 31. maja 1848," in Václav Žáček, ed., *Slovanský sjezd v Praze roku 1848: Sbírka dokumentů* (Prague, 1958), p. 515. This passage on Palacký was deleted in the published version of Moraczewski's account: *Opis pierwszego Zjazdu słowiańskiego* (Poznań, 1848).

8. *The "Confession" of Mikhail Bakunin* (Ithaca, 1977), pp. 70-71.

9. Friedrich Engels, *Germany: Revolution and Counter-Revolution,* in *The German Revolutions,* ed. L. Krieger (Chicago, 1967), pp. 177-180. Engels' work originally appeared in the New York *Daily Tribune* in 1851-52 under Marx's name. See also Roman Rosdolsky, "Friedrich Engels und das Problem der 'geschichtslosen'Völker (Die Nationalitätenfrage in der Revolution 1848-49 im Lichte der 'Neuen Rheinischen Zeitung')," *Archiv für Sozialgeschichte,* IV (1964), 155-164.

10. Štúr's support for Jelačić and the Austrian ministry against the Magyars led to a break with Bakunin. In words remarkably similar to those Štúr himself had used during the congress sessions, Bakunin prophetically warned his Slovak friend in a letter from Berlin in September 1848: "Brother, what are you doing? You are destroying Slavdom. You've lost your senses; you're sacrificing the great Slav enterprise and acting merely in the interests of the emperor and the Austrian aristocracy. You believe that diplomacy will save you, but it will destroy you." *Listy L'udovíta Štúra*, ed. J. Ambruš (Bratislava, 1954-60), III, 116-117, 241.

11. Ed. Josef Jirásek (Bratislava, 1931), pp. 185 ff. Štúr's manuscript was first published in 1867 under the Russian title *Slavianstvo i mir budushchago* and was reprinted in 1909. The Slovak historian Vladimír Matula, on the basis of unpublished correspondence between Štúr and the Russian archpriest M.F. Raevskii, finds an explanation for Štúr's apparent concessions to tsarist absolutism not only in his disillusionment after 1848-49 but, more importantly, in the hopes Štúr attached to the "political thaw" in Russia which accompanied the accession of Alexander II in early 1855. Štúr hurriedly finished his manuscript and sent it to Raevskii in Vienna to be distributed to influential personages in St. Petersburg. "Liudovit Shtur i Rossiia," in *L'udovít Štúr und die slawische Wechselseitigkeit*, ed. L'. Holotík (Bratislava, 1969), pp. 364-365. See also Matula's "L'udovít Štúr a M. F. Rajevskij," *Slovenská literatúra*, XIII (1966), 361-384.

12. See Michael B. Petrovich, "L'udovít Štúr and Russian Panslavism," *Journal of Central European Affairs*, XII, No. 1 (April 1952), 7-8. Although several leading participants of the 1848 congress, notably Palacký, also attended the Moscow gathering, it is incorrect to see the 1867 congress as a direct continuation of the Prague meeting. The Poles, still smarting from their 1863 defeat at Russian hands, of course boycotted the meeting. See Georges Luciani, "Du Congrès de Prague (1848) au Congrès de Moscou (1867)," *Revue des Etudes Slaves*, XLVII (1968), 85-93; Mieczysław Tanty, *Panslawizm, Carat, Polacy: Zjazd Słowiański w Moskwie 1867* (Warsaw, 1970); and Milan Prelog, *Pout' Slovanů do Moskvy 1867* (Prague, 1931).

BIBLIOGRAPHICAL ESSAY:
THE CONGRESS AS HISTORY

Much of the fascination of the Slav Congress for historians derives from the disparate judgments it has evoked. The bitter exchanges which erupted in 1848 in the Slav and German press have continued in polemical brochures, popular and scholarly journals, and monographic studies. Indeed, the historiography of the congress may be viewed as a microcosm of the nationalist sentiments and, more recently, the ideological divisions which have blighted East Central Europe since the 1848-49 upheavals.

After the rupture of the congress its supporters immediately set to the task of providing a scrupulous rectification of its activities and aims, especially in response to continuing criticisms from German and Magyar nationalists and Habsburg officials. Soon after Windischgrätz allowed the Prague newspapers to resume publication, the leading Slav organs issued semi-official (no agreement had been reached on a permanent secretariat before the uprising) reports on the proceedings which emphasized the congress' peaceful and loyal intent.[1]

The decade of reaction which followed the revolutions afforded little encouragement for a dispassionate accounting. The first critical appraisal of the congress against the background of the Austrian revolution was made in the 1860's by the Bohemian-German Anton Springer in his history of Austria in the nineteenth century.[2] In Springer's opinion the congress foundered due to irreconcilable conflicts—between political moderates and a small but vocal radical wing, and among the Slavs themselves due to Polish intransigence—which were reflected in the congress' manifestos. Springer stated his views without rancor or recrimination and rejected the charge that the congress precipitated the abortive June Uprising. Springer's contemporary, the Magyar historian Mihály Horváth, however, in a study of the Hungarian "independence struggle" of 1848-49, still displayed contempt for the reactionary Prague Slavs, who he felt were unquestionably "in secret liaison" with tsarist propagandists.[3]

But almost half a century passed before serious study of the congress was undertaken. In the 1890's the conservative Austrian historian, Baron Josef Alexander von Helfert, published his adulatory biography of Count Leo Thun, the last two sections of which he devoted to the congress and the June Uprising.[4] Basing his account on Thun's personal papers, of which he was executor, Helfert made a sweeping indictment of the congress' politically inept leadership for opening the meeting to non-Austrian subjects and for allowing the radicals to gain the upper hand and provoke the uprising (which ended Thun's political career in Bohemia). In addition to his partisan approach, Helfert gave credence to the unsubstantiated rumors which abounded in Prague after the uprising.

The turn of the century brought renewed interest from Czech historians on the Slav re-awakening and the events of 1848.[5] In 1901 the young Czech historian, Zdeněk V. Tobolka wrote the first scholarly study of the congress based on unpublished sources, chiefly the congress files which were housed in the Czech National Museum. These documents had had an intriguing odyssey. During the June Uprising Josef Jireček removed the files (protocols and correspondence) from the Czech Museum, the secretariat's headquarters during the sessions, to keep them safe from the military. On June 18, 1848, Jireček, together with Šafařík and the Pole Seweryn Celarski, sorted the papers, and Celarski, who was secretary of the Rada Narodowa in Lvov, removed the Polish protocols. At the end of June when Governor Thun, at Windischgrätz's behest, requested Šafařík to turn over the congress files to the Investigatory Commission, Šafařík relinquished only those documents which he believed could not be construed as damaging to the Slavs. The materials not given to Thun or taken by Celarski—first drafts of protocols, minutes of the Preparatory Committee, communications to the secretariat, and lists of congress membership—were eventually returned to the Czech Museum. They became the core documentation for Tobolka's study. The principal shortcoming of Tobolka's study was the absence of the Polish documents (which at the time he believed were lost). This led him to censure the Poles for the changes in the congress agenda that Libelt introduced on June 5.[6] Essentially, Tobolka viewed the congress as the unique achievement of Czech-inspired Austro-Slavism; the contributions of the other Slavs receive only casual mention. Nevertheless, Tobolka's history significantly advanced knowledge about the congress and greatly influenced subsequent accounts, especially those by the French Slavophile historians.[7]

In the decade preceding World War I a quantity of memoirs and correspondence of several principal actors of 1848 was published, making it possible to trace the views and activities of such key figures in the congress as the Poles Floryan Ziemiałkowski and Franciszek Smolka; the Czechs V.V. Tomek, Karel Havlíček, F.L. Čelakovský, and P.J. Šafařík; the Ukrainian Iakiv Hotovats'kyi; and the South Slavs Jovan Subotić,

Stanko Vraz, and Ljudevit Gaj. A major breakthrough of those years was the uncovering of the hitherto missing files of Windischgrätz's Investigatory Commission. In addition to investigatory reports and interrogation protocols of those arrested (which included a number of congress participants), the commission's files also contained several protocols of congress sessions that were not among the records in the Czech Museum.[8] After the war, Anna Bajerová, into whose hands the files first came, painstakingly prepared a comprehensive history of the June Uprising.[9] On the basis of this massive documentation, she argued convincingly what Slav authors had alleged since 1848—that no direct link existed between the congress and the uprising, despite the efforts of the commission to uncover such a tie.[10]

The postwar years saw new interest on the part of Yugoslav, Ukrainian, and, to a lesser degree, Polish historians in the congress. In 1924 the Croat historian, Milan Prelog, published a study of the Slav re-awakening, the last part of which he devoted to the congress.[11] Yet Prelog's account did not go beyond Tobolka's earlier work except in additional detail. Prelog's chief contribution was to position the congress as the culminating point of decades of cultural and political revival.[12] Both Tobolka's and Prelog's writings were relatively free of national recrimination. This was not true, however, of the Ukrainian and Polish writings, in which each side accused the other of bad faith and obstructionism in failing to carry out the congress agreements. The Ukrainian historians Ivan Sozans'kyi and Ivan Bryk denounced the Poles' repeated attempts to sidetrack legitimate Ukrainian demands.[13]

For the most part, Polish students of 1848 paid little attention to the congress, which they treated as a minor episode, choosing rather to concentrate on the European dimensions of Polish involvement in 1848— the Poznań troubles and Polish participation in the revolutionary movements in Hungary and Italy. Not until 1927, when Władysław T. Wisłocki published the Polish documents, was it finally possible to develop a composite picture of the congress.[14] While working at the Ossolineum library in Lvov on a biography of Prince Jerzy Lubomirski, Wisłocki had stumbled onto the missing Polish protocols.[15] Though faithfully reproducing these documents, Wisłocki's interpretive passages were intended to show Polish participation in the most favorable light: it was the Ukrainians, not the Poles, who obstructed the sessions and blocked understanding. Yet Wisłocki rightly pointed to Karol Libelt's major contribution and challenged the assertion, advanced by Tobolka, that blamed Libelt for the congress' shortcomings.

With the fall of the Habsburg empire, the records of the imperial government became available to scholars. From the investigations of the Czech historians Karel Kazbunda and Otakar Odložilík in particular, it was possible to reconstruct the policy of Pillersdorff's ministry toward the congress and to trace official relations between Prague and Vienna.[16]

In Russia the collapse of the tsarist regime brought a new interest in nineteenth-century radicalism. With the opening of the secret files of the Third Department, Mikhail Bakunin's *Confession* to Tsar Nicholas I came to light. For the student of the congress this was truly an intriguing find, for Bakunin devoted considerable attention to his stay in Prague and his opinion of the congress. Bakunin's activities in Prague were examined in detail by the Czech historian, Václav Čejchan.[17]

Non-Slav historians, in general, have made little original contribution to the study of the congress. The main German study of Pan-Slavism, by Alfred Fischel, is based largely on Tobolka's monograph, though lacking the latter's sympathetic interpretation.[18] Nevertheless, Fischel has remained the primary source on the congress for Western authors unversed in Slav languages.

The centenary of the 1848 revolutions brought an unprecedented wave of publishing fury, though the results were of disparate scholarly value. The most significant contribution was Václav Žáček's two-volume study of Czech-Polish relations in 1848.[19] His lengthy researches in Polish and Czech archives produced a comprehensive portrait of the diverse strands of Polish response to the Slav question. Specifically his study sheds new light on the activities of Prince Adam Czartoryski, the democratic *emigracja,* and the Polish Rada Narodowa in Lvov.[20] In 1948 the Slav Institute in Prague issued a volume of lectures commemorating the congress.[21] The collective work suffered, however, from unevenness in methodology and documentation.

Among the numerous contributions to historical journals during the centenary, special mention should be made of Henryk Batowski's seminal essay pointing to unresolved problems regarding the Slavs in 1848.[22] After the war, the first treatment in English of the congress appeared in Lewis Namier's *1848: The Revolution of the Intellectuals.* Though restricted to the resources of the British Museum, due to wartime conditions, Namier advanced well beyond the limited French and German works already cited. His emphasis fell strikingly on the divisions—both national and ideological—that separated the Slav participants. In his judgment the congress manifesto was "an exceedingly vague, verbose and ineffective document." Both Batowski and Namier noted the need for new study of the congress in view of the shortcomings of the existing literature.

The 1848 centenary also attracted the attention of Soviet historians. The leading Russian student of the congress is I.I. Udal'tsov, whose work on Bohemia in 1848 earned him a Stalin prize.[23] Udal'tsov treated the congress as a conspicuous episode of 1848 wherein the fledgling Czech bourgeoisie, led by Palacký and acting out of class self-interest, abandoned the revolutionary cause. As had Marx and Engels a century before, Udal'tsov discounted the danger posed by the more progressive Magyar and German national movements.

As early as 1947 the leading Czech students of the congress, Zdeněk Tobolka and Václav Žáček, collaborated in preparing a comprehensive edition of the major congress documents. Tobolka gathered printed materials, especially contemporary newspaper reports, while Žáček concentrated on unpublished archival sources. Their initial plan to ready the collection for publication during the centenary had to be abandoned due to the vast quantity of materials they had amassed. Moreover, the political changes of 1948 in Czechoslovakia hampered their access to materials located abroad, especially in Vienna and Western Europe, and it was not until 1952 that the fruits of their collaboration were available. Five hundred pages of the first volume, earmarked for professional, non-commercial circulation, covered only the congress preparations, concluding with the delegates' arrival and the congress opening on June 2.[24] Unfortunately, the volume suffered from hasty editing and faulty organization, and the expected companion volumes never appeared.

Following Tobolka's death, Žáček revived the project and in 1958 brought out a one-volume compendium of congress sources.[25] The limitations of the 1952 edition were rectified and the result was an outstanding technical and scholarly achievement.[26]

The appearance of Žáček's work has certainly smoothed the task facing the student of the congress, making it possible to fill in many gaps that have puzzled and eluded historians, and facilitating the preparation of the "new and comprehensive account" that Namier called for.[27]

NOTES TO BIBLIOGRAPHICAL ESSAY

1. Esp. V.V. Tomek's "Historická zpráwa o sjezdu slowanském," in Havlíček's *Národní Nowiny;* and J.P. Jordan's "Aktenmässiger Bericht über die Verhandlungen des ersten Slavenkongresses in Prag," in *Slavische Centralblätter.* Later in the year, both were reissued separately as brochures. More interpretive were the assessments by two Polish participants: Carl [Karol] Malisz, *Der Slaven-Kongress und die neuesten Ereignisse in Prag* (Mannheim, 1848), also in Polish; and Jędrzej Moraczewski, *Opis pierwszego Zjazdu słowiańskiego* (Poznań, 1848).

2. *Geschichte Oesterreichs seit dem Wiener Frieden 1809* (Leipzig, 1863-65), II, 329-352.

3. *Magyarország függetlenségi harczának története 1848 és 1849-ben,* 2d ed. (Pest, 1871-72), I, 97. The first ed. appeared in 1865.

4. "Graf Leo Thun III: Slaven-Congress," *Österreichisches Jahrbuch,* XX (1896), 179-254, also separately as *Slavencongress* (Vienna, 1897); and "Graf Leo Thun IV: Blutige Pfingsten," *Österreichisches Jahrbuch,* XXI (1897), 1-271, and separately as *Der Prager Juni-Aufstand 1848* (Prague, 1897).

5. The fiftieth anniversary of the revolutionary year was celebrated in several Czech studies in a popular vein, most notably Josef Toužimský's richly illustrated *Na úsvitě nové doby,* which depicted the congress as a crowning achievement of Czech leadership.

6. Even after the Polish documents were published, Tobolka continued to view June 5 as the tragic turning point in the deliberations: "The basis of political realism was abandoned and its place taken by political romanticism" (*Politické dějiny československého národa od r. 1848 až do dnešní doby* [Prague, 1932-37], I, 85).

7. Most notably, Ernest Denis, *La Bohême depuis la Montagne-Blanche* (Paris, 1903), II, 283-321; and Louis Leger, *Le Panslavisme et l'intérêt français* (Paris, 1917), pp. 159-201.

8. These were the materials which Thun received from Šafařík and forwarded to the Investigatory Commission.

9. *Svatodušní bouře v Praze r. 1848 ve světle soudního vyšetřování* (Plzeň, 1920). In her preface Bajerová relates the dramatic manner in which the documents came into her possession. In 1909 an order was given to remove and burn a number of old files in the Bohemian Supreme Court in Prague. The court librarian, František Bajer, was apprised, and while examining the materials in question discovered the Investigatory Commission's papers, which apparently had remained there forgotten and untouched for over fifty years. He succeeded in exempting these documents from the destruction order, and after his death they passed to his wife.

10. The commission itself was the subject of a meticulous study by Otakar Odložilík, "Vyšetřovací komise z roku 1848 a jejich registratura," *Sborník Archivu ministerstva vnitra Republiky československé,* II (1929), 1-90.

11. *Slavenska renesansa 1780-1848* (Zagreb).

12. Prelog, who completed his book in 1921, did not use the files of the Investigatory Commission.

13. Sozans'kyi, "Do istorii uchasty halyts'kykh Rusyniv u slovians'kim kongresi v Prazi 1848 r., " *Zapysky Naukovoho Tovarystva im. Shevchenka,* LXXII (1906), 112-121; and Bryk, "Slavians'kyi zizd u Prazi 1848 r. i ukrains'ka sprava," *Zapysky Naukovoho Tovarystva im. Shevchenka,* CXXIX (1920), 141-217.

14. *Kongres słowiański w r. 1848 i sprawa polska* (Lvov; 1927).

15. Although Celarski brought the Polish files back to Lvov, their subsequent fate was unknown. Apparently he turned them over to Lubomirski (a contemporary report in the Lvov press alleged that they were given to the Rada Narodowa [*Gazeta Narodowa*, July 1, 1848, No. 54, p. 216]), but they were not placed at that time with other official records in the Ossolineum. Most likely they were deposited at one of Lubomirski's estates to keep them out of Austrian hands. After Lubomirski's death, his widow gave his personal papers to the Ossolineum, where the congress documents remained buried until 1925.

16. Esp. Kazbunda, *České hnutí roku 1848* (Prague, 1929); and Odložilík, "Slovanský sjezd a svatodušní bouře r. 1848," *Slovanský přehled*, XX (1928), 408-425.

17. Esp. in his *Bakunin v Čechách: Příspěvek k revolučnímu hnutí českému v letech 1848-49* (Prague, 1928); and "Bakunin v Praze roku 1848," *Český časopis historický*, XXXVIII (1932), 564-569.

18. *Der Panslawismus bis zum Weltkrieg* (Stuttgart & Berlin, 1919), pp. 249 ff.

19. *Čechové a Poláci roku 1848* (Prague, 1947-48).

20. Research on Czartoryski's activities in 1848 had begun in the interwar years by the Polish historian Marceli Handelsman. On the Slav question, see esp. his *Ukraińska polityka ks. Adama Czartoryskiego przed wojną krymską* (Warsaw, 1937). The war interrupted Handelsman's work, and his massive three-volume biography of Czartoryski was published posthumously (Warsaw, 1949-50).

21. *Slovanský sjezd v Praze 1848: Sborník přednášek Slovanského ústavu* (Prague, 1948).

22. "Zagadnienia roku 1848 w Słowiańszczyźnie," *Przegląd historyczny*, XXXVIII (1948), 37-60. A condensed version appeared in English: "The Poles and Their Fellow Slavs," *Slavonic and East European Review*, XXVII, No. 69 (May, 1949), 404-413.

23. *Ocherki iz istorii natsional'no-politicheskoi bor'by v Chekhii v 1848g.* (Moscow, 1951). Cf. John Erickson, "Recent Soviet and Marxist Writings: 1848 in Central and Eastern Europe," *Journal of Central European Affairs*, XVII, No. 2 (July 1957), 119-126.

24. *Slovanský sjezd v Praze 1848: Sbírka dokumentů*, Part 1 (Prague: Vydáno jako rukopis Slovanského ústavu v Praze, 1952).

25. *Slovanský sjezd v Praze roku 1848: Sbírka dokumentů* (Prague: Nakladatelství Československé akademie věd, 1958).

26. See Otakar Odložilík's review article, "The Slavic Congress of 1848," *Polish Review*, IV, No. 4 (1959), 3-15.

27. Since Žáček's publication of congress documents, Western scholars have directed particular attention to the confusing preparatory phase of the congress. See Georg Plaschka, "Zur Einberufung des Slawenkongresses 1848," *Archiv für österreichische Geschichte*, CXXV (1966), 196-207; and John Erickson, "The Preparatory Committee of the Slav Congress, April-May 1848," in *The Czech Renascence of the Nineteenth Century*, ed. Peter Brock and H. Gordon Skilling (Toronto, 1970), pp. 176-201. Note should also be made of a succinct account of the congress in Stanley Z. Pech, *The Czech Revolution of 1848* (Chapel Hill, 1969), chap. v.

Despite Batowski's urgings in 1948, Polish historians have paid little attention to the congress.

BIBLIOGRAPHY

Archival Sources

Děčín
  Státní archiv
    Rodinný archiv Thun-Hohensteinů: Archiv des Grafen Leo von Thun, fond.
    A3/XXI C 95-114.

Prague
  Archiv Národního musea (ANM)
    Materiály Slovanského sjezdu v Praze 1848 (SS-1848).
    Materiály i protokoly Lípy slovanské, 1848-1849 (LS).
  Státní ústřední archiv (SÚA)
    Sbírka tisku 1848 (ST 1848): č. 7: Letáky.
    Vyšetřovací komise 1848 (KV):
    Fasc.
      3 Vyšetřování průběhu svatodušních bouří, Slovanského sjezdu a událostí
         v Klementinu. 21. června-11. října.
      5 Dr. Josef Frič, Josef Václav Frič
     10 Jan Arnold
     11 Baron Villani
     50 Hrabě Jiří Buquoi
     51 Dr. Caspar [Kašpar]
     52 Marcel Turánsky
    110 Jan Josef rytíř Neuperg [Neuberg]
    260 P.J. Šafařík, Dr. Gabler, Dr. Rieger, Petrovič
    294 No title given

Warsaw
  Archiwum Głowne Akt Dawnych (AGAD)
    269 Protokoły Rady Narodowej 1848
    276 Rada Narodowa z r. 1848
    277 Akta Rady Narodowej 1848 r.
    278 Akty Rady Narodowej we Lwowie r. 1848

Wrocław
  Biblioteka Zakładu Narodowego im. Ossolińskich (Ossolineum) 13581/II Frag-
  ment materiałów dotyczących Kongresu Słowiańskiego w Pradze w 1848 r.
  zebranych przez Władysława Tadeusza Wisłockiego

Newspapers

Augsburg. *Allgemeine Zeitung*
Brno. *Týdenník*

Bratislava [Prešporok]. *Slovenskje Národňje Novini* (Facsimile reprint of all issues, 1845-48, and literary supplement *Orol Tatránski*, 4 vols. [Bratislava: Slovenské vydavatel'stvo politickej literatúry, 1956]).

Budapest [Pest]. *Sveobšte jugoslavenske i serbske narodne novine*

Cologne. *Kölnische Zeitung; Neue Rheinische Zeitung* (Facsimile reprint of 1848-49 issues, 2 vols. [Berlin, 1928]).

Dresden. *Dresdner Journal*

Heidelberg. *Deutsche Zeitung*

Kraków. *Dziennik Polityczny; Jutrzenka.*

Leipzig. *Deutsche Allgemeine Zeitung; Die Grenzboten; Illustrirte Zeitung; Jahrbücher für slawische Literatur, Kunst und Wissenschaft; Die Reform; Slawische Rundschau.*

Ljubljana [Laibach]. *Illyrisches Blatt; Kmetijske in rokodelske novíce.*

Lvov [Lwów, L'viv]. *Dnewnyk Ruskij; Dziennik Mód Paryskich; Dziennik Narodowy; Gazeta Lwowska; Gazeta Powszechna; Postęp; Rada Narodowa* (beginning 1 June 1848, *Gazeta Narodowa*); *Zoria Halytska.*

Paris. *La Pologne, Journal des Slaves confédérés*

Poznań. *Gazeta Polska*

Prague. *Blahowěst; Bohemia; Constitutionelle Allgemeine Zeitung von Böhmen; Constitutionelles Blatt aus Böhmen; Der Freund des Volkes; Kwěty; Lípa Slovanská* (beginning 2 January 1849, *Noviny Lípy Slovanské*); *Národní Nowiny; Ost und West; Pokrok, Nowiny pro Slowany rakauské; Poutník; Prager Abend-Blatt; Prager Zeitung* (from 23 March-30 June 1848, *Constitutionelle Prager Zeitung); Pražské Nowiny* (beginning 25 April 1848, *Konstituční Pražské Nowiny); Pražský Posel; Pražský Wečerní List; Slavische Centralblätter; Swatowáclawské Poselstwí; Wčela.*

Vienna. *Allgemeine Slawische Zeitung; Die Constitution; Constitutionelle Donau-Zeitung; Der Freimüthige; Gerad'aus; Oesterreichischer Beobachter* (from 31 March-12 April 1848, *Oesterreichische Zeitung;* beginning 13 April 1848, *Allgemeine Oesterreichische Zeitung); Oesterreichisch deutsche Zeitung; Der Radikale; Der Volksfreund; Wahrheit; [Der] Wanderer; Wiener Abendzeitung; Wiener Schnellpost; Wiener Sonntagsblätter; Wiener Tageblatt für alle Stände; Wiener Zeitschrift für Recht, Wahrheit, Fortschritt, Kunst, Literatur, Theater, Mode und geselliges Leben; [Oesterreichisch-Kaiserliche privilegirte] Wiener*

Wrocław [Breslau]. *Allgemeine Oder-Zeitung; Breslauer Zeitung.*

Zadar. *Zora Dalmatinska*

Zagreb. *Novine Dalmatinsko-Hervatsko-Slavonske*

Memoirs, Documents and Correspondence

M.A. Bakunin. *Aufruf an die Slaven.* Köthen, 1848.
——————. *The "Confession" of Mikhail Bakunin.* Trans. Robert C. Howes, with Introduction and Notes by Lawrence D. Orton. Ithaca: Cornell University Press, 1977.
——————. *Sobranie sochinenii i pisem 1828-1876.* Ed. Iu. M. Steklov. 4 vols. 1934-36. Reprint Vaduz: Europe Printing, 1970.

Batowski, Aleksander. *Diariusz wypadków 1848 roku.* Ed. Marian Tyrowicz. Wrocław: Zakład Narodowy imienia Ossolińskich, 1974.

Beneš, K.J., ed. *Rok 1848 v projevech současníků.* 3rd ed. Prague: Melantrich, 1948.

"Die blutige Pfingstwoche des Jahres 1848 in Prag." *Prager Presse,* 17 June 1926, No. 165, p. 4.

Bokes, František, ed. *Dokumenty k slovenskému národnému hnutiu v rokoch 1848-1914.* Vol. 1: *1848-1859.* Bratislava: Vydavateľstvo Slovenskej akadémie vied, 1962.

Borys, Włodzimierz. "Głos z 1848 r. w sprawie zgody polsko-ukraińskiej." *Przegląd historyczny,* 62 (1971), 717-724.

Čejchan, Václav. "Ještě k otázce vztahu polských účastníků Slovanského sjezdu k červnovému povstání v Praze roku 1848." *Slovanský přehled,* 52 (1966), 241-243.

Čelakovský, F.L. *Korrespondence a zápisky.* Ed. F. Bílý. Vol. 3. Prague, 1915.

Černý, Jan M. *Boj za právo: Sborník aktů politických u věcech státu a národa českého od roku 1848.* Prague, 1893.

Chaloupecký, Václav. "Hrabě Josef Matyáš Thun a slovanský sjezd v Praze r. 1848." *Český časopis historický,* 19 (1913), 84-91.

Chojecki, Edmund. *Rewolucyoniści i stronnictwa wsteczne w 1848 roku.* Vol. 3 Ed. Leon Zienkowicz. Leipzig, 1865.

Cocles, Horatius. *Die Prager Pfingstwoche.* Prague, 1848.

Dębicki, L. *Portrety i sylwetki z dziewiętnastego stulecia.* Ser. 2, vol. 2. Kraków, 1907.

Deželić, Velimir, ed. *Pisma pisana Dru. Ljudevitu Gaju i njeki njegovi sastavci (1828-1850).* Zagreb, 1909.

Documents diplomatiques du Gouvernement Provisoire et de la Commission du Pouvoir Exécutif. 2 vols. Paris: Imprimerie Nationale, 1953-54.

Engels, Friedrich. *Germany: Revolution and Counter-Revolution.* In *The German Revolutions,* ed. L. Krieger. Chicago: University of Chicago Press, 1967.

Ernst [K.]. *Die Prager Juni-Ereignisse in der Pfingstwoche des Jahres 1848, Nach den Ergebnissen der hierüber geflogenen gerichtlichen Untersuchung.* Vienna, 1849.

Fischel, Alfred, ed. *Materialien zur Sprachenfrage in Österreich.* Brno, 1902.

————. *Das österreichische Sprachenrecht: Eine Quellensammlung.* Brno, 1901.

Franko, Ivan. "Osnovy novoi slavians'koi polityky Bakunina." *Zapysky Naukovoho Tovarystva imeny Shevchenka,* 106 (1912), 155-165.

Frantsev, V.A. "Priglashenie russkikh na slavianskii s"ezd v Prage." *Golos Minuvshago,* no. 5 (1914), pp. 238-240.

Frič, Josef Václav. *Paměti.* 4 vols. Prague, 1885-87.

Glücklich, Julius. "Dopis Poláka ze slovanského sjezdu 1848." *Časopis Matice moravské,* 49 (1925), 417-421.

Grada za istoriju srpskog pokreta u Vojvodini 1848-1849. Ser. 1, Book 1: *Mart-Juni 1848.* Belgrade, 1952.

Halla, J. "Die Opfer der Prager Pfingsten." *Vierteljahrschrift für die praktische Heilkunde,* 5, No. 4 (1848), 141-154.

Havlíček-Borovský, Karel. *Politické spisy.* Ed. Z.V. Tobolka. 3 vols. in 5. Prague, 1900-03.

Ilešič, Fran, ed. "Korespondenca dr. Jos. Muršca." *Zbornik znamstvenih in poučnih spisov (Zbornik Slovenské Matice),* 6 (1904), 102-168; and 7 (1905), 1-210.

Jirečková, Svatava, ed. "K událostem r. 1848: Listy z r. 1848 Josefa a Hermenegilda Jirečka." *Osvěta,* 44 (1914), 252-259, 348-354.

Jordan, Jan Petr. *Aktenmässiger Bericht über die Verhandlungen des ersten Slaven-*

kongresses in Prag. Prague, 1848.

Kabelík, Jan, ed. *Korrespondence a zápisky Jana Helceleta.* Brno, 1910.

"Ke vzniku myšlenky slovanského sjezdu r. 1848." *Pokroková revue,* 1 (1905), 200-201.

Kleinschnitzová, Flora. "Josefa Dobrovského řeč: 'Über die Ergebenheit und Anhänglichkeit der Slawischen Völker an das Erzhaus Östreich' z r. 1791." *Listy filologické,* 45 (1917), 96-104.

Kollár, Jan. *Rozpravy o slovanské vzájemnosti.* Ed. Miloš Weingart. Knihovna Slovanského ustavu v Praze, vol. 1. Prague, 1929.

_____. *Spisy.* 4 vols. Prague, 1862-64.

Kopp, Ferdinand. *Die Ereignisse der Pfingstwoche des Jahres 1848 in Prag und in dessen nächster Umgebung.* Prague, 1848.

Korespondence Pavla Josefa Šafaříka s Františkem Palackým. Ed. V. Bechyňová and Z. Hauptová. Prameny k dějinám české literatury, vol. 4. Prague: Nakladatelství Československé akademie věd, 1961.

Krasiński, Valerian [Waleryn]. *Panslavism and Germanism.* London, 1848.

Malisz, Karol. *Sobór słowiański i najświeższe zdarzenia w Pradze.* Lvov, 1848. Published in German as *Der Slaven-Kongress und die neusten Ereignisse in Prag.* Mannheim, 1848.

"Manifesto of the First Slavonic Congress to the Nations of Europe." Trans. William Beardmore. *Slavonic and East European Review,* 26, No. 67 (April 1948), 309-313.

Matula, Vladimír. "L'udovít Štúr a M.F. Rajevskij (Nové materiály k otázke slovensko-ruských vzt'ahov v 40.-50. rokoch 19. stor.)." *Slovenská literatúra,* 13 (1966), 361-384.

Menčík, F. "Ein Prager Polizist über die Junitage 1848." *Mitteilungen des Vereins für Geschichte der Deutschen in Böhmen,* 54 (1916), 320-345.

Moraczewski, Jędrzej. *Opis pierwszego Zjazdu słowiańskiego.* Poznań, 1848.

_____. "Pamiętnik Jędrzeja Moraczewskiego." In *Wizerunki polityczne dziejów państwa polskiego,* vol. 4: *Polska w kraju w 1848 roku.* Ed. Leon Zienkowicz. Leipzig, 1865.

Müller, J. *Die merkwürdigsten Tage Prag's in der Pfingstwoche des Jahres 1848.* Prague, 1848.

Naše národní minulost v dokumentech. Vol. 2: *Od zrušení nevolnictví do revoluce roku 1848.* Ed. František Kutnar. Prague: Státní pedagogické nakladatelství, 1962.

Nikolajewskij, B. "Prag in den Tagen des Slavenkongresses 1848." *Germanoslavica,* 1 (1931-32), 300-312.

Novotný, Miloslav, ed. *Letáky z roku 1848.* Prague: Nakladatelství Elk, 1948.

Palacký, Franz [František]. *Gedenkblätter.* Prague, 1874.

Palacký, František. "Letter Sent by František Palacký to Frankfurt." Trans. William Beardmore. *Slavonic and East European Review,* 26, No. 67 (April 1948), 303-308.

_____. *Politisches Vermächtniss.* Prague, 1872.

_____. *Spisy drobné.* Vol. 1: *Spisy a řeči z oboru politiky.* Ed. Bohuš Rieger. Prague, [1898].

Paul, Karel, ed. *Dopisy československých spisovatelů St. Vrazovi a L. Gajovi.* Prague, 1923.

Pejaković, Stephan. *Aktenstücke zur Geschichte des kroatisch-slavonischen Landtages und der nationalen Bewegung vom Jahre 1848*. Vienna, 1861.

Petrè, Fran, ed. "Zahteva po 'Kraljevini Sloveniji' 1. 1848 v praških dokumentih." *Glasnik Muzejskega društva za Slovenijo*, 21 (1940), 38-59.

Polonskii, V. *Materialy dlia biografii M. Bakunina*. 3 vols. Moscow & Petrograd, 1923-33.

Quis, Ladislav, ed. *Korrespondence Karla Havlíčka*. Prague, 1903.

Rapant, Daniel. *Slovenské povstanie roku 1848-49*. 5 vols. in 13. Turčiansky Svätý Martin & Bratislava: Matica slovenská & Vydavateľstvo Slovenskej akadémie vied, 1937-72.

Řeči Františka Palackého a Pavla Josefa Šafařika na Slovanském sjezdě v Praze roku 1848. Ed. Arne Novák. Prague, 1928.

Rezek, A. "Zápisky faráře Jana Arnolda r. 1848 a o době reakční." *Sborník historický*, 3 (1885), 350-360.

Robert, Cyprien. "Les deux panslavismes: Situation actuelle des peuples slaves vis-à-vis de la Russie." *Revue des Deux Mondes*, n.s., 16 (1846), 452-483.

Rok 1848 w Polsce: Wybór źródeł. Ed. Stefan Kieniewicz. Wrocław: Zakład Narodowy im. Ossolińskich, 1948.

Rudel, J. *Die Barikaden Prags in der verhängnissvollen Pfingstwoche 1848*. Prague, 1848.

Šafařík, Pavel Josef. *Slovanský národopis*. 4th ed. Prague: Nakladatelství Československé akademie věd, 1955.

Sapieha, Leon. *Wspomnienia z lat od 1803 do 1863 r*. Ed. B. Pawłowski. Lvov & Warsaw, n.d.

Schopf, F.J. *Wahre und ausführliche Darstellung der am 11. März 1848 zur Erlangung einer constitutionellen Regierungs-Verfassung in der königlichen Hauptstadt Prag begonnenen Volks-Bewegung und der hierauf gefolgten Ereignisse, als ein Beitrag zur Geschichte, und ein Andenken an die verhängnisvolle Zeit chronologisch verfasst, auch mit allen Urkunden*. 6 vols. Leitmeritz [Litoměřice], 1848.

Schulz, Václav. "Průkaz vyslance lidu moravského, sběratele pohádek M. Mikšíčka, k Sjezdu Slovanskému r. 1848 v Praze." *Český lid*, 7 (1898), 383-384.

Shcherbatov, A.P. *General-fel'dmarshal kniaz' Paskevich, ego zhizn' i deiatel'nost'*. 7 vols. in 8. St. Petersburg, 1888-1904.

Smolka, Stanisław, ed. *Dziennik Franciszka Smolki 1848-1849 w listach do żony*. Warsaw & Lvov, 1913.

Springer, Anton, ed. *Protokolle des Verfassungs-Ausschusses im Oesterreichischen Reichstage 1848-1849*. Leipzig, 1885.

Starčević, Veselin. "Dopis Přípravného výboru slovanského sjezdu chorvatskému bánu J. Jelačicovi z dne 21. května 1848." *Slovanský přehled*, 51 (1965), 165.

Steier, Lajos, ed. *A tót nemzetiségi kérdés 1848-49-ben*. 2 vols. Budapest, 1937.

Stenographischer Bericht über die Verhandlungen der deutschen constituirenden Nationalversammlung zu Frankfurt. Ed. Franz Wigard. 9 vols. Frankfurt a/M, 1848-49.

Studyns'kyi, K., ed. *Korespondentsiia Iakova Holovats'koho v litakh 1835-49*. Lvov, 1909.

————. "Materialy do istorii kul'turnoho zhyttia v Halychyni 1795-1857." *Ukrains'ko-Rus'kyi arkhiv*, 13-14 (1920).

Štúr, L'udovit. *K přátelům, k bratrům*. Prague: Státní nakladatelství krásné literatury, hudby a umění, 1956.

Štúr, L'udovit. *Listy L'udovíta Štúra.* Ed. J. Ambruš. 3 vols. Bratislava: Vydavatel'-stvo Slovenskej akadémie vied, 1954-60.

_____. *Das Slawenthum und die Welt der Zukunft.* Ed. Josef Jirásek. Bratislava, 1931.

Subotić, Jovan. "Zápisky dra Subotiće, účastníka slovanského sjezdu." *Naše doba,* 10 (1902-03), 887-893.

_____. *Život Dra Jovana Subotića, Avtobiografija.* 5 vols. Novi Sad, 1901-10.

Szalay, Ladislaus [Laszlo]. *Diplomatische Aktenstücke zur Beleuchtung der Un-garischen Gesandtschaft in Deutschland.* Zürich, 1849.

Thim, József, ed. *A Magyarországi 1848-49-iki szerb fölkelés története.* 3 vols. Budapest, 1930-40.

Thomas, Alexandre. "La Praguerie de 1848." *Revue des Deux Mondes,* n.s., 23 (1848), 708-740.

Thun, Leo. *Betrachtungen über die Zeitverhältnisse, insbesondere im Hinblicke auf Böhmen.* Prague, 1849.

_____. *Die Stellung der Slowaken in Ungarn.* Prague, 1843.

_____. *Über den gegenwärtigen Stand der böhmischen Literatur und ihre Be-deutung.* Prague, 1842.

Tobolka, Zdeněk, and Žáček, Václav, eds. *Slovanský sjezd v Praze 1848: Sbírka dokumentů.* Part 1 (all printed). Prague: Slovanský ústav, 1952.

Tomek, Václav Vladivoj. *Paměti z mého života.* 2 vols. Prague, 1904-05.

Traub, H. "O přípravách k Slovanskému sjezdu v Praze r. 1848." *Časopis Musea království českého,* 92 (1918), 247-255, 319-326.

Verhandlungen der deutschen verfassunggebenden Reichsversammlung zu Frankfurt am Main. Ed. K.D. Hassler. 6 vols. Frankfurt a/M, 1848-1849.

Verhandlungen des Deutschen Parlaments. Ed. F. Jucho. 2 vols. Frankfurt a/M, 1848.

Verhandlungen des österreichischen Reichstages nach der stenographischen Auf-nahme. 5 vols. Vienna, 1848-49.

Vocel, J.E. "O čem by se mělo jednati na Slowanském sjezdu?" *Časopis českého Museum,* 22, No. 1 (1848), 544-545.

_____. "Slowo o slowanském sjezdu." *Časopis českého Museum,* 22, No. 1 (1848), 642-646.

Winter, Eduard. "Eine grundlegende Urkunde des Austroslawismus: Der Brief B. Kopitars an Metternich vom 7. April 1827 mit bibliothekarischen Bericht." *Zeitschrift für Slawistik,* 3 (1958), 107-124.

Wisłocki, Władysław T. *Kongres słowiański w r. 1848 i sprawa polska.* Lvov, 1927.

Žáček, Václav, ed. *Slovanský sjezd v Praze roku 1848: Sbírka dokumentů.* Prague: Nakladatelství Československé akademie věd, 1958.

Zíbrt, Čeněk. "Pobyt P.J. Šafaříka v Berlíně r. 1841 a ve Vídni r. 1848 i 1851 v novém světle dopisů choti Julii." *Osvěta,* 39 (1909), 451-457, 543-550, 617-623, 707-712.

_____. "Život a činnost P.J. Šafaříka ve světle dopisů synovi Janovi (1834-1859)," *Časopis Musea království českého,* 84 (1910), 53-129.

Ziemiałkowski, Floryan. *Pamiętniki.* 4 vols. Kraków, 1904.

Zpráwa o sjezdu slowanském. Prague, 1848. Also published in *Časopis českého Museum,* 22, No. 2 (1848), 1-66.

Selected Secondary Works

Andics, E. *Das Bündnis Habsburg-Romanow: Vorgeschichte der zaristischen Intervention in Ungarn im Jahre 1849.* Studia Historica Academiae Scientiarum Hungaricae, vol.52. Budapest: Akadémiae kiadó, 1963.

Anon. "Die Revolution von 1848-1849 und die Sudetendeutschen." *Archiv für Politik und Geschichte,* 7 (1926), 430-470.

Apih, Josip. *Slovenci in 1848 leto.* Ljubljana, 1888.

————. "Die Slovenen und der constituirende Reichstag 1848/49." *Österreichisches Jahrbuch,* 18 (1894), 15-35.

————. "Die Slovenen und die Märzbewegung von 1848." *Österreichisches Jahrbuch,* 14 (1890), 79-106.

————. "Die slovenische Bewegung im Frühjahr und Vorsommer 1848." *Österreichisches Jahrbuch,* 16 (1892), 175-208.

Auty, R. "Jan Kollár, 1793-1852." *Slavonic and East European Review,* 31, No. 76 (December 1952), 74-91.

————. "The Linguistic Revival Among the Slavs of the Austrian Empire, 1780-1850." *Modern Language Review,* 53 (1958), 392-404.

Bajerová, Anna. *Svatodušní bouře v Praze r. 1848 ve světle soudního vyšetřovani.* Plzeň, 1920.

————. *Z české revoluce 1848.* Prague, 1919.

Batowski, Henryk. "Adam Mickiewicz a Čechové v revolučních letech 1848 a 1849." *Československý časopis historický,* 6 (1958), 32-46.

————. "The Poles and Their Fellow Slavs." *Slavonic and East European Review,* 27, No. 69 (May 1949), 404-413.

————. *Przyjaciele Słowianie: Szkice z życia Mickiewicza.* Warsaw: Czytelnik, 1956.

————. "Zagadnienia roku 1848 w Słowiańszczyźnie." *Przegląd historyczny,* 38 (1948), 37-60.

Bělič, Jaromír. *Karel Havlíček Borovský a Slovanstvo.* Prague: Nakladatelství M. Stejskal, 1947.

Beneš, Edvard. *Úvahy o slovanství: Hlavní problémy slovanské politiky.* London: Lincolns-Prager, n.d. French translation by G. Aucouturier, *Où vont les Slaves?* Paris: Editions de Notre Temps, 1948.

Beneš, Václav L. "Bakunin and Palacky's Concept of Austroslavism." *Indiana Slavic Studies,* 2 (1958), 79-111.

Berlin, Isaiah. "Russia and 1848." *Slavonic and East European Review,* 26, No. 67 (April 1948), 341-360.

Birke, Ernst. *Frankreich und Ostmitteleuropa im 19. Jahrhundert.* Cologne & Graz: Böhlau Verlag, 1960.

Bittner, Konrad. "J.G. Herders 'Ideen zur Philosophie der Geschichte der Menschheit' und ihre Auswirkungen bei den slavischen Hauptstämmen." *Germanoslavica,* 2 (1933), 453-480.

Black, C.E. "Poznań and Europe in 1848." *Journal of Central European Affairs,* 8, No. 2 (July 1948), 191-206.

Boemus, A.H. "Der tschechische Panslawismus im Jahre 1848." *Oesterreich: Zeitschrift für Geschichte,* 1 (1918-19), 506-536.

Bogdanov, Vaso. *Društvene i političke borbe u Hrvatskoj 1848/49.* Zagreb: Jugoslavenska akademija znanosti i umjetnosti, 1949.

_____. *Hrvatska ljevica u godinama revolucije 1848/49.* Zagreb: Matica Hrvatska, 1949.

Boháč, Antonín. *Hlavní město Praha: Studie o obyvatelstvu.* Knihovna statistického věstníku, vol. 3. Prague, 1923.

Bohachevsky-Chomiak, Martha. *The Spring of a Nation: The Ukrainians in Eastern Galicia in 1848.* Philadelphia: Shevchenko Scientific Society, 1967.

Borys, V. "Deiaki pytannia pol'sko-ukrains'kykh vidnosyn pid chas revoliutsii 1848 r. v Halychyni." *Ukrains'ke slov'ianoznavstvo,* 6 (1972), 74-87.

Bosl, Karl. "Deutsche romantisch-liberale Geschichtsauffassung und 'slawische Legende': Germanismus und Slawismus, Bemerkungen zur Geschichte zweier Ideologien." *Bohemia,* 5 (1964), 12-52.

Brock, Peter. "Ivan Vahylevych (1811-1866) and the Ukrainian National Identity." *Canadian Slavonic Papers,* 14 (1972), 153-190.

_____. "J.P. Jordan's Role in the National Awakening of the Lusatian Serbs." *Canadian Slavonic Papers,* 10 (1968), 312-340.

_____. *The Slovak National Awakening: An Essay in the Intellectual History of East Central Europe.* Toronto: University of Toronto Press, 1976.

_____. "Smoler's Idea of Nationality." *Slavic Review,* 28 (1969), 25-47.

Brock, Peter, and Skilling, H. Gordon, eds. *The Czech Renascence of the Nineteenth Century.* Toronto: University of Toronto Press, 1970.

Bryk, Ivan. "Slavians'kyi zizd u Prazi 1848 r. i ukrains'ka sprava." *Zapysky Naukovoho Tovarystva imeny Shevchenka,* 129 (1920), 141-217.

Burian, Peter. *Die Nationalitäten in Cisleithanien und das Wahlrecht der Märzrevolution 1848/49.* Cologne & Graz: Verlag Hermann Böhlaus Nachf., 1962.

Butter, Oskar. "Rozbor čtyř zachovaných čísel Tomkova 'Pokrok'." *Duch novin,* 3 (1930), 181-201.

Butvin, Jozef. *Slovenské národnozjednocovacie hnutie (1780-1848).* Bratislava: Vydavatel'stvo Slovenskej akadémie vied, 1965.

Carr, E.H. *Michael Bakunin.* 1937. Reprint New York: Vintage Books, 1961.

Čejchan, Václav. *Bakunin v Čechách: Příspěvek k revolučnímu hnutí českému v letech 1848-49.* Prague, 1928.

_____. "Dozvuky slovanských sjezdů v Praze 1848 a v Moskvě 1867." *Český časopis historický,* 38 (1932), 374-379.

_____. "Ke vzniku myšlenky slovanského sjezdu roku 1848." *Slovanský přehled,* 20 (1928), 401-408.

_____. "M. Bakunin v Praze roku 1848." *Český časopis historický,* 38 (1932), 564-569.

_____. "Přípravy k svatodušním bouřím v Praze roku 1848." *Zprávy Vojenského archivu a musea RČS,* 5 (1929), 61-72.

Čejchan, Václav, et al. *Slovanský sjezd v Praze 1848: Sborník přednášek Slovanského ústavu.* Prague: Orbis, 1948.

Čepelák, Václav. "Opavsko a Slovanský sjezd 1848." *Věstník Matice opavské,* 36 (1931), 15-25.

Černý, Adolf. "Dr. Jan Petr Jordan." *Zlatá Praha,* 8 (1891), 415, 427-428, 435, 438.

Černý, Jan M. *Slovanský sjezd v Praze roku 1848.* Prague, 1888.

Červinka, František. *Český nacionalismus v XIX. století.* Prague: Svobodné slovo, 1965.

Clementis, Vladimir [Vlado] . *"Panslavism" Past and Present.* London, 1943.

Ciągwa, Józef. "Słowackie koncepcje wzajemności słowiańskiej w XIX. w." *Kwartalnik historyczny,* 77 (1970), 137-149.

Danilák, M. "Ukrajinci a slovanský zjazd v Prahe roku 1848." *Slovanské štúdie,* 10 (1968), 5-28.

Denis, Ernest. *La Bohême depuis la Montagne-Blanche.* 2 vols. Paris, 1903.

————. *La Question d'Autriche: Les Slovaques.* Paris, 1917.

Despalatović, Elinor M. *Ljudevit Gaj and the Illyrian Movement.* Boulder: East European Quarterly, 1975.

Divéky, Andrjan. *Węgrzy a Polacy w XIX stuleciu.* Warsaw, [1918].

Drechsler, Branko. *Stanko Vraz: Studija.* Zagreb, 1909.

Droz, Jacques. *L'Europe Centrale: Evolution historique de l'idée de 'Mitteleuropa.'* Paris: Payot, 1960.

Dziewanowski, M.K. "1848 and the Hotel Lambert." *Slavonic and East European Review,* 26,No.67 (April 1948), 361-373.

Eisenmann, Louis. *Le compris austro-hongrois de 1867.* 1904. Reprint Hattiesburg, Miss.: Academic International, 1971.

Erickson, John. *Panslavism.* London: Historical Association, 1964.

————. "Recent Soviet and Marxist Writings: 1848 in Central and Eastern Europe." *Journal of Central European Affairs,* 17, No. 2 (July 1957), 119-126.

Evreinov, B.A. "Bakunin i slavianskii s"ezd 1848 goda v Prage." *Zapiski russkago nauchnago instituta v Belgrade,* 13 (1936), 131-160.

Eyck, Frank. *The Frankfurt Parliament 1848-1849.* New York: St. Martin's Press, 1968.

Fadner, Frank. *Seventy Years of Pan-Slavism in Russia, Karazin to Danilevskii, 1800-1870.* [Washington] : Georgetown University Press, 1962.

Fejtö, François, ed. *The Opening of an Era 1848: An Historical Symposium.* 1948. Reprint New York: Howard Fertig, 1966.

Felczak, Wacław. *Węgierska polityka narodowościowa przed wybuchem powstania 1848 roku.* Kraków: Zakład Narodowy im. Ossolińskich, Wydawnictwo PAN, 1964.

Feldman, Józef. *Sprawa polska w roku 1848.* Kraków, 1933.

Feldman, Wilhelm. *Geschichte der politischen Ideen in Polen seit dessen Teilungen (1795-1914).* 1917. Reprint Osnabrück: Otto Zeller, 1964.

————. *Stronnictwa i programy polityczne w Galicyi 1846-1906.* 2 vols. Kraków, 1907.

Feyl, Othmar. "Exkurse zur Geschichte der südosteuropäischen Beziehungen der Universität Jena." *Wissenschaftliche Zeitschrift der Friedrich Schiller Universität Jena,* 4 (1954-55), 399-442.

————. "Die führende Stellung der Ungarländer in der internationalen Geistesgeschichte der Universität Jena." *Wissenschaftliche Zeitschrift der Friedrich Schiller Universität Jena,* 3 (1953-54), 399-445.

Fischel, Alfred. *Der Panslawismus bis zum Weltkrieg.* Stuttgart & Berlin, 1919.

Flack, Michael J. "The Slav Congresses and Pan-Slavism, 1848-1914." Ph.D. dissertation, Fletcher School of Law and Diplomacy, 1953.

Frantsev, V.A. *Cheshko-slovenskyi raskol i ego otgoloski v literature sorokovykh godov.* Warsaw, 1915.

Frančić, M. *Sprawa polska w publicystyce Karola Hawliczka-Borowskiego.* Kraków: Biblioteka studium słowiańskiego Uniwersyteta Jagiellońskiego, 1948.

Fricz [Frič], Joseph, and Leger, Louis. *La Bohême historique, pittoresque et littéraire*. Paris, 1867.

Friedjung, Heinrich. *Österreich von 1848 bis 1860*. 2 vols. Stuttgart & Berlin, 1908.

Geist-Lányi, Paula. *Das Nationalitätenproblem auf dem Reichstag zu Kremsier 1848/1849*. Munich, 1920.

Gogolák, Ludwig. *Beiträge zur Geschichte des slowakischen Volkes*. Vol. 2: *Die slowakische nationale Frage in der Reformepoche (1790-1848)*. Buchreihe der Südostdeutschen Historischen Kommission. Vol. 21. Munich: Verlag R. Oldenbourg, 1969.

Goláň, Karol. "Štúrove reči na slovanskom sjazde roku 1848." *Slovenské pohľady*, 52 (1936), 417-429.

_____. "Príspevok k vývoju slovenskej politickej myšlienky." *Historica Slovaca*, 1-2 (1940-41), 270-277.

Grajewski, Henryk. *Komitet Emigracji Polskiej z 1848 roku: Nieznana karta z dziejów Wielkiej Emigracji*. Łódź: Zakład Narodowy im. Ossolińskich, 1960.

Grim, E. *Paweł Stalmach: Jego życie i działalność w świetle prawdy*. Cieszyn [Teschen], 1910.

Haas, Arthur G. "Metternich and the Slavs." *Austrian History Yearbook*, 4-5 (1968-69), 120-149.

Hafner, Stanislaus. "Das austro-slawische kulturpolitische Konzept in der ersten Hälfte des 19. Jahrhunderts." *Österreichische Osthefte*, 5 (1963), 435-444.

_____. "Sprache und Volkstum bei den Slawen im Vormärz." *Südost-Forschungen*, 24 (1965), 138-165.

Hanák, J. "Slovaks and Czechs in the Early 19th Century." *Slavonic and East European Review*, 10, No. 30 (April 1932), 588-601.

Handelsman, Marceli. *Adam Czartoryski*. 3 vols. in 4. Warsaw: Nakładem Towarzystwa Naukowego Warszawskiego, 1948-50.

_____. *Ukraińska polityka ks. Adama Czartoryskiego przed wojną krymską*. Prace ukraińskiego institutu naukowego, No. 35. Warsaw, 1937.

_____. "La politique slave de la Pologne aux XVIIIe et XIXe siècles." *Le Monde Slave*, n.s., 13 (1936), 427-455.

Hantsch, Hugo. *Die Nationalitätenfrage im alten Österreich*. Wiener historische Studien, vol. 1 Vienna: Verlag Herold, 1953.

_____. "Pan-Slavism, Austro-Slavism, Neo-Slavism: The All-Slav Congresses and the Nationality Problems of Austria-Hungary." *Austrian History Yearbook*, 1 (1965), 23-37.

Hartl, Antonín. "Slovanství Františka Palackého." *Slovanský přehled*, 18 (1926), 318-324, 413-423.

Hawgood, John A. "1848 in Central Europe: An Essay in Historical Synchronisation." *Slavonic and East European Review*, 26, No. 67 (April 1948), 314-328.

Heidler, Jan. *Antonín Springer a česká politika v letech 1848-1850*. Prague, 1914.

_____. *Čechy a Rakousko v politických brožurách předbřeznových*. Prague, 1920.

Helfert, Josef Alexander. *Fürst Alfred Windisch-Grätz und Graf Leo Thun in den Prager Juni-Tagen 1848*. Munich, 1886.

_____. *Geschichte der österreichischen Revolution im Zusammenhange mit der mitteleuropäischen Bewegung der Jahre 1848-1849*. 2 vols. Freiburg im Bresgau & Vienna, 1907-09.

————. "Graf Leo Thun, III: Slaven-Congress." *Österreichisches Jahrbuch*, 20 (1896), 179-254. Published separately as *Slaven-Congress*. Vienna, 1897.

————. "Graf Leo Thun, IV; Blutige Pfingsten." *Österreichisches Jahrbuch*, 21 (1897), 1-271. Published separately as *Der Prager Juni-Aufstand 1848*. Prague, 1897.

————. *Die Wiener Journalistik im Jahre 1848*. Vienna, 1877.

Helin, Leo. "Die slawische Wiedergeburt unter besonderer Berücksichtigung des Prager Slawenkongresses im Jahre 1848." Ph.D. dissertation, University of Vienna, 1926.

Henry, R. "Le Congrès slave de Prague (1848)." *Annales des Sciences politiques*, 18 (1903), 225-250.

Hepner, Benoît-P. *Bakounine et le panslavisme révolutionnaire*. Paris: Marcel Rivière, 1950.

Hodža, Milan. *Československý rozkol: Príspevky k dejinám slovenčiny*. Turčiansky Svätý Martin, 1920.

Horák, Jiří, ed. *Slovanská vzájemnost 1836-1936: Sborník prací k 100. výročí vydání rozpravy Jana Kollára o slovanské vzájemnosti*. Prague, 1938.

Horváth, Mihály. *Magyarorszag függetlenségi harczának története 1848 és 1849-ben*. 2nd ed. in 3 vols. Pest, 1871-72.

Hostička, Vladimír. "K.V. Zap a haličtí Ukrajinci." *Kapitoly z dějin vzájemných vztahů národů ČSR a SSSR*, 1 (1958), 69-115.

————. *Spolupráce Čechů a haličských Ukrajinců v letech 1848-1849*. Rozpravy Československé akademie věd, vol. 75, No. 12. Prague: Nakladatelství Československé akademie věd, 1965.

————. "Vznik českého austroslavismu a jeho vztah k obrozenskému slovanství." *Slovanský přehled*, 54 (1968), 225-232.

Hroch, Miroslav. *Die Volkämpfer der nationalen Bewegung bei den kleinen Völkern Europas: Eine vergleichende Analyse zur gesellschaftlichen Schichtung der patriotischen Gruppen*. Acta Universitatis Carolinae, Philosophica et Historica, No. 24. Prague: Universita Karlova, 1968.

Hugelmann, Karl Gottfried, ed. *Das Nationalitätenrecht des alten Österreich*. Vienna & Leipzig, 1934.

Hurban, J.M. *L'udovít Štúr: Rozpomienky*. Bratislava: Slovenské vydavatel'stvo krásnej literatúry, 1959.

Ivantyšynová, Tatjana. "L'udovít Štúr a Michail Bakunin v revolúcii 1848-1849." *Zborník Filozofickej Fakulty Univerzity Komenského—Historica*, 21 (1970), 9-25.

Janáček, Josef, et al. *Dějiny Prahy*. Prague: Nakladatelství politické literatury, 1964.

Jelavich, Charles. "Garašanins *Načertanije* und das grossserbische Program." *Südostforschungen*, 27, (1968), 131-147.

Jeřábek, Luboš. "Slovanský sjezd v Praze roku 1848, jeho průběh a výsledky." *Rozhledy*, 7 (1897-98), 961-969, 1061-1069, 1089-1107.

Jílek, F. "Pražská polytechnika a jeji studenti v revolučním roce 1848." *Sborník Národního technického muzea*, 4 (1965), 268-366; 5 (1968), 337-508.

Jirásek, Josef. *Rusko a my: Dějiny vztahů československo-ruských od nejstarších dob až do roku 1914*. 2nd rev. ed. in 4 vols. Prague & Brno, 1945-46.

Jireček, Josef. "Paul Joseph Šafařík: Ein biographisches Denkmal." *Österreichische Revue*, 8 (1965), 1-73.

_____. "Vzpomínky na události r. 1848." *Světozor*, 12 (1878), 592-595, 603-604, 606.

Jurčić, Hrvoje. "Das ungarisch-kroatische Verhältnis im Spiegel des Sprachenstreites 1790-1848." *Ungarn-Jahrbuch*, 3 (1971), 69-87.

J.F. *Frič a demokratické proudy v české politice a kultuře: Sborník statí*. Ed. Václav Žáček and Karel Kosík. Prague: Nakladatelství Československé akademie věd, 1956.

Kann, Robert A. *The Multinational Empire: Nationalism and National Reform in the Habsburg Monarchy 1848-1918*. 2 vols. 1950. Reprint New York: Octagon Books, 1964.

Kapper, S. *Die serbische Bewegung in Südungarn*. Berlin, 1851.

Karásek, J. "Karel Libelt, účastník Slovanského sjezdu." *Moravská Orlice* (Brno), 7 June 1908, No. 131.

Kazbunda, Karel. *České hnutí roku 1848*. Prague, 1929.

Kieniewicz, Stefan. *Społeczeństwo polskie w powstaniu poznańskiem 1848 roku*. Rozprawy historyczne Towarzystwa Naukowego Warsawskiego, vol. 14, No. 1. Warsaw, 1935.

Kimball, Stanley B. *The Austro-Slav Revival: A Study of Nineteenth-Century Literary Foundations*. Transactions of the American Philosophical Society, n.s., 63, Part 4. Philadelphia, 1973.

Kiszling, Rudolf. *Die Revolution im Kaisertum Oesterreich 1848-1849*. 2 vols. Vienna: Universum Verlag, 1949.

Klarnerówna, Zofia. *Słowianofilstwo w literaturze polskiej lat 1800 do 1848*. Warsaw, 1926.

Klíma, Arnošt. *Revoluce 1848 v českých zemích*. Prague: Státní pedagogické nakladatelství, 1974.

_____. *Rok 1848 v Čechách*. 2nd ed. Prague: Svoboda, 1949.

Koberdowa, Irena. *Polska Wiosna Ludów*. Warsaw: Wiedza Powszechna, 1967.

Koberg, Gerda. "*Die Grenzboten* 1842-1848 und ihr Verhältnis zu Böhmen." Ph.D. dissertation, Deutsche Universität, Prague [1938].

Kočí, Josef. "Karel Havlíček Borovský a počátky austroslavismu." *Slovanský přehled*, 62 (1971), 191-201.

_____. *Naše národní obrození*. Prague: Státní nakladatelství politické literatury, 1960.

Koch, Hans. "Slavdom and Slavism in the Polish National Consciousness 1794-1848." In *Eastern Germany: A Handbook*. Vol. 2: *History* Ed. Goettingen Research Committee. Würzburg: Holzner Verlag, 1963.

Kohn, Hans. *Pan-Slavism: Its History and Ideology*. 2nd ed. rev. New York: Vintage Books, 1960.

Kolejka, Josef. *Slavianskie programmy i ideia slavianskoi solidarnosti v XIX i XX vekakh*. Opera Universitatis Purkynianae Brunensis, Facultas Philosophica, vol. 98. Prague: Státní pedagogické nakladatelství, 1964.

Kosík, Karel. *Česká radikální demokracie*. Prague: Státní nakladatelství politické literatury, 1958.

Kozik, Jan. *Między reakcją a rewolucją: Studia z dziejów ukraińskiego ruchu narodowego w Galicji w latach 1848-1849*. Warsaw & Kraków: Państwowe Wydawnictwo Naukowe; Nakładem Uniwersytetu Jagiellońskiego, 1975.

_____. *Ukraiński ruch narodowy w Galicji w latach 1830-1848*. Kraków: Wydawnictwo Literackie, 1973.

Kreibich, Karel. *Němci a česká revoluce v roce 1848.* Brno: Rovnost, 1950.

Křížek, Jaroslav. *Národní gardy v roce 1848.* Prague: Naše vojsko, 1954.

Krnjević, Juraj. "The Croats in 1848." *Slavonic and East European Review,* 27, No. 68 (December 1948), 106-114.

Krofta, Kamil. *Byli jsme za Rakouska: Úvahy historické a politické.* Prague, 1936.

Labuda, Gerard. "The Slavs in Nineteenth-Century German Historiography." *Polish Western Affairs,* 10 (1969), 177-234.

Lades, Hans. *Die Nationalitätenfrage im Karpatenraum 1848/49.* Vienna, 1941.

––––––. *Die Tschechen und die deutsche Frage.* Erlanger Abhandlungen zur mittleren und neueren Geschichte, n.s., vol. 1. Erlangen, 1938.

Lednicki, W. "Poland and the Slavophil Idea." *Slavonic and East European Review,* 7, No. 19 (June 1928), 128-140; 7, No. 21 (March 1929), 649-662.

Leger, Louis. *Le Panslavisme et l'intérêt français.* Paris, 1917.

––––––. *La renaissance tchèque au dix-neuvième siècle.* Paris, 1911.

Leshchilovskaia, I.I., and Freidzon, V.I. "Revoliutsiia 1848-1849 godov i ugnetennye narody avstriiskoi imperii." *Sovetskoe Slavianovedenie,* No. 6 (1973), pp. 29-50.

Lewak, Adam. "Dozór polski w Genewie w r. 1848." *Kwartalnik historyczny,* 33 (1919), 45-60.

Lisicki, Henryk. *Antoni Zygmunt Helcel 1808-1870.* 2 vols. Lvov, 1882.

Locher, T.J. G. *Die nationale Differenzierung und Integrierung der Slovaken und Tschechen in ihrem geschichtlichen Verlauf bis 1848.* Haarlem, 1931.

Luciani, Georges. "Du Congrès de Prague (1848) au Congrès de Moscou (1867)." *Revue des Etudes Slaves,* 47 (1968), 85-93.

––––––. "Polonais et Ruthènes (Ukrainiens) de Galicie au Congrès Slave de Prague (1848)." *VIIᵉ Congrès International des Slavistes, Varsovie, 21-27 août 1973: Communications de la délégation française.* Paris: Institut d'Etudes Slaves, 1973.

L'udovít Štúr und die slawische Wechselseitigkeit: Gesamte Referate und die integrale Diskussion der wissenschaftlichen Tagung in Smolnice 27.-29.Juni 1966. Ed. L'udovít Holotík. Bratislava: Vydavateľstvo Slovenskej akadémie vied, 1969.

Macartney, C.A. *The Habsburg Empire 1790-1918.* New York: Macmillan, 1969.

Macůrek, Josef. "The Achievements of the Slavonic Congress." *Slavonic and East European Review,* 26, No. 67 (April 1948), 329-340.

––––––. *Rok 1848 a Morava.* Brno: Zemská osvětová rada, 1948.

Maršan, Robert. *Čechové a Němci r. 1848 a boj o Frankfurt.* Prague, 1898.

Marx. Julius. *Die wirtschaftlichen Ursachen der Revolution von 1848 in Österreich.* Graz & Cologne: Verlag Hermann Böhlaus Nachf., 1965.

Masaryk, Tomáš G. *Česká otázka.* 4th ed. Prague, 1936.

––––––. *Karel Havlíček.* Prague, 1896.

Matoušek, Josef. *Karel Sladkovský a český radikalism za revoluce a reakce.* Prague, 1929.

Mattausch, Rudolf. "Geistige und soziale Voraussetzungen der nationalen Wiedergeburt in Böhmen vor 1848." *Bohemia,* 14 (1973), 155-178.

Matula, Vladimír. "L'udovít Štúr und Russland." *Jahrbücher für Geschichte Osteuropas,* n.s., 15 (1967), 29-58.

––––––. "Slovanská vzájemnost', národnooslobodzovacia ideológia slovenského národného hnutia." *Historický časopis,* 8 (1960), 248-264.

Mérei, G. "Über die Möglichkeiten eines Zusammenschlusses der in Ungarn lebenden Völker in den Jahren 1848-1849." *Acta Historica Academiae Scientiarum Hungaricae,* 15 (1969), 253-298.

BIBLIOGRAPHY 175

Mésároš, Július. "Magyaren und Slovaken: Zur Frage des Panslavismus in der Vormärzzeit." *Jahrbücher für Geschichte Osteuropas*, n.s., 15 (1967), 393-414.
————. "Slovanská otázka v politike slovenskej buržoázie v druhej polovici 19. storočia." *Historický časopis*, 8 (1960), 324-359.
Mikoláš, J.L. "Slezsko a slovanský sjezd v Praze roku 1848." *Věstník Matice opavské*, 33-34 (1927-28), 22-28.
Mommsen, Wilhelm. *Grösse und Versagen des deutschen Bürgertums: Ein Beitrag zur politischen Bewegung des 19. Jahrhunderts, insbesondere zur Revolution 1848/49*. 1949. Reprint Munich: R. Oldenbourg, 1964.
Mosely, Philip E. "A Pan-Slavist Memorandum of Liudevit Gaj in 1838." *American Historical Review*, 40 (1935), 704-716.
Müller, Paul, *Feldmarschall Fürst Windischgrätz: Revolution und Gegenrevolution in Oesterreich*. Vienna & Leipzig, 1934.
Münch, Hermann. *Böhmische Tragödie: Das Schicksal Mitteleuropas im Lichte der tschechischen Frage*. Braunschweig: G. Westermann, 1949.
Murko, Matthias. *Deutsche Einflüsse auf die Anfänge der böhmischen Romantik*. Graz, 1897.
Namier, Lewis. *1848: The Revolution of the Intellectuals*. London: Oxford University Press, 1946.
The Nationality Problem in the Habsburg Monarchy in the Nineteenth Century: A Critical Appraisal. In *Austrian History Yearbook*, 3 (1967), 3 parts.
Navalovs'kyi, M. *Ukrainci i slovians'kyi kongres u Prazi 1848 r*. Kharkov, 1930.
Nifantov, A.S. *1848 god v Rossii: Ocherki po istorii 40-kh godov*. Moscow & Leningrad, 1931. Rev. ed., *Rossiia v 1848 godu*. Moscow, 1949. German translation of 1949 ed., *Russland im Jahre 1848*. Berlin: Rütten & Loening, 1953.
Novák, Arne. "Politické myšlenky v Kollárově spise 'O literární vzájemnosti mezi kmeny a nářečími slovanskými'." *Slavia*, 3 (1924-25), 65-74.
Novák, M. "Austroslavismus, příspěvek k jeho pojetí v době předbřeznové." *Sborník archivních prací*, 6 (1956), 26-50.
Nikitin, S. "Slovanské národy v revolúcii r. 1848." *Historica Slovaca*, 6-7 (1948-49), 21-42.
Novotný, Jan. "Češi a Slováci v národně politických bojích od slovanského sjezdu do porážky revoluce 1848-1849." *Historický časopis*, 16 (1968), 299-331.
————. *Češi a Slováci za národního obrození a do vzniku československého státu*. Prague: Svobodné slovo, 1968.
————. "K některým problémům slovanské myšlenky v českém národním hnutí v době předbřeznové." *Historický časopis*, 8 (1960), 265-290.
————. "K politickej činnosti Pavla Jozefa Šafárika za revolúcie 1848-1849." *Historický časopis*, 18 (1970), 544-565.
————. *O bratrské družbě Čechů a Slováků za národního obrození*. Prague: Státní nakladatelství politické literatury, 1959.
————. "Příspěvek k vzájemným vztahům Čechů a Slováků v první etapě revoluce roku 1848." *Historický časopis*, 11 (1963), 366-388.
Odložilík, Otakar. "A Czech Plan for a Danubian Federation 1848." *Journal of Central European Affairs*, 1, No. 3 (October 1941), 253-274.
————. "The Czechs on the Eve of the 1848 Revolution." *Harvard Slavic Studies*, 1 (1953), 179-217.
————. Review of *Slavenska renesansa 1780-1848* by Milan Prelog. *Časopis Matice moravské*, 51 (1927), 329-347.
————. "Neue Dokumente über den Prager Slavenkongress." *Prager Presse*, 16 October 1927, No. 285, p. 10.

_____. "Pokus o soudní vyšetřování Fr. Palackého r. 1848." *Národní Osvobození*, 26 May 1926, No. 143.

_____. "The Slavic Congress of 1848." Review of *Slovanský sjezd v Praze roku 1848: Sbírka dokumentů*, ed. Václav Žáček. *Polish Review*, 4, No. 4 (1959), 3-15.

_____. "Slovanský sjezd a svatodušní bouře." *Slovanský přehled*, 20 (1928), 408-425.

_____. "Vyšetřovací komise z roku 1848 a jejich registratura." *Sborník Archivu ministerstva vnitra Republiky Československé*, 2 (1929), 1-90.

Orton, Lawrence D. "Bakunin's Plan for Slav Federation, 1848." *Canadian-American Slavic Studies*, 8 (1974), 107-115.

_____. "Did the Slavs Speak German at Their First Congress?" *Slavic Review*, 33 (1974), 515-521.

_____. "The Investigation of the June 1848 Uprising in Prague: The Strange Case of Marcel Turánsky." *East European Quarterly*, 8 (1974), 57-69.

Pascal, Roy. "The Frankfurt Parliament, 1848, and the *Drang nach Osten*." *Journal of Modern History*, 18 (1946), 108-122.

Pashaeva, N.M. "Otrazhenie natsional'nykh i sotsial'nykh protivorechii v Vostochnoi Galichine v 1848 g. v listovkakh Russkogo Sobora." In *Slavianskoe vozrozhdenie*. Moscow: Nauka, 1966.

Paul, Karel. *Pavel Josef Šafařík: Život a dílo*. Prague: Nakladatelství Československé akademie věd, 1961.

Pech, Stanley Z. "Czech Political Parties in 1848." *Canadian Slavonic Papers*, 15 (1973), 462-486.

_____. *The Czech Revolution of 1848*. Chapel Hill: University of North Carolina Press, 1969.

_____. "The Czech Revolution of 1848: Some New Perspectives." *Canadian Journal of History*, 4 (1969), 47-72.

_____. "The Czech Working Class in 1848." *Canadian Slavonic Papers*, 9 (1967), 60-73.

_____. "The June Uprising in Prague in 1848." *East European Quarterly*, 1, No. 4 (January 1968), 341-370.

_____. "The Nationalist Movements of the Austrian Slavs in 1848: A Comparative Sociological Profile." *Histoire sociale/Social History*, 9 (1976), 336-356.

_____. "The Press of the Habsburg Slavs in 1848: Contribution to a Political Profile." *Canadian Journal of History*, 10, No. 1 (April 1975), 35-49.

Petrovich, Michael B. *The Emergence of Russian Panslavism 1856-1870*. New York: Columbia University Press, 1956.

_____. "Ľudovít Štúr and Russian Panslavism." *Journal of Central European Affairs*, 12, No. 1 (April 1952), 1-19.

Peukert, Herbert. "Zur Struktur der interslawischen Beziehungen der Štúr-Generation." *Wissenschaftliche Zeitschrift der Friedrich-Schiller-Universität Jena, Gesellschafts- und Sprachwissenschaftliche Reihe*, 8 (1958-59), 575-580.

Pfitzner, Josef. *Bakuninstudien*. Prague, 1932.

_____. "Zur nationalen Politik der Sudetendeutschen in den Jahren 1848-1849." *Jahrbuch des Vereins für Geschichte der Deutschen in Böhmen*, 3 (1930-33), 210-243.

Picht, Ulrich. *M.P. Pogodin und die slavische Frage: Ein Beitrag zur Geschichte des Panslavismus*. Kieler historische Studien, vol. 8. Stuttgart: Ernst Klett Verlag, 1969.

Piechowiak, Alojzy. "Jędrzej Moraczewski w kręgu zagadnień słowiańskich." *Slavia Occidentalis*, 28-29 (1971), 173-186.

Piotrowski, Bernard. "Delegacja wielopolska na Zjeździe Słowiańskim w Pradze (1848 roku)." *Zeszyty Naukowe Uniwersytetu im. Adama Mickiewicza w Poznaniu*, No. 47: *Historia*, No. 6 (1964), 103-123.

Plaschka, Richard G. "The Political Significance of František Palacký." *Journal of Contemporary History*, 8 (1973), 35-55.

_____. "Zur Einberufung des Slawenkongresses 1848." *Archiv für österreichische Geschichte*, 125 (1966), 196-207.

Pogodin, A.L. "Ocherki iz istorii slavianskoi vzaimnosti, II: Slavianskii s"ezd v Prage v 1848 godu." *Moskovskii Ezhenedel'nik*, 5, No. 15 (1910), 31-46.

Polišenský, Josef. *Revoluce a kontrarevoluce v Rakousku 1848*. Prague: Svoboda, 1975.

Popiołek, Kazimierz, and Popiołek, Franciszek. "1848 in Silesia." *Slavonic and East European Review*, 26, No. 67 (April 1948), 374-389.

Pražák, Albert. *Dějiny spisovné slovenštiny po dobu Šturovu*. Prague, 1922.

_____. "The Slavonic Congress of 1848 and the Slovaks." *Slavonic and East European Review*, 7, No. 19 (June 1928), 141-159.

_____. "Slováci na slovanskom sjazde v Prahe r. 1848." *Slovenská politika*, 1 June 1920, No. 74, pp. 1-2; and 2 June 1920, No. 75, pp. 2-3.

_____. "The Slovak Sources of Kollár's Pan-Slavism." *Slavonic and East European Review*, 6, No. 18 (March 1928), 579-592.

Prelog, Milan. "Mihailo Bakunin i Jugosloveni na sveslovenskom kongresu u Pragu god. 1848." *Srpski Književni Glasnik*, n.s., 12 (1924), 195-204.

_____. *Slavenska renesansa 1780-1848*. Zagreb, 1924.

Prinz, Friedrich. *Prag und Wien 1848: Probleme der nationalen und sozialen Revolution im Spiegel der Wiener Ministerratsprotokolle*. Munich: Robert Lerche Verlag, 1968.

_____. "Die Sudetendeutschen im Frankfurter Parlament." In *Zwischen Frankfurt und Prag*. Munich: Robert Lerche Verlag, 1963.

Rapant, Daniel. "Slovak Politics in 1848." *Slavonic and East European Review*, 27, No. 68 (December 1948), 67-90; 27, No. 69 (May 1949), 381-403.

Rath, R. John. "The Viennese Liberals of 1848 and the Nationality Problem." *Journal of Central European Affairs*, 15, No. 3 (October 1955), 227-239.

_____. *The Viennese Revolution of 1848*. Austin: University of Texas Press, 1957.

Raupach, Hans. *Der tschechische Frühnationalismus: Ein Beitrag zur Gesellschafts- und Ideengeschichte des Vormärz in Böhmen*. 1939. Reprint Darmstadt: Wissenschaftliche Buchgesellschaft, 1969.

Rebro, Karol. "Attempts at a Rightful Solution of the Slovak National Question in the Revolutionary Years 1848-1849." *Studia Historica Slovaca*, 4 (1966), 109-138.

Redlich, Josef. *Das österreichische Staats- und Reichproblem: Geschichtliche Darstellung der inneren Politik der habsburgischen Monarchie von 1848 bis zum Untergang des Reiches*. Vol. 1, 2 parts in 3. Leipzig, 1920.

Revoljucii 1848-1849. Ed. F.V. Potemkin and A.I. Molok. 2 vols. Moscow: Izdatel'-stvo Akademii Nauk SSSR, 1952.

Řezníček, Václav. *František Palacký, jeho život, působení a význam*. 3rd ed. Prague, 1923.

Riasanovsky, Nicholas. *Nicholas I and Official Nationality in Russia 1825-1855.* 1959. Reprint Berkeley & Los Angeles: University of California Press, 1967.

Rosdolsky, Roman. "Friedrich Engels und das Problem der 'geschichtslosen' Völker: Die Nationalitätenfrage in der Revolution 1848-1849 im Lichte der 'Neuen Rheinischen Zeitung'." *Archiv für Sozialgeschichte,* 4 (1964), 87-282.

Rothenberg, Gunther E. "Jelačić, the Croatian Military Border, and the Intervention Against Hungary in 1848." *Austrian History Yearbook,* 1 (1965), 45-68.

Rothfels, Hans. "1848—One Hundred Years After." *Journal of Modern History,* 20 (1948), 291-319.

Roubík, František. *Časopisectvo v Čechách v letech 1848-1862.* Prague, 1930.

————. *Český rok 1848.* 2nd rev. ed. Prague, 1948.

Russjan, L. *Polacy a sprawa polska na Węgrzech w roku 1848-1849.* Warsaw, 1934.

Saitl, Vilém. *Dozvuky pražské revoluce na nádraží v Běchovicích 17. června 1848.* Prague: Ministerstvo dopravy, 1948.

Schlesinger, Rudolf. *Federalism in Central and Eastern Europe.* London: Kegan Paul, Trench, Trubner & Co., 1945.

Šidak, Jaroslav. "Austroslavizam i Slavenski kongres u Pragu 1848." *Historijski pregled,* 6 (1960), 204-218.

Šimeček, Zdeněk. "Slavista J. Dobrovský a austroslavismus let 1791-1809." *Slovanský přehled,* 62 (1971), 177-190.

Šišić, Ferdo. "Hrvati i Madžari uoči sukoba 1848." *Jugoslavenska njiva,* 7, Part 2 (1923), 409-419, 453-462.

————. *Jugoslovenska misao.* Belgrade, 1937.

————. "Kako je Jelačić postao banom." *Jugoslavenska njiva,* 7, Part 2 (1923), 169-183.

Skene, Alfred. *Entstehen und Entwickelung der slavischnationalen Bewegung in Böhmen und Mähren im XIX. Jahrhundert.* Vienna, 1893.

Skowronek, Jerzy. *Polityka bałkańska Hotelu Lambert (1833-1856).* Warsaw: Wydawnictwo Uniwersytetu Warszawskiego, 1976.

Škultéty, Jozef. "Slovanský sjazd v Prahe roku 1848." *Slovenské pohl'ady,* 21 (1901), 452-463, 523-526, 658-674.

————. "Slovanský sjazd v Prahe roku 1848." *Slovenské pohl'ady,* 44 (1928), 455-462.

Slavíček, Karel. *Tajná politická společnost Český Repeal v roce 1848.* Prague: Nakladatelství pragnostik, 1947.

Slovanství v národním životě Čechů a Slováků. Ed. V. Šťastný et al. Prague: Melantrich, 1968.

Sozans'kyi, Ivan. "Do istorii uchasty halyts'kykh Rusyniv u slovians'kim kongresi v Prazi 1848 r." *Zapysky Naukovoho Tovarystva imeny Shevchenka,* 72 (1906), 112-121.

Spira, G. "The National Minorities Policy of the Pest Revolution's Left in March 1848." *Studia Slavica,* 16 (1970), 81-91.

Springer, Anton. *Geschichte Oesterreichs seit dem Wiener Frieden 1809.* 2 vols. Leipzig, 1863-65.

Stälin, R. "Die Entstehung des Panslavismus." *Germanoslavica,* 4 (1936), 1-24, 237-262.

Stranjaković, D. "La Collaboration des Croates et des Serbes en 1848-49." *Le Monde Slave,* 12, No. 2 (June 1935), 394-404.

_____. "Misja Franciszka Zacha w Zagrzebie w 1848 roku." *Przegląd historyczny*, 52 (1961), 297-325.

Sundhaussen, Holm. *Der Einfluss der Herderschen Ideen auf die Nationalbildung bei den Völkern der Habsburger Monarchie*. Munich: R. Oldenbourg, 1973.

Szyjkowski, Marjan. *Polská účast v českém národním obrození.* 3 vols. Práce Slovanského ústavu v Praze, vols. 3, 15, 19. Prague, 1931-46.

Tamborra, Angelo. "Panslavismo e solidarietà slava." *Questioni di Storia Contemporanea*, 2 (1952), 1777-1873.

Tanty, Mieczysław. *Panslawizm, Carat, Polacy: Zjazd Słowiański w Moskwie 1867 roku*. Warsaw: Państwowe wydawnictwo naukowe, 1970.

Thienen-Adlerflycht, Christoph. *Graf Leo Thun im Vormärz: Grundlagen des böhmischen Konservativismus im Kaisertum Österreich*. Graz, Vienna & Cologne: Hermann Böhlaus Nachf., 1967.

Thim, Josef R. "Die Gründungsversuche Jugoslaviens 1848-49." *Ungarische Jahrbücher*, 1 (1921), 22-35.

Thomson, S. Harrison. "A Century of Phantom Pan-Slavism and the Western Slavs." *Journal of Central European Affairs*, 11, No. 2 (1951), 57-78.

Tkadlečková, J. "Názory a činnost Karla Havlíčka Borovského z hl'adiska vývoja česko-slovenských vzt'ahov." *Historický časopis*, 6 (1958), 32-47.

Tobolka, Zdeněk V. "Česká otázka v jednáních frankfurtského parlamentu roku 1848." *Časopis Matice moravske*, 30 (1906), 155-162, 220-228.

_____. "Der Panslavismus." *Zeitschrift für Politik*, 6 (1913), 215-235.

_____. *Počátky dělnického hnutí v Čechách*. Rev. ed. Prague, 1923.

_____. *Politické dějiny československého národa od 1848 až do dnešní doby*. 4 vols. in 5. Prague, 1932-37.

_____. "Politika Slovanského klubu v Kroměříži r. 1848-1849." *Slovanský přehled*, 8 (1906), 199-206, 263-271.

_____. *Slovanský sjezd v Praze roku 1848*. Prague, 1901.

Tóth, Zoltán I. "The Nationality Problem in Hungary in 1848-1849." *Acta Historica*, 4 (1955), 234-277.

_____. "Quelques problèmes de L'état multinational dans l'Hongrie d'avant 1848." *Acta Historica*, 4 (1955), 123-149.

Tourtzer [Turcerová], H. *Louis Stúr et l'idée de L'indépendance slovaque*. Paris, 1913.

Toužimský, Josef J. *Na úsvitě nové doby: Dějiny roku 1848 v zemích českých*. Prague, 1898.

Traub, Hugo. *Květnové spiknutí v Čechách r. 1849*. Prague, 1929.

_____. "Příspěvek k svatodušním událostem v Čechách roku 1848." *Osvěta*, 44 (1914), 112-118.

_____. "Zum Slavenkongresse in Prag im J. 1848." *Union* (Prague), 25 September 1913, No. 263.

Traub, R. *Kabinetní listy z 23. března a 8. dubna 1848 s hlediska práva jazykového*. Prague, 1919.

Tůma, Karel. *Karel Havlíček Borovský*. Kutná Hora, 1885.

Tyrowicz, Marian. *Polski kongres polityczny w Wrocławiu 1848 r*. Kraków: Czytelnik, 1946.

Udal'tsov, I.I. "Iz istorii slavianskogo s"ezda v Prage 1848 godu." *Uchenye zapiski Instituta slavianovedeniia*, 1 (1949), 57-84.

180 BIBLIOGRAPHY

_____. *Ocherki iz istorii natsional'no-politicheskoi bor'by v Chekhii v 1848 godu.* Moscow: Izdatel'stvo Akademii Nauk SSSR, 1951. Translated into Czech as *Z dějin národních a politických bojů v Čechách roku 1848.* Prague: Státní nakladatelství politické literatury, 1954. Translated into German as *Aufzeichnungen über die Geschichte des nationalen und politischen Kampfes in Böhmen im Jahre 1848.* Berlin: Rütten & Loening, 1953.

Usznula, Ludwig. "Wien und die Slawenfrage von 1848: Das Problem dargestellt aus der Wiener Presse des Jahres 1848." Ph.D. dissertation, University of Vienna, 1937.

Valentin, Veit. *Geschichte der deutschen Revolution 1848-49.* 2 vols. 1930-31. Reprint Aalen: Scientia Verlag, 1968.

Vigh, Károly. "A pragai szláv kongresszus centenáriumára." *Századok,* 82 (1948), 235-251.

Vochala, Josef. *Rok 1848 ve Slezsku a na severovýchodní Moravě.* Opava: Slezský studijní ústav, 1948.

Vomáčková, Věra. "K národnostní otázce v buržoazní revoluci 1848 v českých zemích." *Československý časopis historický,* 9 (1961), 1-16.

Vucinich, Wayne S. "Croatian Illyrism: Its Background and Genesis." In Stanley B. Winters and Joseph Held, eds., *Intellectual and Social Developments in the Habsburg Empire from Maria Theresa to World War I: Essays Dedicated to Robert A. Kann.* Boulder: East European Quarterly, 1975.

Ward, David. "Windischgrätz and the Bohemian Revolt, 1848." *History Today,* 19 (1969), 625-633.

Warnier, R. "Illyrisme et le nationalisme croate." *Le Monde Slave,* 12, No. 3 (July 1935), 27-75.

Weber, O. "Die Prager Revolution von 1848 und das Frankfurter Parlament." In *Festschrift des Vereins für Geschichte der Deutschen in Böhmen.* Prague, 1902.

Weingart, Miloš. "Joseph Dobrovský, the Patriarch of Slavonic Studies." *Slavonic and East European Review,* 7, No. 21 (March 1929), 663-675.

_____. *Slovanská vzájemnost: Úvahy o jejích základech a osudech.* Bratislava, 1926.

Wendel, Hermann. *Aus dem südslawischen Risorgimento.* Gotha, 1921.

_____. *Der Kampf der Südslawen um Freiheit und Einheit.* Frankfurt a/M, 1925.

_____. "Der Prager Slawenkongress von 1848." *Die Gesellschaft, Internationale Revue für Sozialismus und Politik,* 3 (1926), 459-469.

Wereszycki, Henryk. *Pod berłem Habsburgów.* Kraków: Wydawnictwo Literackie, 1975.

Widmann, Karol. *Franciszek Smolka, jego życie i zawód publiczny od roku 1810 do 1849.* Rev. ed. Lvov, 1890.

Wierer, Rudolf. "F. Palackýs staatspolitisches Programm." *Zeitschrift für Ostforschung,* 6 (1957), 246-258.

Winter, Eduard. *Frühliberalismus in der Donaumonarchie: Religiöse, nationale und wissenschaftliche Strömungen von 1790-1868.* Berlin: Akademie-Verlag, 1968.

_____. *Revolution, Neoabsolutismus und Liberalismus in der Donaumonarchie.* Vienna: Europa Verlag, 1969.

Wisłocki, Władysław T. *Jerzy Lubomirski 1817-1872.* Lvov, 1928.

Wolfgramm, Eberhard. "Der böhmische Vormärz, im besonderen die böhmischen Arbeiterunruhen des Jahres 1844 in ihren sozialen und politischen Zusammenhängen." In *Aus 500 Jahren deutsch-tschechoslowakischer Geschichte.* Ed. K. Obermann and J. Polišenský. Berlin: Rütten & Loening, 1958.

Wollman, Frank. *Slavismy a antislavismy za jara národů*. Prague: Academia, 1968.

—————. *Slovanství v jazykově literárním obrození u Slovanů*. Prague: Státní pedagogické nakladatelství, 1958.

—————. "Terminologie slovanské součinnosti." *Slovanský přehled*, 34 (1948), 126-140.

W stulecie Wiosny Ludów 1848-1948. Ed. N. Gąsiorowska. 5 vols. Warsaw: Państwowy Institut Wydawniczy, 1948-53.

Wurmová, Milada. "Morava 1848-1849: Slovanský sjezd a kroměřízsky sněm." Ph.D. dissertation, Masaryk University, Brno, 1948.

Žáček, Václav. "Andrija T. Brlić v Čechách r. 1848." *Slovanský přehled*, 56 (1970), 241-251.

—————. *Čechové a Poláci roku 1848*. 2 vols. Práce Slovanského ústavu v Praze, vols. 22, 23. Prague: Nákladem Slovanského ústavu a Slovanského výboru Československa, 1947-48.

—————. "České a jihoslovanské Slovanské lípy v roce 1848." *Literární archiv*, 6 (1971), 195-239.

—————. "Česko-polská diskuse o austroslavismu r. 1842-1843." *Slavia*, 32 (1963), 227-239.

—————. "K dějinám austroslavismu rakouských Slovanů." *Slovanské historické studie*, 7 (1968), 129-179.

—————. "Moravský účastník svatodušních bouří 1848: Příspěvek k životu a působení Matěje Mikšíčka." *Časopis Matice moravské*, 57 (1933), 180-210.

—————. "Pokusy o slovanské sjezdy po r. 1867." *Slovanský přehled*, 54 (1968), 202-211.

—————. *Z revolučních a politických pol'sko-slovenských stykov v dobe predmarcovej*. Bratislava: Vydavateľstvo Slovenskej akadémie vied, 1966.

—————, ed. *Češi a Poláci v minulosti*. Vol. 2: *Období kapitalismu a imperialismu*. Prague: Academia, 1967.

—————, et al. *Češi a Jihoslované v minolosti: Od nejstarších dob do roku 1918*. Prague: Academia, 1975.

Zaionchkovskii, P.A. *Kirillo-Mefodievskoe obshchestvo*. Moscow: Izdateľstvo Moskovskogo universiteta, 1959.

Zawadzki, Władysław. *Dziennikarstwo w Galicji w roku 1848*. 1878. Reprint as *Pamiętniki życia literackiego w Galicji*. Kraków: Wydawnictwo literackie, 1961.

Zwitter, Fran. *Les problèmes nationaux dans la Monarchie des Habsbourg*. Belgrade: Comité national yugoslave des sciences historiques, 1960.

EAST EUROPEAN MONOGRAPHS

The *East European Monographs* comprise scholarly books on the history and civilization of Eastern Europe. They are published by the *East European Quarterly* in the belief that these studies contribute substantially to the knowledge of the area and serve to stimulate scholarship and research.

1. *Political Ideas and the Enlightenment in the Romanian Principalities, 1750–1831.* By Vlad Georgescu. 1971.

2. *America, Italy and the Birth of Yugoslavia, 1917–1919.* By Dragan R. Zivojinovic. 1972.

3. *Jewish Nobles and Geniuses in Modern Hungary.* By William O. McCagg, Jr. 1972.

4. *Mixail Soloxov in Yugoslavia: Reception and Literary Impact.* By Robert F. Price. 1973.

5. *The Historical and National Thought of Nicolae Iorga.* By William O. Oldson. 1973.

6. *Guide to Polish Libraries and Archives.* By Richard C. Lewanski. 1974.

7. *Vienna Broadcasts to Slovakia, 1938–1939: A Case Study in Subversion.* By Henry Delfiner. 1974.

8. *The 1917 Revolution in Latvia.* By Andrew Ezergailis. 1974.

9. *The Ukraine in the United Nations Organization: A Study in Soviet Foreign Policy. 1944–1950.* By Konstantin Sawczuk. 1975.

10. *The Bosnian Church: A New Interpretation.* By John V. A. Fine, Jr. 1975.

11. *Intellectual and Social Developments in the Habsburg Empire from Maria Theresa to World War I.* Edited by Stanley B. Winters and Joseph Held. 1975.

12. *Ljudevit Gaj and the Illyrian Movement.* By Elinor Murray Despalatovic. 1975.

13. *Tolerance and Movements of Religious Dissent in Eastern Europe.* Edited by Bela K. Kiraly. 1975.

14. *The Parish Republic: Hlinka's Slovak People's Party, 1939–1945.* By Yeshayahu Jelinek. 1976.

15. *The Russian Annexation of Bessarabia, 1774–1828.* By George F. Jewsbury. 1976.

16. *Modern Hungarian Historiography.* By Steven Bela Vardy. 1976.

17. *Values and Community in Multi-National Yugoslavia.* By Gary K. Bertsch. 1976.

18. *The Greek Socialist Movement and the First World War: the Road to Unity.* By George B. Leon. 1976.
19. *The Radical Left in the Hungarian Revolution of 1848.* By Laszlo Deme. 1976.
20. *Hungary between Wilson and Lenin: The Hungarian Revolution of 1918–1919 and the Big Three.* By Peter Pastor. 1976.
21. *The Crises of France's East-Central European Diplomacy, 1933–1938.* By Anthony J. Komjathy. 1976.
22. *Polish Politics and National Reform, 1775–1788.* By Daniel Stone. 1976.
23. *The Habsburg Empire in World War I.* Robert A. Kann, Bela K. Kiraly, and Paula S. Fichtner, eds. 1977.
24. *The Slovenes and Yugoslavism, 1890–1914.* By Carole Rogel. 1977.
25. *German-Hungarian Relations and the Swabian Problem.* By Thomas Spira. 1977.
26. *The Metamorphosis of a Social Class in Hungary During the Reign of Young Franz Joseph.* By Peter I. Hidas. 1977.
27. *Tax Reform in Eighteenth Century Lombardy.* By Daniel M. Klang. 1977.
28. *Tradition versus Revolution: Russia and the Balkans in 1917.* By Robert H. Johnston. 1977.
29. *Winter into Spring: The Czechoslovak Press and the Reform Movement 1963–1968.* By Frank L. Kaplan. 1977.
30. *The Catholic Church and the Soviet Government, 1939–1949.* By Dennis J. Dunn. 1977.
31. *The Hungarian Labor Service System, 1939–1945.* By Randolph L. Braham. 1977.
32. *Consciousness and History: Nationalist Critics of Greek Society 1897–1914.* By Gerasimos Augustinos. 1977.
33. *Emigration in Polish Social and Political Thought, 1870–1914.* By Benjamin P. Murdzek. 1977.
34. *Serbian Poetry and Milutin Bojić.* By Mihailo Dordevic. 1977.
35. *The Baranya Dispute 1918–1921: Diplomacy in the Vortex of Ideologies.* By Leslie Charles Tihany. 1978.
36. *The United States in Prague, 1945–1948.* By Walter Ullmann. 1978.